24319465

Capitalism in Colonial Puerto Rico

University of Florida Social Sciences
Monograph 78

Capitalism in Colonial Puerto Rico

Central San Vicente in the Late Nineteenth Century

Teresita Martínez-Vergne

University Press of Florida
Gainesville Tallahassee Tampa Boca Raton Pensacola
Orlando Miami Jacksonville

Copyright 1992 by the Board of Regents
of the State of Florida
Printed in the U.S.A. on recycled, acid-free paper ∞

The University of Florida Press is the scholarly publishing
agency for the State University System of Florida, comprised of
Florida A&M University, Florida Atlantic University, Florida
International University, Florida State University, University of
Central Florida, University of Florida, University of North
Florida, University of South Florida, and University of West
Florida.

University Press of Florida, 15 NW 15th St., Gainesville, FL
32611

Chapter 5 previously appeared as "New Patterns for Puerto
Rico's Sugar Workers: Abolition and Centralization at San
Vicente, 1873–1892" in *Hispanic American Historical Review*
68, no. 1. Copyright 1988 by Duke University Press. Reprinted
by permission.

Library of Congress Cataloging in Publication data can be
found on the last printed page of the book.

Contents

Plates

Figures

Preface

I visited the ruins of Central San Vicente for the first time in 1981. Its fields were sown with rice. There was no machinery to be seen anywhere. All that remained of one of the largest sugar producers on the island was the skeleton of two huge buildings that evidently had housed the mill and the sugar-making equipment. At a distance, an old man pushed a cart full of all sorts of scrap. I stopped my car in the middle of the road and asked, "Excuse me, is that San Vicente?" "That *was* San Vicente," was the solemn response.

I have never forgotten my encounter with the old man. It pointed to the emotions that "sugar" stirs up in Puerto Rico, as the slow disappearance of the industry during the last half of this century has made it ever more present in the collective Puerto Rican experience. The foundation for everything Puerto Rican; the cause of rural poverty; a symbol of colonialism and backwardness; standing proof of the inadvisability of nationalization—Puerto Ricans of all age groups and social backgrounds will voice impassioned opinions about the sugar industry.

Older folk will remember the harsh treatment of rural laborers in the early decades of the twentieth century and the paternalism that accompanied their exploitation—although they would hardly use these words. They will tell stories of widespread ignorance, rampant disease, and limited opportunities for self-improvement in the rural areas, blaming large U.S. companies for the appearance of these conditions and eulogizing small-scale Puerto Rican landowners for mitigating them. The younger generation—or perhaps the more formally educated—will take on a more rational air and speak of agriculture as a lost cause, singing the praises of industrialization and the modernization that it has brought. They will undoubtedly refer to the continued existence of the sugar industry before 1990 as an anachronism, shamelessly subsidized by the government to provide employment for a few thousand. Most nonhistorians feel free to contrast their observations with what they understand to have been the situation in the nineteenth century—a prosperous sugar industry run by an honorable landed gentry and worked by fairly treated and conscientious slaves or free laborers.

In this book I attempt to correct this vision, popularly held by most nonspecialists. I describe the vicissitudes of Puerto Rico's sugar industry—from the perspectives of landowners and workers—in the last decades of the nineteenth century. The heated debate over the problems of producing agricultural commodities for export has not changed much since 1850. Sugar producers then, as now, identified as their concerns the accessibility of investment capital, the need for improving the quality and lowering the costs of production, and the reliability of the labor force. This short volume, then, places in a historical context a theme long familiar in Puerto Rican history.

In so doing, my work fits in with a fairly recent historiographical past. Beginning in the 1970s, a group of historians—dissatisfied with traditional narratives and political explanations of events—introduced new concepts and perspectives to the study of Puerto Rico's past. Gervasio L. García Rodríguez, Fernando Picó, the late Andrés Ramos Mattei, Angel G. Quintero Rivera, and Francisco Scarano were the pioneers of social and economic history for nineteenth-century Puerto Rico. Coffee and sugar, slaves and wage laborers, landowners and merchants, even Liberals and Conservatives were placed in the context of an incipient capitalism, complete with class conflict and political unrest. Soon, other scholars followed in their footsteps and broadened the scope of subjects worthy of inquiry. Juan José Baldrich, Guillermo Baralt, Laird W. Bergad, Astrid Cubano, and Pedro San Miguel shifted the focus of attention to minor crops, peasant-squatters, urban professional groups, and the nonparty affiliated. The interpretations offered by the "new historiography" have gained wide recognition on the island and abroad.

The kinds of issues I address here will contribute to the efforts of this new generation of historians at reconstructing Puerto Rico's nineteenth century. I pay particular attention to the influences of the international market in an export economy, the impact of "modernization" in the sugar industry, the changes in the social relations of production with the introduction of wage labor, and the power play between merchants and landowners for economic and political predominance. As do most "younger" historians, I tend to deemphasize 1898, the year that marks the beginning of U.S. control of the island, as a watershed in the social, economic, and even political life of Puerto Rico.

Scholars of Caribbean and Latin American plantation societies will also recognize the thrust of the questions I ask. The external pressures faced by planters; their attempted alliances with the politically powerful in the face of crisis; the forms of worker control—short of coerced labor—they adopted; the ways of resistance from below—these themes have been developed in other contexts by Michael Craton, Warren Dean, Peter L. Eisenberg, Michael Gonzales, Franklin W. Knight, Sidney W. Mintz, Manuel Moreno Fraginals, Walter Rodney, and Rebecca Scott, among others just as well known, for Jamaica, Brazil, Peru, Cuba, and Guyana. My work is inspired by their scholarship and dedication.

The argument I develop in the pages that follow is that the disappearance of Puerto Rico's first modern sugar factory resulted ultimately from the clash between the owner's ambitious plans and the context in which he launched the novel project. A noble Creole merchant turned landowner/entrepreneur—Don Leonardo Igaravídez, Marqués de Cabo Caribe—tried to set up a rational system of sugar production in the municipality of Vega Baja. The agricultural-industrial complex known as Central San Vicente after 1873 established modern methods of cane cultivation, used the latest technology for the manufacture of sugar, and managed its labor force most efficiently. Unfortunately for its visionary founder, the requirements for capital of such an enterprise could not be satisfied by the limited resources of credit institutions controlled by a commercial class with a narrow vision of the future. San Vicente filed for bankruptcy in 1879.

The story of the evolution and demise of plans to revive Puerto

Rico's economy followed a similar course. As the island's sugar industry faced imminent crisis in the last three decades of the nineteenth
century, Puerto Rico's economic leaders adopted a broadly defined
"capitalism" as their goal. Centralization, the separate organization of
field activities in cane plantations and the manufacture of sugar in
modern industrial *centrales*, became their shibboleth. Through mechanization, proletarianization, and large-scale capital investment, they
hoped to increase productivity and reduce costs. They failed to understand that the success of their plans depended on Spain's commitment
to build infrastructure. What's more, even if their plans succeeded, the
sugar industry would still remain at the mercy of the world market.
Puerto Rico's economic future, like San Vicente's, depended on forces
well outside its control.

Although the story of the first central on the island parallels in
many ways the insistent call for change, it would be a mistake to conclude that the enterprise failed because it did not follow the blueprint
for centralization. What destroyed San Vicente was the limited access
to investment capital for a project of its dimensions and the personal
animosities that grew out of its owner's and manager's insistence on
saving the enterprise, *not* the inability to separate the agricultural from
the manufacturing processes as agricultural analysts recommended.
One could argue further that the transformations suggested were, in
fact, misguided in that they included as a primary goal the production
of refined sugar, a development that would have resulted in the loss of
a most important and relatively secure client: U.S. refineries. It is
ironic, then, that San Vicente's failure to centralize could have actually
saved it from total ruin—had it not been for the other complications
mentioned above.

Distinguishing between San Vicente's particular experience and
tragic fate and those of the nineteenth-century sugar industry is important. Nineteenth-century economic analysts interpreted the central's
disappearance as the death knell of the sugar industry. Historians have
picked up the cue and have argued that Puerto Rico's sugar industry
had to centralize or perish. The success of the heavily capitalized U.S.
sugar centrales after 1900 adds weight to their contention. But the
sugar industry did not have to centralize to survive, nor did U.S. investments have to flood the island for capitalism to become estab-

lished. San Vicente stood—for a very short while—as an example that this was (and would be in the future) a fallacious argument.

In the first chapter of this study I provide the setting for changes proposed in the island's sugar economy. I describe Puerto Rico as moving slowly out of Spain's economic orbit during the eighteenth century until the possibilities for growth via cane plantations became apparent. From the beginning of the nineteenth century onward, the island's economic, political, and social structures rapidly developed around the production of sugar for export. Although coffee began to become important at midcentury (precisely when the price of sugar went down), cane planters remained an outspoken if not influential minority in island affairs. It is no surprise that, as the market price of sugar continued to fall, a sense of crisis and the conviction that change was urgently needed spread rapidly among planters and other agriculturalists.

The background to the solutions proposed to face the critical situation is my subject in the second chapter. I argue that the perceived needs of agriculture—in terms of land, labor, and capital—were embraced in the concept of centralization. Speakers for change focused their efforts on the adoption of modern, rational, scientific views regarding economic and social organization at the local and island level. A radical departure from previous methods of production, centrales offered a better product at a lower cost. Their promise, however, proved highly illusory. The reorganization of production might have offered some protection against violent market fluctuations, but the desired concomitant changes—such as reductions in export duties and the creation of banks—belonged to the distant future. More importantly, Puerto Rico would gain little by producing refined sugar, the dream of many. Its natural market, it was already evident, was U.S. refineries, which required raw sugars.

In the third chapter I deal with the purchase of lands surrounding the old Hacienda San Vicente by Leonardo Igaravídez. Using all instruments available, the noble merchant-turned-entrepreneur from Vega Baja planned to establish the first modern sugar factory on the island. In doing so, he fulfilled the highest expectations of the ardent advocates of centralization. But he had to accumulate lands if he was to mobilize social and financial resources for the project, given the values and premises of Puerto Rican nineteenth-century society. Owning such vast expanses, though, was actually detrimental to the interests of his enterprise, not because the proposal for centralization was not implemented to the letter, but because high land-related expenses made it impossible for Igaravídez to meet his financial obligations. Although he could have eventually resolved the problem to his and his creditors' satisfaction, time ran out all too quickly.

I address the question of the central's capital requirements in chapter 4. I pay particular attention to Igaravídez's methods of obtaining credit to establish and maintain his ambitious project and to the attack of creditors once he defaulted on a number of obligations. San Vicente could count only on small-scale financial mechanisms and Igaravídez felt comfortable using them creatively. Creditors and judges were likely to be less imaginative and were less moved by business considerations than by personal interests. Igaravídez was jailed for fraud, and parts of Central San Vicente were distributed among its creditors in 1892.

Chapter 5 contains a statistical analysis of San Vicente's work force within and outside the sugar complex. Just as in earlier chapters I attempt to shed light on the sugar industry by following the story of one enterprise, in this chapter I try to reconstruct the trajectory of the working class through the experiences of as many of its members as possible. My findings here suggest that Igaravídez's relations with his workers were characteristic of a man of his time. He fluctuated between the impersonal, uniform incentives that he believed would attract laborers in a modern wage system and the individual, exceptional, case-by-case treatment of workers characteristic of earlier face-to-face contacts. The sudden emergence of the central in the small town of Vega Baja, then, did not result in the establishment of capitalist relations of production, did not transform workers into a proletariat, and consequently did not produce the types of class conflict associated with capitalism. Ways of life, places of residence, and regularity of habits remained unaffected, probably as a result of the brevity of the experiment. The best evidence for the project's ultimate inability to conform to the blueprint for change is—precisely—its limited impact upon the working class.

The experience of San Vicente is far from representative of events in the sugar industry. The rise and decline of the enterprise—a result of its owner's enterprising spirit and personal failures—were unequaled in nineteenth-century Puerto Rico because of the scope of the project. The division of labor, the installation of the most modern machinery, and the application of advanced management techniques reflected the highest expectations of contemporaries. The forces that stood as obstacles to the success of the project were also particular to the case at hand.

Yet San Vicente's trajectory generally reflects occurrences in Puerto Rico and can be used to illuminate some of the processes that characterized the end of the century. Its response to crisis—modernization—followed the patterns dictated by time and place. The circumstances of its demise—the failure to mobilize resources held by merchants—were commonplace in the sugar industry. Most important, San Vicente constitutes a bona fide example of an attempt to establish capitalist relations of production in the nineteenth century.

What follows, then, is a study of business activity in a context shaped by considerations external to the enterprise itself—the limited and concrete reality that was Puerto Rico in the nineteenth century. My work challenges interpretations that identify the arrival of capitalist relations of production with the establishment of large U.S. corporations. In addition, it provides a more solid base to the largely theoretical efforts of a number of labor historians, while following the pattern set by a number of monographs on sugar and coffee haciendas. The specificity of its scope and its particular focus are themselves part of my contribution to the growing literature on nineteenth-century Puerto Rico.

As all history books, this study is the result of years of researching and verifying data, thinking and rethinking concepts, writing and rewriting arguments, and revising them again and again. I would have run out of energy had it not been for the support of many people and institutions at different stages of the book's development. It is easy to acknowledge the help of the most visible and almost impossible to thank those who have always offered their encouragement. But my gratitude goes to all alike.

It seems appropriate to begin with friends who shared my concerns and listened patiently, at times only because I asked them to. Richard and Sandra Graham, Sarita Brown, Lesley Williams, Alida Metcalf, and Julia Curry played important roles during my years in Austin. During the course of my research in Puerto Rico, Luis de la Rosa, Peggy McLeod, Raymond Morales, and Blanca Silvestrini tried very hard to look interested when I mentioned San Vicente and its workers. I always appreciated it. At Colgate University, Nigel and Ellie Bolland, Fred Luciani, Julia Meyerson, Mary Moran, Lourdes Rojas, Lynn Rugg, Nancy Tucker, and Gary Urton offered me their friendship, which I treasure. A number of colleagues at the University of Puerto Rico–Río Piedras—Astrid Cubano, Barbara Southard, Francisco Moscoso, Javier Figueroa, María de los Angeles Castro, Gervasio García, María Dolores Luque, Fernando Picó, and Pedro San Miguel—also encouraged me. I have been fortunate to have counted on the long-distance support of Franklin Knight and Blanca Silvestrini at several critical moments and I am forever grateful to them. My sincere thanks go also to Steve Stern, from whom I learned much during a summer at the University of Wisconsin–Madison.

I have an intellectual debt to a number of historians who have read my work and criticized it carefully. Richard Graham, Franklin Knight, Francisco Scarano, Rebecca Scott, Nigel Bolland, Luis de la Rosa, Nettie Lee Benson, Carolyn Boyd, and Henry Dietz fought with me, suggested new ways of looking at old issues, forced me to read some more, and generally taught me how to be a better historian. I hope I will do justice to their efforts.

Other people and institutions helped with the technical aspects of the project. I used the research facilities at the Benson Latin American Collection (UT–Austin), the Colección Puertorriqueña (UPR), the Archivo General de Puerto Rico, and the Archivo Municipal de Vega Baja. My thanks go to their respective staffs. The Computation Center at UPR and at UT–Austin made possible the coding of data and their analysis. I borrowed freely from the expertise of Juan José Baldrich, Diana Macken, Gloria Vecchini, Edna Pizarro, and Nyrma García at this stage of the project.

The Inter-American Foundation, the Graduate School at UT–Austin, and Colgate's Department of History and its Research Council funded my research throughout the years. I hope they are pleased with the results of their investment.

I dedicate my work to Irene Toro Martínez, una niñita muy especial.

1

The Setting

Puerto Rico in the Nineteenth Century

Puerto Rico played a rather unimportant role within Spain's empire for most of its colonial life. In the early years of colonization, it existed as a military fortress, with isolated pockets of subsistence farming and smuggling activity. Little by little, the island developed—outside of Spain's sphere of influence—a limited economy based on cattle ranching and farming for local consumption. Coffee, tobacco, and some sugar production contributed to population growth and to the expansion of the island's economy by the end of the eighteenth century. But despite these developments, rural landholders and their urban providers continued to demand little from the metropolis and remained oblivious to its exigencies.

By 1850, however, the island's economic, social, and political life revolved around the production of sugar for export. A shift in policy on the part of Spain and external economic stimuli in the early 1800s explain the radical change. Motivated by threats to its American empire in the second decade of the nineteenth century, Spain set out to "reconquer" the colony, to use John Lynch's apt phrase, through liberalizing measures designed to increase imperial control. Supporting Spain's new attitude were the opportunities for economic growth provided by the destruction in the 1790s of Haiti, the world's largest sugar producer. In the first decades of the nineteenth century, then, Puerto

Rico became a sugar colony, island planters rose to social prominence, and political activity centered on keeping internal order.[1]

This interpretation appears radically different from that offered by Francisco Scarano in his seminal work, *Sugar and Slavery in Puerto Rico. The Plantation Economy of Ponce, 1800–1850*, and deserves further clarification for that reason. In his introduction, Scarano rejects traditional (political) explanations for the economic growth experienced in the early nineteenth century and argues convincingly that Spain's actions were not a departure from previous policies, that Puerto Rico's economy had been growing steadily since the eighteenth century, that the stimulus received in the early nineteenth century came in the form of favorable external conditions (and not legislation), and that Puerto Rico did not become a plantation society the way Cuba did. While all of this is true, it is also undeniable that the early nineteenth century marked a change in the mother country's attitude toward Puerto Rico, in the island's capacity to generate income, and in the activities of its dominant classes in various local, metropolitan, and even worldwide circles. The transformations required cannot be readily dismissed, and I have chosen to emphasize them because I believe they dwarf the continuities Scarano highlights. While not negating the value of Scarano's objections to the facile arguments of traditional historiography, I hold that the sugar industry, as it appeared in the early years of the nineteenth century, defined and dominated political, economic, and social developments for decades to come.[2]

The patterns of political activity in nineteenth-century Puerto Rico conformed to the island's renewed colonial status.[3] Spain regarded its colony with interest when it showed economic promise or when the possibility of disaffection arose. Otherwise, it preferred to concentrate all its efforts in stabilizing the political scene at home, especially after 1833 when the Carlist movement became a powerful threat to the Bourbon line. That the colonial relationship needed invigorating—because war had depleted Spain's treasury during the eighteenth century and because the old colonial formula had lost its force among other American possessions—became evident in the early years of the nineteenth century. The Cédula de Gracias of 1815, then, stimulated economic growth in the previously ignored colony through a number of concessions regarding immigration, agriculture, trade, and industry. The efforts of enlightened politicians—such as Ramón Power y Giralt, vice-president of the constituent Spanish Cortes of 1812, and Alejandro Ramírez, intendant in the colony after 1816—found a hospitable environment in these early decades, as the mother country redirected the island's economy and afforded it special treatment.

An integral element of Spain's effortless policy except when self-interest required action was the delegation of authority to local officials in the day-to-day operation of the colonial pact. Beginning in the twenties, the captain-general's supreme control over island affairs was asserted through the issuance of *facultades omnímodas*—extraordinary powers that remained a permanent feature of colonial life. Repressive measures designed to protect the colony from the influence of the Latin American independence movements became commonplace. The continuous possibility of violent repression limited the scope of changes in Puerto Rico's political life throughout the century. Whether Liberal or Moderate, then, governments in Madrid were committed to stabilizing politics in the peninsula and keeping internal order abroad through the means selected by colonial officials.

Yet several measures taken during the century offered to counterbalance the absolute rule of island governors. The establishment of civil institutions in Puerto Rico beginning in 1831 and the promise of special laws for the island in the Spanish constitution of 1837 filled many Puerto Ricans with hope. The creation of the Audiencia Territorial, a high court of appeals, and the introduction of *ayuntamientos* (town councils) offered to decentralize authority. The Junta de Información in 1866—a commission elected to discuss the much-awaited special laws of 1837 before the metropolitan government—opened up debate among the Puerto Rican delegates with respect to badly needed political, economic, and social reforms. After Spain's Glorious Revolution of 1868 and during the Republic (1873–74), Puerto Rico enjoyed the same rights as any Spanish province.

But without a master plan with respect to colonial administration, liberalizing institutions and practices was vulnerable to the frequent power struggles between political factions in the mother country and to the whims of reactionary local governors. Colonial arguments for reform were not fully debated in 1866, for example, because the overseas minister who called the meetings was replaced when his party fell out of favor. In the 1880s, reacting to the increased mobilization of political forces on the island, the governor felt free to embark on a campaign of persecution against autonomist elements on the southern coast. It was clear that in the last decades of the nineteenth century as well as in the earlier ones, Spanish rule on the island was marked by indifference except in the face of political threats and economic gain and by inaction except through the figure of the governor.

The emphasis I have placed on Spain's primary interest in political stability at home and its decision to delegate authority to local officials for the routine aspects of colonial administration is not original. Josep Fradera fully documents a similar thesis for Cuba.[4] But Puerto Rican scholars have traditionally pointed to the seemingly aimless trajectory of nineteenth-century politics to argue either that the island was the victim of the rotative nature of metropolitan politics or that Spain changed policies constantly in order to better exploit the colony and so advance its position before the European community. I hold that Spain, did, in fact, *decide* to concentrate its efforts at home and so relegated colonial affairs to a secondary position. Its desire to milk the colonies became irrelevant in the face of local unrest; administering the colonies effectively seemed a distant objective when compared to normalizing internal politics. Puerto Rico's political development, then, suffered not from its dependence on the party in power or from Spain's evil intentions, but from the absence of any continuous colonial policy.

Puerto Rico's economic life was equally influenced by metropolitan considerations. The sugar industry, initially stimulated by the elimination of Haiti as a major competitor in the 1790s, flourished after 1815 because of legislation granting land and tax exemptions to immigrants, removing all trade regulations with Spain, and reducing export duties and tariffs on goods imported from friendly countries. In the early decades of the nineteenth century, agricultural machinery entered the colony duty-free from Spain, export taxes were minimal, and customs duties were reduced to encourage trade with Spanish colonies as well as with friendly nations. Agriculturalists took advantage of the favorable circumstances and concentrated their efforts on making sugar. They planted cane on land previously dedicated to minor crops for internal consumption as well as on uncultivated tracts. The island's economy shifted gears to participate fully in agricultural production for export.

But the mother country changed course at midcentury to promote its own fiscal well-being. Spain decided to protect metropolitan manufactures by raising customs duties on U.S. goods—also imported by the colony—and began to tax island sugar exports. It was an unfortunate coincidence that the steady drop in market prices caused by the introduction of subsidized European beet sugar hit with full force in 1840. Planters avoided imminent disaster simply by increasing output. At times helped by fortuitous events—such as the market disruptions caused by the Civil War in the United States and the Ten Years' War in Cuba—Puerto Rico's sugar industry had nevertheless already encountered the negative effects of the vagaries of the market in the absence of protection. Coffee slowly replaced sugar as the island's major export crop beginning in the 1850s, only to follow a similar course by the end of the century.[5]

The description of Spain's role in the rise and demise of the Puerto Rican sugar industry, as outlined above, appears to gloss over the important influence of the market in the expansion and contraction of local production. Yet, it is not my intention to suggest that Spain was responsible for Puerto Rico's economic growth—based on sugar as well as on other products for export and for local consumption—during the nineteenth century. Nor is it to attribute the difficulties the sugar industry faced solely to Spain's withdrawal of support. I simply wish to recognize the impact of Spain's actions on the island's economy. Just as it would be irresponsible to dismiss market conditions as irrelevant to an analysis of local successes and failures, to emphasize what Spain did and did not do to help the sugar industry become firmly established is imperative. To anticipate my argument, the plans of agricultural analysts in Puerto Rico to weather market crises invariably depended on the commitment of the mother country to build infrastructure for the sugar industry. The extent to which Spain responded, then, directly affected the success of the projects proposed.[6]

Puerto Rico's social organization reflected the changes in the relationship between metropolis and colony, too. The dominant classes came to be readily identified by their participation in colonial institutions: merchants, landowners, government officials, urban professionals, military men. These groups, however, were generally content to promote the status quo on the island and, consequently, Puerto Rico's association with Spain. They constituted a force only when they joined their efforts to secure their own position vis-à-vis that of those they controlled: urban artisans, domestic servants, rural laborers, peasants, slaves. Just as the elites of Latin American republics allied themselves to political power groups that promised to safeguard their interests, the dominant classes of Puerto Rico supported—quite literally—the relationship with Spain wholeheartedly. As they failed to establish more-than-immediate goals, they limited severely their chances of be-coming a powerful force in the decision-making process at the top level. In short, Puerto Rico's elite not only reflected but also made possible the subordination of its class interests by Spain.[7]

At the bottom of the social scale, the oppressed had not defined their interests vis-à-vis those of the oppressor either. In the urban cen-ters, artisans and domestic servants provided necessary services for city dwellers—a rising professional class, the securely established merchant group, and rural landed gentry with urban residences. In the rural areas, slaves and full-time *jornaleros* (day laborers) found themselves subjected to the demands of production for export, while the *jíbaros* (peasants) and others with access to land tilled the soil for subsistence purposes and for local markets. Racial differences became blurred in both urban and rural areas as the number of whites roughly equaled the number of nonwhites. The Reglamento de Jornaleros of 1849, a semicoerced wage labor system, effectively eliminated social distinc-tions in the rural areas as it provided for free men the same harsh treatment afforded slaves. Given these conditions, the lower strata of Puerto Rican society could hardly have articulated their interests in a coherent manner. Not having yet had the opportunity to face the enemy squarely, these groups remained classes-in-the-making for most of the nineteenth century.[8]

Puerto Rican historians have been fond of speculating on the causes for evident conflict between social groups. They tend to link political activism, economic activity, and national origins with the same enthu-siasm that contemporaries did in the nineteenth century. Many schol-ars explain social divisions as the result both of the marked Spanish immigrant presence among merchants, allied inextricably to the Span-ish cause on the island as a function of their occupation, and of the supposed predominance of the native-born among landowners, who favored autonomy in economic and social matters as a result of their activity. More recently, María Isabel Bonnín Orozco has reiterated the point by presenting Ponce merchants as a dominant social group through its control of credit and as an obstacle to economic progress through its monopoly of the limited currency that circulated on the island. Her conclusions are confirmed by Pedro San Miguel, who demonstrates convincingly that Vega Baja immigrant planters, who had been previously tied to commerce, had more resources to invest in technology than did those born on the island, whose previous experience was more often in land. In Lares and Yauco, Laird Bergad highlights the resentment of local coffee planters, small traders, and coffee pickers against "a powerful immigrant merchant class" as underlying the Grito de Lares, Puerto Rico's failed attempt at gaining its independence in 1868.[9]

The identification of peninsular merchants with conservative politics and native-born landowners with the Liberal party has been challenged. Astrid Cubano found in Arecibo plenty of conservative landowners and Liberal merchants. She established convincingly, moreover, the existence of a marriage of convenience between planters and Spanish authorities. Other studies have regarded the division between planters and merchants as artificial. Cruz Ortiz Cuadra ignores the dichotomy altogether and treats Humacao's merchants and landowners indiscriminately as businesspeople who shift the focus of their attention according to circumstances. These interpretations are consonant with my contention that both planters and merchants had much to gain by the maintenance of the status quo. They also implicitly recognize that other groups were dominant in Puerto Rico's political, economic, and social life.[10]

Puerto Rico, to repeat, took a sharp turn to join the ranks of exploitation colonies during the nineteenth century. A culmination perhaps of limited growth under Spain's neglectful wing in the previous century, the island's new course nevertheless demanded increased attention. The organization of labor and the large-scale production of sugar for the international market became the concern of the local elite and of the metropolitan government. The island's ad hoc society, as that of many plantation areas, changed only when self-preservation required it. Metropolitan concerns and island politics narrowed to the maintenance of stability, that is, of the economic and social status quo.[11]

The sugar industry, the subject of this work, embodied the principal features of Puerto Rico's redefined status. From the early 1800s until the midcentury crisis, Puerto Rico gained recognition as the world's second largest producer of sugar. The land dedicated to cane cultivation increased fivefold from 1830 to 1860. Production rose from 19,554 *quintales* (one *quintal* equals 100 pounds) in 1814 to 419,897 quintales in 1834. The value of sugar exports reached three million *pesos* (one *peso* is roughly equal to a U.S. dollar) in the 1840s. As the century progressed, Puerto Rico sent more and more of its sugar to the United States for processing. Spain, of course, enjoyed the benefits of increased trade indirectly by collecting export taxes and customs duties.[12]

But the economic premises of export production for the commodities market began to exert their negative influence by midcentury. Spain's gradual neglect of the island, or rather its primary interest in preserving its own fiscal, political, and economic well-being, made evident to Puerto Rican cane planters the dangers of monoculture for export. Lower prices, higher taxes, decreases in labor and capital, and scant protection alarmed sugar producers. The industry was not prepared to sustain the pattern of growth of earlier decades in the face of pure competition in the international market.[13]

The interaction of social forces within the sugar industry shaped and was shaped by the patterns of society at large. Merchants and planters worked together, at opposite ends, to place agricultural commodities in international markets in exchange for manufactured goods not available in the colony. But their business partnership remained unequal and laden with uncertainty. Landowners could only borrow money from merchants to finance their operations and import expensive machinery at high interest rates, while merchants, dependent on overseas market conditions, hoped for a high return on investment in sugar exports and imported consumer goods to compensate for perceived risks.

The relationship of planters and laborers rested on similar predicaments: each depended on the other, but at different levels and intensities. Workers tilled the soil, cut the cane, and processed it to support their families, but they also stayed home to tend their gardens and socialize with friends. Planters complained bitterly about the irregular patterns of attendance of their workers and used every means, short of good wages, to attract them to the workplace. From the perspective of the rural working population, the Reglamento de Jornaleros appeared abusive in its demands. As the abolition of slavery approached inevitably, planters found the reglamento also ineffective in providing them with the labor they required. The microcosm of sugar reflected the patterns of society at large: planters and merchants, landowners and laborers had ill-defined objectives in the context of mutual dependence and in the absence of clear-cut conflict.[14]

Because of the importance of the sugar industry on the island's economy and the dominant position of planters in Puerto Rican society, it is not surprising that politics after 1870 quickly focused on the plight of agriculturalists, especially the cane planters. Progressive leaders denounced the use of slaves and deplored the absence of banks for agricultural credit, blaming Spain for the island's backwardness. As factors that would foster the island's development, they called for the establishment of modern methods in the cultivation process and the introduction of sophisticated machinery for the manufacture of sugar. The advocates of progress, identified with political and economic liberalism as they were, directed their efforts to providing Puerto Rico with the elements necessary to compete on an equal footing with modern industrial nations.

The *hacienda*, the dominant socioeconomic unit of the period, was quite ready to modernize. The various characterizations of nineteenth-century sugar estates that circulate today promote this view. Sidney W. Mintz, although labeling haciendas "capitalistic," emphasizes their traditionalist features: forced labor, few technological improvements, face-to-face contact between workers and owner, and even a nonprofit orientation on the part of the planter. José Curet presents an even more static picture, as he emphasizes the "self-sufficiency" of sugar estates, almost as if they existed in isolation and operated independently of outside forces. Even Eugenio Fernández Méndez, who argues for the existence of "agrarian capitalism" on the island in the nineteenth century, makes reference to the seigneurial life-style of the sugar lords. The general consensus among historians, as well as among contemporaries, was that the island's sugar industry could use some reorganization.[15]

Planters themselves saw their business units as backward. They longed to produce more efficiently and would have willingly exchanged the seigneurial life-style for industrial advances. Many accepted the inevitable transition to a system of wage labor and aggressively fought for a larger degree of control in the commercial and political affairs of the island. The efforts of late-century activists reflected a general shift in the mood of island planters as well.[16]

The institutionalization of patterns of capitalist production, as defined by agricultural analysts and described fully below, appeared to offer the solution to the crisis in the sugar industry. The rational exploitation of the soil, the establishment of technological innovations, and the transition to wage labor represented the first steps toward joining the ranks of industrial nations. With centralization—the separation of the agricultural from the manufacturing aspects of sugar production—came modernity and, by extension, economic success. Capitalism, then, encompassed all of the internal changes necessary to save Puerto Rico from crisis and thus became the medicine for all economic ills.[17]

Yet advocates of change misjudged the importance of some of their proposals. As will be demonstrated in the following chapter, the internal reorganization of the sugar industry was not by itself enough to weather the crisis faced by sugar planters. The unpredictability of the market threatened to victimize commodities producers permanently. What was worse, improving the quality of Puerto Rican sugar, as agricultural analysts recommended, might only close the doors of U.S. refineries on island planters without any assurances of alternative markets. The success of these plans, moreover, necessitated Spain's commitment to build infrastructure—transportation and communications networks—as well as to provide the financial apparatus that would sustain the ambitious projects proposed and the muscle to negotiate better terms of exchange with Puerto Rico's trading partners. Such plans were a far cry, then, from providing what the appeals for change suggested: the solution to the sugar industry's crisis.

2

The Concept of
Centralization

Land, Labor, and Capital

The establishment of sugar factories (centrales) appeared in Puerto
Rico after 1870 as the embodiment of urgently needed change. The
midcentury crisis, set off by a decline in sugar prices after the introduction in the world market of subsidized beet sugar and prolonged
by the failure to transform the sugar industry, had long suggested the
need for alternative courses of action. The abolition of slavery in 1873
and the transition to wage labor through a three-year apprenticeship
period forcefully prescribed transformations of deeply rooted institutions. Island leaders mobilized their resources to publicize learned local and imported opinions on the solutions to the crisis. Translating
their vision of a perfect order into a broadly defined capitalism, they
published newspaper articles, debated current issues, and printed agricultural manuals and journals.

The men who took up the cause of agricultural reform were an as-
sorted lot. I refer to them as a "group"—of reformers, of progressive
thinkers, of agricultural analysts—because they collectively kept alive
the public discussion of critical issues. Their commitment to expose
the situation in the agricultural areas and to propose necessary changes
might even suggest a concerted effort. But their individual ideas cannot be considered part of a coherent whole. Some of them dedicated
all their energies to researching and writing on only one aspect of a
larger situation—say, the limited amount of money in circulation as a

problem that affected landowners. Others, even when they took up several related issues at once, failed to comment on their cumulative effect. Although a good number openly defended the Liberal party program, not all of them did. Their discourse, then, varied greatly in form and in content.

Their connections to leading *hacendados* are also tenuous. Because of their participation in colonial institutions, these government officials, lawyers, and academics doubtless had frequent social contact with planters and merchants involved in the agricultural export business. The McCormick family name, for example, appears frequently in newspapers of the period as well as on the documentation relating to the loans necessary to establish Central San Vicente, the object of this study. Francisco del Valle Atiles and Salvador Brau, as active members of the Liberal party, must have on more than one occasion exchanged views with Julián Blanco, the right-hand man of Central San Vicente's owner and a veteran power broker. Apart from these speculative insights, though, nothing suggests that reformers had monolithic goals or that their ties with the landowning elite could be used to serve them.

It is simply impossible—and it would be incorrect—to reconcile the views of agricultural analysts into an unequivocal line of reasoning and pattern of opinion. These men, as suggested above, were likely to write from the perspective of their field or occupation, that is, as the sociologists, economists, agronomists, planters, and government officials that they were. In addition, one can seldom find an argument that can be traced to a previous alliance with a particular planter based on personal considerations or mutual interest. But in order to clarify a series of perceptions on the issues debated, I have grouped similar lines of thought when independently developed by several authors. I have specifically cited the sources of information and opinion in each case.[1]

Perhaps because of its composition, this motley group failed to acknowledge that a large part of the problem that occupied their attention was outside their control. Obsessed with upgrading Puerto Rico's economy to the advanced levels of those of industrial nations, they spoke of using land more rationally, investing in modern technology, and employing skilled salaried laborers. Puerto Rico, they argued, should adopt more modern, capitalist, methods of production. They did not stress sufficiently, however, that certain infrastructural changes were also in order—for example, banks, roads, and communications networks—all of which depended on Spain's initiative and good will. Even more important, they overlooked the gigantic unknown that was the market. Because of their incomplete assessment of the situation and their faulty ordering of priorities, the concept of centralization in the sugar industry ultimately became meaningless to Puerto Rico's future development.

Description of Conditions in the Agricultural Areas

Everyone in 1870 agreed that Puerto Rico's agricultural industry still suffered the consequences of the precipitous decline in sugar prices. The difficulties encountered after 1850 shook the foundations of many early sugar establishments and threatened to displace those hacendados unable or unwilling to meet the demands of a new age of competition. Borrowing capital to purchase equipment proved onerous for small landowners. Moreover, the Reglamento de Jornaleros of 1849, established to counteract the effects of abolishing the slave trade, remained ineffective in providing a steady, disciplined, and abundant work force.[2]

To be sure, some planters withstood the hard times by partially mechanizing existing units of production and enlarging their work forces. More efficient mills, widespread use of wage laborers, more intense exploitation of slaves, and increased planted acreage resulted in greater production. Others developed creative combinations of economic activities on their estates to diffuse the shock: producing molasses and renting lands as pasture, for example, or buying even more land to increase cultivation and to use existing trees as fuel for machinery. The solutions adopted resulted in neither a new understanding of technology nor a different organization of labor. Most haciendas offset the fall in prices by increasing output without changing the basic structures of production. The efforts of those fortunate enough to weather the crisis resulted in the large-scale reproduction of the hacienda system and left untouched traditional patterns of cane cultivation and sugar manufacturing.[3]

In the eyes of the late-century reformers, this dire state of affairs threatened the very existence of the sugar industry. The price of sugar had fallen to around two cents per pound, compared to 15 cents in 1815 and five cents on the average in the 1840s.[4] Output fluctuated considerably: 100,000 tons were produced in 1870, 83,000 in 1878; from a record 170,000 tons in 1879, the count fell to 60,000 tons in 1880.[5] The number of active haciendas fell from nearly 1,550 in the 1820s, to 550 in 1860, to around 450 in 1888. In 1870, most of these depended on oxen to grind the cane and on open kettles to ferment the juice; steam engines and vacuum pans seldom constituted an element of Puerto Rican haciendas. Sucrose yield remained at only 5 percent, when the sucrose content of cane was known to be as high as 17 to 18 percent.[6]

These figures were not so alarming, however, when compared to those for the sister colony, Cuba. Market prices for the sugars produced there were comparable to those obtained for Puerto Rican sugars. True, the best grade sugar in Cuba, Derosne evaporator white, obtained an average price in 1859 of just over seven cents per pound. But the price of standard muscovado, the sugar commonly produced in Puerto Rico, stood at three cents at that early date, not far from the two cents per pound that reformers complained about in the 1870s. Annual tonnage of sugar in Cuba, although much larger than Puerto Rico's, showed variations similar to those of its smaller sister island: records for the same years indicate 726,000 tons were produced in 1870, 533,000 in 1878, 670,000 in 1879, and 530,000 in 1880.[7] The number of production units there—called *ingenios* for the milling machinery they held—fell just as markedly throughout the century.[8] And even though 70 percent of Cuba's mills had steam engines as early as 1863, both islands obtained equally low figures for yield and productivity, the true measures of efficiency. Depending on the type of mill, a sucrose yield of 5 to 6 percent of the weight of the cane was considered high in Cuba. Whereas Puerto Rican planters produced on the average 3,000 to 3,500 pounds of sugar per acre of cane planted, the most productive mill in Cuba obtained only 4,071 pounds per acre.[9] Either because they ignored these facts or because the facts appeared detrimental to their cause, reformers never acknowledged that Puerto Rico's sugar industry fared relatively well under adverse circumstances.

Agricultural analysts were adamant in their conviction that the situation called for drastic change. As far as they were concerned, circumstances such as external conditions and recent trends had to be separated from the organizational structure of the sugar industry and the solidity, or lack thereof, of its internal base. The turn of events had spoken loudly enough. Puerto Rican cane planters had initially met with success because of the juncture of high prices, more external markets, and favorable legislation.[10] But the hacendados had enjoyed this prosperity only as long as circumstances remained favorable. By midcentury, Puerto Rico lost the favor of the mother country, and subsidized European beet, U.S. beet, and Cuban cane sugar came to dominate the market. Seeing that Puerto Rico's sugar industry could not stand up to more competitive producers, reformers concluded that only internal reorganization would strengthen it against external conditions. The alternative to depending on circumstances for economic growth was to restructure the sugar industry to increase productivity and reduce costs.

That late nineteenth-century social reformers should have reached this conclusion is not surprising. The influence of European positivism on the patterns of thought of island leaders is clearly evident. The infallibility of the rational was a major component of the positivist world view, as it was of these reformers' plans. The conviction of positivists that human beings could understand, manipulate, and ultimately control the variables that affected their existence found a reflection in the belief of reformers that their analysis of the situation and the solutions they proposed were correct. The wide circulation of these postulates as a body of thought reinforced reformers' notions of what constituted order and progress.[11]

The assessment of the situation, unfortunately, was faulty. True, Puerto Rico's sugar industry could have used a complete overhaul. Island planters had undoubtedly become accustomed to producing inefficiently when the price of sugar was high, land and machinery cheap, and slaves readily available. But the reorganization of production would not by itself automatically translate into a safeguard against future losses. Revamping communications and transportation networks could well have been listed as a prerequisite, given the ambitious marketing plans progressive thinkers had for the high quality sugar they hoped Puerto Rico would produce. The absence of credit institutions for investment capital, they should have complained more forcefully, was also a hindrance to their projects.

Furthermore, agricultural analysts failed to recognize that the biggest enemy of sugar producers was the market, which dictated prices and determined the amounts sold with no regard to the industry's internal changes. To complicate matters, reformers insisted on producing refined sugar (thus alienating Puerto Rico's largest buyer, the United States, which required the raw product) and ignored altogether the possibilities of negotiating better terms of trade via Spain. More efficient production could perhaps have put off the devastating effects of violent market fluctuations, but it left untouched many of the ailments of Puerto Rico's sugar economy.

Contemporaries did not possess the hindsight to make these evaluations. Caught up as they were with the decline of agriculture, reformers listed the ills that Puerto Rico's sugar industry suffered without understanding their relative weight, mutual effect, and cumulative impact. Unavailability of capital, instability of the work force, declining production, decreasing prices of sugar, rising export duties, unfavorable Spanish protectionist policies, and Cuban competition were all issues debated separately from 1870 on.[12] Influenced as they were by the idea of progress that underlay positivist philosophy, they were convinced that the solution to these problems was within their reach. A more thorough analysis would have revealed the futility of their efforts.

The Issue of Land

The critics of rural production methods selected as their first target the routinism with which agriculturalists performed their tasks. Convinced as many were that sugar constituted "the axis of the island's wealth and the pivot on which rested and depended the province's contribution to the government's treasury," one writer argued that Puerto Rican planters did not even produce half as much as the fertility of the soil warranted; their canes yielded less than a third of the juice they contained. In an attempt to explain this, he recalled the isolation in which farmers "vegetated," a factor that prevented them from transcending the limitations imposed by existing conditions and from aspiring to more ambitious goals. Another author singled out wasteful practices as the reason for Puerto Rico's inability to withstand the competition of efficient U.S. production at lower costs.[13] Writers accused planters of appropriating fertile lands from the jíbaros, only to carry out extensive cultivation in an irresponsible manner.[14] Agricultural experts argued that their obsession with exploiting the soil without improving it had resulted in depreciation, depopulation, and uncertainty.[15] This type of discourse built itself around, and constantly made reference to, Puerto Rico's alleged ability to produce better quality sugar at lower cost than any other country.[16] The first goal to be achieved, then, was a more rational exploitation of its rich, but undeveloped land.

Just as now, many held that Puerto Rico did not take full advantage of its fertile soil. Geographic conditions on the island, the smallest of the Greater Antilles, support such a position. Fifty sizable rivers flow from the mountainous interior to form valleys on all four coasts. Twenty-five percent of the 3,500-square-mile land surface is level, 40 percent is occupied by mountains, and 35 percent is hilly. Although fertile valleys are especially characteristic of the North, agricultural activity has been carried out successfully in the drier southern coast and in the mountains. Favored by a mild climate and abundant rainfall year-round, a variety of crops—beans, citrus fruits, coffee, corn, rice, roots, sugar, tobacco, vegetables—grow easily. The percentage of total land area under cultivation, most of it dedicated to export crops, increased only minimally throughout the nineteenth century: 6 percent in 1830 and only 14 percent as late as 1897.[17] Since the land seemed to have so much potential, contemporaries found its inefficient use especially objectionable.

These highly critical views would quickly transform themselves into a glorification of science. Comparing the scientific manufacture of sugar in the factory to the "making" of cane in the fields, agricultural planners urged farmers to adopt more rational methods of cultivation. The proper use of fertilizers and pesticides, for example, became a factor in the formula for success.[18] Agriculture, then, became a science: the prosperity of the island began to be viewed as depending solely on human endeavor, on the foresight and know-how of the farmer.[19]

These new attitudes logically fanned out to include the dissemination of scientific knowledge. The institution of practical schools, where industrious men would share their experiences in the cultivation of the soil, was only one element in this effort. Journals spread news regarding government policies, mechanical innovations, and upcoming events, and promoted agricultural interests in editorials and critical analyses of current issues. Some authors advocated the establishment of agricultural associations, as well as of experimental and model field stations for conducting scientific inquiries, as a means to acquire more exact agricultural knowledge. Others considered the need to train hired hands important; the ignorance of jornaleros could negatively affect the progress that could be achieved using the latest developments.[20]

Such views and proposals for action no doubt attempted to incorporate the ideals of order and progress into Puerto Rico's economic future. In line with the optimism and confidence in science that characterized positivist philosophy, they emphasized the advantages that would result from rational applications of science to production. As did other Latin American reformers, progressive leaders in Puerto Rico considered the practical formulation of intellectual concerns to be the most productive of all human activities. The application of scientific investigation reduced the time and cost, and improved the quality, of production.[21]

In the minds of these self-proclaimed reformers, then, the separation of the cultivation of cane from the process of manufacturing sugar became a rational objective.[22] Success was as predetermined as for a mathematical formula: since both required specialization, once the two processes were separated, farmers could obtain greater savings, produce better-quality goods, and use labor more efficiently.[23] Critics condemned the practice of growing cane and making sugar in the same hacienda precisely because they believed that resources had to be concentrated on only one activity.[24] If cane growers paid more attention to their land and its products, it followed, they would be well under way toward attacking one of the basic problems of agricultural life on the island.

Most observers of the rural environment were convinced that planters carried out the exploitation of the soil in a highly irregular manner. This general agreement on the issue made the ideal of scientific progress an appropriate mold within which reformers could cast their arguments. They insisted on replacing traditional methods of cultivation with the advanced notion of specialization by dividing work into field and factory activities. They hoped these modern concepts of land management and new cultivation techniques would transform a basically traditional economy and society.

The Labor Force

Extending their preoccupations to other factors, agricultural planners focused on the organization of the labor force as an important aspect of the weaknesses of the sugar industry. The debate turned on the alleged difficulty planters faced in obtaining a steady supply of workers after the abolition of the slave trade and the failure of the *libreta* system. Contemporary writers usually portrayed the rural population as "lazy," "immoral," and "given to gambling," and explained or justified these imputations in varied and often contradictory ways.[25] Proposals for solutions went from regeneration through limited educational programs for the lower classes to strict control through official mechanisms.

Proclivity to idleness was the most common complaint about the rural worker. Most observers agreed that the laborer had no love of work or concept of duty and frequently conspired against the interests of the planter. Unreliable when he signed a contract to perform certain services, he worked only to cover his most basic needs (and a few whims) and interrupted his labors soon afterwards. Not used to regular work, the field laborer often ignored criticism from above and performed tasks incorrectly on purpose. Planters often complained of having to redo entire projects because workers had been careless. The unreliability of the work performed made labor that should have been considered cheap by any standard a source of loss for the hacendado.[26]

The landed elite also worried about gambling and sexual promiscuity among the rural population. Contemporaries reported that the rural worker frequently spent his daily wage of 50 to 63 cents in drink and cockfights at the local gathering place. They believed the absence of family and social responsibilities aggravated the situation; supposedly a man's "errant existence" explained his "immoral behavior." Other contributing factors were "the instability of settlements" and "the moral laxity" of priests in the rural areas.[27]

These impressions, though at first glance exaggerated, doubtless resulted from a real clash between preindustrial workers and landowners in need of their services. The push to increase production in the absence of modern industrial methods required either a larger labor force or a more intense labor effort. Rural workers with ready access to land, either in an estate or in some distant backland, were certainly not prepared to till somebody else's soil unless forced to do so. When they were so forced, under the *régimen de libretas*, they preserved their nominal freedom by carrying on as usual: working at the customary pace, deciding when to take the day off, meeting friends informally, and ignoring social mandates imposed from above. Hacendados, of course, must have found much of this behavior objectionable. Reformers, given their fixed views of a sound social order, rushed to correct it.

When they engaged in a more profound analysis, the very proponents of this negative picture of the Puerto Rican rural population felt compelled to qualify it in various ways. The most rudimentary explanation for the rural worker's sluggishness was heredity. The Andalusian conquerors that populated the island, the argument went, had been precisely those who sought an easy life and avoided the harsh existence awaiting them in the rest of America. Other exponents of this view went further and attributed certain qualities of the rural population to the three racial groups that mixed on the island: the Taíno had provided the Puerto Rican with his characteristic indolence, taciturnity, lack of enthusiasm, and hospitable nature; the African, with physical endurance, sensuality, superstition, and fatalism; the Spaniard gave him the grave temper and pride of the gentleman, a festive humor, austere devotion, perseverance in adversity, love for his country, and an independent nature.[28] The heritage theory, then, negated the possibility of "improvement" among the rural workers through material incentives, as it suggested that their habits were inherent to their nature. It suggested that the only way to get the rural population to work was through force.

A second view explained the rural population's propensity to idleness as a function of the environment. A visitor insisted, for example, that the bounty of nature on the island allowed its inhabitants to "exist"—that is, to live—without the necessity to work. The ease with which manioc grows and pigs multiply in Puerto Rico's mountains provided ample evidence for this axiom. Others extended the argument and singled out access to that nature (land) as the condition that determined whether an individual would have to work for pay or not. Clearly, wide differences separated the jornalero who lived in town or close to a hacienda and the peasant who inhabited distant neighborhoods. The latter had the choice of performing other economic activities, like growing crops or raising animals on his own or somebody else's unclaimed piece of land, and worked irregularly on an hacendado's property.

The differences between individuals who operated in a natural economy and those who sold their force of labor as a commodity were obviously not lost on island reformers. So ingrained was their belief in a direct correlation between working for pay and the need to do so that they were convinced that jornaleros developed particular "vices" when unemployed. Jíbaros, on the other hand, were "blessed with health and high moral standards" because, one supposes, their needs were always met by their natural surroundings.[29] The notion that the environment determined the rural population's proclivity to work must have led directly to the conviction that if access to land was curtailed, more people would seek work in the haciendas.

The laid-back attitude of rural folk was also explained as a human reaction to particular developments in the island's social, economic, and political life. The jíbaro commonly abandoned his duties, this view claimed, because he found no stimulus in a system where getting ahead depended not on hard work but on the protection of a patron, personal contacts, and family connections. The experience of slavery, this group further contended, had led to the antithesis of forced labor; rural ex-slaves had reacted to abolition by refusing to work.[30] A bit more progressive in that it recognized the connections between what were perceived as social ills and the way society was organized, this argument suggested the possibility of reform through a regeneration of society.

A related current in the analysis of the alleged lackadaisical nature of workers challenged the authority of the propertied to pass judgment on the rural population. Public opinion, this minority charged, only concerned itself with indolence when the accused appeared to pose a material or immediate threat to the establishment. The double standard was obvious to them: concern over economic inactivity only applied to poor jornaleros and artisans, and not to the wealthy who lived off rents and did not work. The rich, they concluded, were dissipated and set poor examples of social obligation; they were in no position to criticize.[31] As did the immediately preceding view, this one also tended toward self-criticism. The solution to "the labor problem" lay not with the rural worker but with society itself.

Finally, a few openly denied that the rural worker was lazy. One essayist cited production statistics, and the output attributed to both slaves and wage laborers during the sugar boom, as examples of the hardworking nature of the Puerto Rican. Some in this group held the advanced notion that workers were not lazy or scarce when they were paid well, basing their opinion on the correlation that existed between work to be performed, wages offered, and labor available. The rewards for work continued to be so limited in Puerto Rico, one argued, that it mattered little to the average *peón* whether or not he had a job. The same author alleged that if wages significantly increased, hordes of immigrants would pour in from the neighboring islands.[32]

The notion that workers were willing to work if conditions were appropriate must have pleased reformers. Surely it was more appealing than the "lazy-by-nature" argument, whose only solution was the not very modern one of enslaving the rural population. Artificially limiting the rural population's access to land also ran counter to the idea of free labor; reformers would have wanted wage workers to be the independent agents who sought the most favorable conditions that classical economists often described. Reforming society was simply not feasible. It was much more convenient and modern to provide incentives in the form of high wages, material rewards for special skills, opportunities for advancement, and other labor organization devices of the industrial system.

Most observers readily accepted the common accusations against the worker regarding gambling and promiscuity, but a few examined the social contexts that made these traits manifest. One thorough analyst pointed an accusatory finger at the "responsible" classes, the owners of stores, and official authorities themselves for making available to the worker opportunities to make money through gambling without having to work. These conditions constituted a tacit encouragement and indirectly lured many to indulge in gambling. Some boldly stated that all human beings, workers and landowners alike, were responsible for their own actions; what one wished to do with one's own money should be nobody else's business, especially when everybody participated in gambling activities.[33]

The prevalence of concubinage became harder to justify, and writers resorted to climatic and historical considerations when advancing their arguments. Rural folk were given to living outside of marriage ties, they explained, because of the (sensual) tropical heat and the frailty of their (moral) constitutions. Manuals listed malnutrition and an aberrant sense of religion as factors possibly accentuating this inclination. In addition, writers argued, an isolated existence in the mountains drove many to seek sexual companionship, as corrupt life-styles imported from nearby urban centers influenced their inclinations. The authors of these pieces, however, exempted rural women from their condemnation, since they would frequently "wait for their wandering men as faithfully as if they were bound by the sacrament of marriage."[34]

Explanations for the rural population's propensity to gambling and sex suggest a desire to regulate the lower ranks of society according to ideal norms. It is curious that only rural folk were offered guidance with respect to the benefits of an orderly life. As reformers themselves made clear, nobody recommended to wealthy gamblers that they mend their ways. Even more telling, the probability that the upper class also neglected to keep their vows of fidelity was not even considered. The emphasis, in any case, lay on making the worker take an interest in settling down and adopting family responsibilities. If such values could be instilled in the rural population, hacendados would enjoy the benefits of a steadier work force.

Sincere as they were, efforts to understand the underlying causes for the characteristic behavior of the rural working population were framed by inflexible moral definitions of "the good society." Explanations pretended to be modern, scientific, rational, and objective. The most advanced attitudes placed a high value on justice, morality, orderliness, and equality. The result could only be a self-righteous campaign for the betterment of society based on the cooperation of all social groups— that is to say, for the economic progress of the island through the imposition of the touted mores of one group upon another to produce a disciplined working class.

As part of this movement, reformers advocated education to give the rural population the means for self-improvement, "awakening in the student new energies, re-directing his feelings, will, ideals, aspirations, morality, and character." They believed that, because of the jíbaro's alleged docility, careful tutelage would be enough to bring him onto the path of "civilization." Taking into consideration the island's heavy racial intermixing, some reformers thought it best to build on the present generation in order to develop a "race" adapted to the demands of climate and environment: the black population would be "fused into the superior (white) race that [would absorb] it and [would be modified] by it in turn." Under the sound influence of a progressive education, they concluded, Puerto Rican society could find material, intellectual, and moral conditions for its existence without having to look up to the neighboring Anglo-Saxon community.[35]

The advantages to be obtained from the tutelage of rural folk were numerous. If trained in agricultural endeavors, they could help eradicate the routinism prevalent in the island's fields and diversify crops for subsistence purposes. Steered away from superstition, they would begin to understand that prayer and success in gambling had no connection and would abandon wagering. Once instructed in sanitary and preventive medical practices, the jíbaro would be alerted to the importance of continuing his pursuit of "good habits and sound moral principles," which "must precede and accompany material progress."[36] A broad understanding of what education should be for the rural population permitted nineteenth-century reformers to convince themselves that the solutions to the most basic problems facing the island's agricultural sector were at hand.

One analyst gave special attention to the education of the 36 percent female "proletarian" population, which remained at a standstill because of lack of resources and traditional attitudes toward gender. Reformers generally recommended that Puerto Rico adopt the model developed in the United States, establishing mixed schools with female teachers ("even black ones") instead of all-male schools.[37] This suggestion should not be construed as one that implied equality of the sexes. Quite the contrary, the ideal, plainly stated, was that a woman's instincts as wife and mother be accentuated by instruction. Marital and family stability, achieved through education, would contribute to the island's intellectual development. Teaching women how to read became an instrument for achieving moral rectitude and, by extension, social order.

Side by side with education, religion played an important role in presenting jornaleros with the reformers' vision of their role in the regeneration of society. Pamphlets defined life on this earth as an "inescapable reality" for workers; suffering and work, considered essential for human beings to carry out their mission on earth and an obligation imposed by God himself, bound them in this world. Idealizing country life and activity, this view stressed that happiness and peace of mind could be achieved as one carried out one's duty. It equated an idle existence with poison in one's soul, and held that only the worker with a pure heart and good intentions would receive God's blessing—in addition to the daily wage earned from an employer. It proclaimed, in short, that "to work was to produce, and to produce was to become God's partner."[38]

Some basic tenets of the Catholic Church became useful in presenting the worker with a view of his role in life that coincidentally furthered the interests of his employer. The notion that human beings owed God respect and veneration as creator of all things fit with the passive function of prayer (thanking God for his blessings) and discouraged asking him for favors. The understanding of this world as a valley of tears condemned material wealth as an end; one's actions should be directed toward attaining the true gifts of faith, hope, and love. The jornalero, in short, had no right to complain about his lot, since the soul of the poorest person could achieve greatness by the power of virtuous behavior and enjoy pure happiness through the experience of being loved by God.[39]

A series of recommendations pretended to integrate the worker into a mainstream vision of what was desirable. In connection with family life, pamphlets advised the jornalero to marry so as to have the steady guidance of a woman, save on his daily expenses, and avoid worldly dangers and self-inflicted temptations such as depravity and incest. These writings exhorted poor heads-of-household to work incessantly, save continuously, and make careful plans as to their future needs, since work, they warned, would not always be available. In addition, pamphlets urged workers not to acquire habits that might augment their daily expenditures.[40]

Planters had a role to play in helping the worker adapt to the norms established by reformers' plans for the rural population's civic and religious rehabilitation. Reformers called on "the respectable classes" (property holders in general and, more specifically, landowners) to foster, protect, and supervise cooperative organizations among workers. Employers were to participate directly in the regeneration of the worker, since they had more contact with the laborers and were most affected by their patterns of behavior. Planters were requested not to abuse their authority and to set aside a day for rest, since "incessant work could lead the worker to abandon godly ways" and could affect negatively the interests of hacendados. The authors of these plans believed that as hacendados acted as fatherly figures, presenting themselves as "models of virtue," they would receive God's blessing and win humanity's appreciation.[41]

In the minds of these reformers, appealing to both worker and landowner resolved the conflict between capital and labor. In their own words, class conflict had its origin in the relationship between wages and needs: if remuneration for the work performed proved inadequate, the worker would be forced into a miserable existence and would always be dissatisfied. If rewards happened to be excessive, however, wealth acquired by hard work would soon be dissipated and labor would become erratic. They thought it fortunate that human beings had an insatiable nature, so the poor had no choice but to work to cover their basic needs, and the rich, to increase their luxuries.[42] Assured that their needs were covered, both rich and poor would be satisfied with their situation.

Just to make sure there were no misunderstandings, the premises on which this set of notions rested were carefully stated. The doctrine of rights, reformers would argue, fostered hatred and worldly pleasures. They preferred to consolidate the concepts of freedom and duty into one ideal, and so they held that the freedom of workers to dispose of their labor—their only property—constituted their wealth, or capital, and that the decision to work remained their duty. Thus, there were no exploiters and exploited on the island. Once worker-capitalist cooperation became a reality, they hoped, all society would benefit, since, as they rightly pointed out, the progress of each class depended on the other. The argument rested, then, on the conviction that as capitalists enriched themselves, they also contributed to improving the level of life generally and to reducing inequality.[43]

Reformist views with respect to education and religion loudly proclaimed interclass harmony based on a self-imposed sense of duty to be developed through the inculcation of high moral standards. These efforts, their proponents were convinced, aimed at producing a situation agreeable and beneficial to all. But progress as defined by reformers was predicated on the establishment of a utopic order. Stripped of its convoluted verbiage, this view merely proposed the adoption of an upper-class vision of society. For the rural population to participate in the progress to come, then, the values and interests of the economically powerful would have to be effectively served first. Religion and education, both instruments of this transfer of mentality, performed the same function: they prepared the rural population for upper-class economic objectives.

Other solutions openly pretended to control the rural population and depended heavily on official measures. One author, for example, defended the institution of agricultural colonies as a way of curbing the independent and free nature of the rural population. As applied in Cuba and the Philippines, the law for the establishment of these communities provided tax exemptions to landowners who followed government guidelines, making land available to a fixed number of *colonos* (agricultural tenants). Tenants would carry out specific economic activities in plots purposely located at some distance from nearby centers of population. Landowners who took advantage of these incentives were also required to grow certain crops and breed a variety of animals. The setup would make haciendas more productive units and improve the nature and behavior of the island's agricultural population through steady labor on the soil. The existence of such farming communities promised to attract others and thus raise the value of surrounding lands. If rural folk enjoyed the opportunity to work and live comfortably without incursions on their autonomy through superfluous demands, they would be bound by social obligations and directed toward thrift and hard work. Workers were thus called upon to improve their own and all of society's lot by their labor on the land, which would be considered their active contribution to the task of civilization. Incidentally, the author concluded, the establishment of rural colonies would aid the government in the collection of taxes, an ineluctable social responsibility.[44]

In many ways, debates over the "rural population problem" permitted nineteenth-century reformers to air freely their views regarding Puerto Rico's future economic organization. No doubt their projections revolved around transforming the rural population into a proletariat; the freedom of the self-sufficient was offensive to their economic interests. At the same time, they sought to "improve" rural folk by the most insistent paternalism: a patronizing religion and education. Most probably, they were confused as to how "modernization" would take place. Obsessed with economic progress and social order, they pretended that Puerto Rico could fit into a capitalist mold overnight.

The Problem of Capital

The most serious obstacle to reformers' plans ended up being, ironically enough, the absence of investment capital, often expressed simply as "the lack of capital" resulting from the farmer's difficulty in obtaining cash advances for the successful completion of the agricultural cycle. The problem was less access to money than the terms under which planters borrowed investment capital. Agricultural credit throughout the nineteenth century was, in fact, readily available. Plenty of merchants were willing to provide the money needed for the cultivation of a given crop. These loans, however, quickly proved a burden to the producer and an easy profit for the *refaccionista*, or factor. They were generally short-term loans for a period of six months to a year and accrued interest at a rate of 12 to 18 percent per year. Merchants usually provided warehousing facilities and marketing arrangements, charging a commission of around 2.5 percent of the total value of the product and requiring borrowers to sell their product through them. Planters had little choice but to accept these harsh terms: in order to obtain the money needed to begin the agricultural cycle, they had to pay creditors for the risk connected with "investment" during the early stages of agricultural undertakings.[45]

Intimately related to the difficulty of borrowing money was the instability produced by the absence of legal titles to land, a product of the vague definitions of land ownership and tenure inherited from earlier times and maintained throughout the nineteenth century. Four types of landowners or landholders received de facto or legal recognition: (1) those who held legal property titles to land that had been surveyed; (2) those who held titles, but whose land had not been surveyed; (3) those who, through a grant, had possession of land that had not been surveyed; and (4) those who held land in usufruct. Only landholders with property titles could place their land as guarantee on a loan; others used their slaves as collateral. Both the end of slavery and the drop in land under cultivation in hard-pressed haciendas, causing depreciation in the value of the estate, limited even more the possibilities for obtaining loans.[46]

The complex nature of the problem of agricultural credit became obvious as interested parties offered suggestions for its solution. Obtaining the capital needed to begin cultivation, some said, would remain difficult for the producer so long as he could not show favorable conditions for the success of the enterprise.[47] How the farmer was to overcome the many difficulties he encountered in securing capital at the local, metropolitan, and international levels, however, was not as clearly stated. The solution, others argued, lay not in increasing output, but rather in producing less using more efficient and exact methods.[48] But then, one author was quick to point out, how were farmers going to cover the costs of initial investment and production if they had less to sell at falling prices?

The establishment of an agricultural credit institution presented itself as an attractive alternative. Such an institution would restore the confidence of investors in international financial circles, an ambitious goal in itself. Conceivably, putting together the necessary operating capital could be achieved once the spirit of association was enhanced in both planter and merchant classes. Savings could then be invested in productive economic activities, to the benefit of the whole economy. An 1877 project advanced by a group of leading citizens went as far as suggesting that the cash compensation to be received from the government for the loss of slaves through abolition could serve as the initial capital investment of three million pesos they considered necessary to begin operations. In fact, the Banco Español de Puerto Rico was founded in 1888 through the government's issuance of one share per slave held, rather than cash, as indemnification to slaveholders. This institution, however, served as a bank for current commercial business and did not provide land and agricultural credit. As late as 1893, then, Julián Blanco, a member of the Asociación de Agricultores de Puerto-Rico, proposed the establishment of a bank for agricultural and land credit that would use native capital as its initial investment.[49]

As did many of the issues in the island's economic sphere, the problem of agricultural credit became enmeshed in political wrangles. As one author complained, "The concept . . . has been introduced by a number of Puerto Ricans, who are very Spanish, but some wealthy men, who call themselves unconditional Spaniards, have opposed it." Liberals either criticized the Spanish government for lending an ear to members of the conservative Partido Español Incondicional, dominated by powerful merchants, in its opposition to a credit institution or asked for Spain's benign interference in providing the colony with financial backing as a means to foster the introduction of foreign capital into the island. Faced with insurrection in Cuba and instability at home, the mother country did nothing.[50]

The currency issue presented similar difficulties. The Mexican coins that circulated on the island had been depreciated by close to 25 percent of their face value through constant wear. Whereas the devaluation was not evident in internal transactions, Puerto Ricans who imported expensive goods—for example, agricultural machinery—had to pay for them at internationally accepted rates. This condition exacerbated the producer's disadvantageous position in the face of merchant/exporters. Hacendados purchased imported machinery and nondurable goods at inflated prices through the same merchants who exported their agricultural products. Merchants who bought agricultural goods at "local" cost sold them profitably at foreign exchange rates.[51]

Agriculturalists, of course, generally favored proposals to change this state of affairs. Melting the silver Mexican pesos and transforming them into national currency would not only prevent the further victimization of producers at the hands of merchants but also permit planters to meet their obligations on much easier terms.[52] Such plans, however, were tainted with political considerations, and Spain, which was itself divided and busy with Cuba's insurrections, ignored the plight of the colony for most of the last three decades of the nineteenth century.

Publications of the period frequently mentioned several other impediments to the success of agricultural enterprises. They complained often, for example, about taxation. Export duties, they argued, harmed both producers and consumers of colonial products; such charges placed the producer's goods in a disadvantageous position in foreign markets that had cheaper suppliers and forced price increases for the consumer even in Spain. Journals also condemned the establishment of protective tariffs on foreign imports, which only contributed to the fiscal well-being of the mother country, prevented the colony from buying inexpensive manufactures or consumer goods, and could result in retaliation by other nations. Spain was also requested to support international efforts to abolish export subsidies on beet sugar especially, as had most European powers, so that there would be more regularity in price fluctuations. Other proposals included abolishing duties on machinery imported into the island, establishing a free trade zone to encourage the circulation of capital, decreasing agricultural taxes, and increasing trade with the Latin American republics.[53]

The reformers' discussion of the problems of land, labor, and capital form a coherent, if not express, program for change. Economic leaders aspired to Puerto Rico's entry into the ranks of industrial nations through a broadly defined capitalism. They called for modernization through mechanization and the adoption of the scientific method, a wage labor system through the proletarianization of the rural population, and the development of investment capital. They hoped that these transformations would allow the island's sugar industry to increase productivity and reduce costs, and consequently succeed as a first-class industrial producer.

This formula for capitalism, however, did not own up to the fact that the success of any producer of agricultural commodities depended on a number of variables that were outside the control of Puerto Rico's economic and political elite. Regardless of how many internal transformations the island's sugar industry underwent, Puerto Rico would never be in full control of its economic future. First, not only did market fluctuations in supply and price dictate the margin of profits for agricultural exporters, but markets for one's products could not simply be created. Producing high quality sugar was quite a risky proposition for Puerto Rican planters, who had a basically secure market for their raw product in the form of U.S. refineries. Second, Spain's indifference to participating in infrastructure projects, as well as its ineffectiveness in promoting a more advantageous position for Puerto Rico vis-à-vis its trade partners, made the plans of reformers chimerical. External conditions limited the island's possibilities and would prove largely responsible for the difficult path ahead.

The Concept of Centralization

That the ideal of building sugar factories (centrales) should have captured the minds of reformers was to be expected, given their attitudes with respect to the desired social and economic order. Centrales responded to many of the concerns of island leaders. The basic argument used to advocate their establishment was the advantage of separating the agricultural from the manufacturing process. Both aspects of production would operate as rational enterprises, based on the division and specialization of labor, the use of modern equipment, and the application of the latest techniques both on the land and in the factory. Investments would flow more readily to an industrial enterprise while landowners, no longer burdened by debts for manufacturing equipment, could concentrate on improving land management methods. As the factors of production became integrated through the cooperation of landowners and industrialists, the island's social, economic, and political organization would, perforce, change. Society would acquire a more modern outlook; economic benefits would be forthcoming; and elite participation in the island's political development would be unavoidable. In characteristic fashion, reformers presented a perspective devoid of conflict or difficulties; they maintained that, as economic needs and resources grew and all social classes were called to participate in the process of production, the new factory system would extend its material and moral benefits to all.[54]

Most manuals presented the separation of the cultivation from the manufacturing phase as necessary to both farmer and manufacturer. In the sphere of cultivation, specialization implied an effective exploitation of available land; it meant obtaining higher yields in a shorter time by concentrating on growing cane, not on producing sugar. The objective included effectively dealing with unpredictable obstacles such as excessive rainfall and reduced exposure to the sun, both of which retarded or prevented the transformation of glucose into sucrose. Concentrating on the agricultural aspect would also permit timing the planting and cutting seasons so that they did not coincide. Specialization assured the farmer that the entire cycle would take no more than twelve months, so that bagasse, the dry fiber that is the byproduct of crushed cane, could be used as fertilizer when new canes were being planted.[55] The goals of exploiting the soil rationally and scientifically by controlling all variables spoke directly to the values of the new agriculturalists.

Separating the two processes would also reduce the capital requirements of agricultural operations. The farmer would avoid expensive machinery repairs, his capital investment would decrease by 30 to 35 percent, and general operating expenses and government taxes would be reduced considerably. As growers of cane, not producers of sugar, planters would be technically freed of worries over market fluctuations.

Their business was limited to supplying good-quality raw material, for which factory owners paid cash on receipt. Growers would be primarily concerned, then, with increasing the sucrose content of their canes, which could be accurately determined immediately after they were cut and upon which the selling price depended.[56] The heavy dependence of planters on refaccionistas for capital would be transformed to an interdependent relationship with the *centralista*, a partner in the business of making sugar.

Quality and availability of field labor would also improve. That the processes of abolition and mechanization occurred almost simultaneously did not escape the attention of rural planners. They rushed to conclude that this timely liberation of resources would result in a greater availability of field labor because advantageous conditions in modern centrales would attract workers, just as unfavorable circumstances now repelled them. Another change that would free a number of workers for other tasks was the establishment of railway systems by the factory itself. Reformers also expected that, as conditions improved and labor became more skilled, workers would specialize in particular tasks, most important among which was cutting cane during the harvest, a job that required not only speed but also accuracy.[57] In as scientific and businesslike a way as they knew, then, reformers advocated the rational exploitation of increasing numbers of workers under the guise of progress for all.

The benefits to be obtained by separating cultivation from manufacturing were also high in the industrial aspects of production. Factories would be run by full-time technicians, scientifically trained to obtain higher yields of better-quality sugar from state-of-the-art machinery, and not by ad hoc appointees who acquired experience from harvest to harvest. By concentrating on technological improvements for the manufacture of sugar, a central could produce as much as 4,500 tons in four months. Puerto Rico, the newly converted believers in industrialization stressed, should not satisfy itself with providing North American refineries with muscovado, but rather aspire to producing white crystallized sugar directly. Since these improvements would bring high profits, returns on large initial investments by a few proprietor/stockholders would be generously distributed as dividends.[58] Centrales offered practical applications of long-time aspirations regarding labor

specialization, market competitiveness, and the organization of investment capital. The projects proposed presented centralization as the
perfect combination of individual strengths and abilities in separate
spheres of activity.

If implemented, these elaborate plans would have had only a limited
impact on Puerto Rico's possibilities as an industrial producer. Island
leaders had appraised the obstacles to be overcome in an unrealistic
manner. The double objective of increasing sugar production and quality did not take into consideration that markets for such an output
hardly existed. More sugar would only mean lower prices; better quality would alienate Puerto Rico's largest customer: refineries in the
United States.[59] The dependence of the sugar industry on external
conditions, unquestionably unfavorable at the time, would render the
plans of agricultural reformers largely ineffective. The limited perspective of island leaders sharply contrasted with their ambitious goals.

A large number of individuals, nevertheless, were caught up in the
enthusiasm of the moment and became standard-bearers for the cause.
They calculated Puerto Rico's chances for success by comparing the island to beet and other cane sugar producers such as Martinique, Ha-
waii, Guadeloupe, Antigua, and Demerara in terms of the raw materials
needed for manufacturing, type of machinery used, cost and reliability
of the work force, and transportation facilities. Eagerly participating in
the push for change, a group of planters publicly commended one Luis
Engel for representing Puerto Rico in a universal exposition in Vienna.
Articles reporting the progress or failure of central projects, for example in Mayagüez and Ponce, appeared frequently in the local press.[60]

Island newspapers published different projects and gave them pub-
licity. Wenceslao Borda presented his project in a meeting called by
the governor-general on 26 June 1873. The Plan Borda reported that,
as of that date, manufacturing absorbed one-half of the refacción costs
of an hacienda as a result of the money spent on machinery, oxen,
carts, and wages. The central, it argued, would concentrate on the
processing of sugar, producing 9 to 10 pounds of refined sugar for
every 100 pounds of cane and offering the cane supplier 5 percent of
the weight of the cane in sugar at the current market price. The right
of farmers to dividends was also assured; centrales in Puerto Rico
could easily be committed to a 20 percent profit margin, given that

factories in the French Antilles obtained a 32 percent profit margin. The plan called for an initial investment for eighteen centrales of seven million pesos to be obtained from the French house Moitessier, Neveu & Co., using as collateral the indemnification papers of ex-slaves. Finally, Borda also advocated the establishment of the Compañía Azucarera de Puerto-Rico as a complement to the central system.[61]

Another project, presented to the Provincial Deputation, was elaborate and carefully laid out. It rested on the assumption that foreign capital could easily be attracted to Puerto Rico because of the fertility of its soil, the vast amounts of cultivated land, clean and abundant water sources, a dense and docile population, strict public discipline, and political stability. Foreign industrial capitalists, farmer-planters from the island itself, and professional factory administrators would all participate as stockholders in the profits and decisions affecting their interests directly. An additional advantage to the foreign capitalist resulted from Puerto Rico's strategic position, to be reinforced by the construction of an isthmian canal.[62] Most details had been calculated carefully. Optimal conditions, under which the interdependent partnership of agriculturalist and industrialist would come into its own, included 300–500 acres under cultivation, a density grade of nine for cane juice, and a return of 5.5 to 6 percent of the weight of the cane supplied by the planter in sugar. The increase in quantity of production would be 25 to 30 percent; quality would improve 25 percent. Proponents also calculated the costs per harvest as the number of centrales increased until they reached twenty and the number of workers 3,200. Significantly, the project pushed for the commercialization of sugar by the company itself, in order to avoid the costs of exporting through a middle person.[63]

A third plan, wider in scope and more definitive in its aims, made its appearance in 1882. The Sociedad de Empresas de Factorías Centrales de Puerto-Rico had been founded in late 1881 by Enrique Delgado y Ortega with the aid of Governor Laportilla, who served as president. By mid-1882, the organizing committee succeeded in obtaining initial capital of 114,000 pesos from an eastern district, where the joint-stock company would build the first central. Shares would be worth 100 pesos apiece, and the 226 founding members were expected collectively to contribute 226,000 of the 400,000 pesos needed to begin operations. The Provincial Deputation itself would invest 10,000 pesos, thus providing the corporation with added worth and a larger degree of legitimacy.

The stated purposes of the association reflected the island's needs and aspirations as perceived by its founding members. The corporation would be dedicated to the production of crystallized sugar, using perfected centrifugal and vacuum machinery, and to the administration of centrales established for such a purpose. It would be in charge of buying land and establishing repair shops for machinery from the initial returns on investment, once four centrales had been established. The company would also review the applications of hacendados interested in sharing 10 percent of the costs of establishing a factory and would procure moderate interest rates on the credit obtained. Finally, a clearing agency would regulate the exchange of draft bills, issue obligations, and provide farmers with insurance.[64] The central formula, then, embodied solutions to many of the concerns of old-time hacendados: it assured them of improved product quality, advanced technology, increased capital investment, more liberal credit—all possible because of the association of interests and resources.

Because these plans complemented the objectives and ideals of the island's leaders, their limited chances for success were ignored. Puerto Ricans had long aspired to a modern industrial economy, resistant to external conditions precisely because of its internal efficiency. But an update of the island's productive apparatus and a reorganization of its labor force were not by themselves going to improve Puerto Rico's situation. To take hold, the transformations proposed required banks, roads, maritime connections, telegraph lines, and other facilities for conducting business that only Spain could provide. Reformers overlooked the mother country's indifference to promoting these projects, as well as the absence of a market for the high-quality product they aspired to put out. Their inability to place proposals for change in a more realistic context was reflected in Puerto Rico's twisted attempts to discard the old and enter the capitalist mainstream.

Yet the concept of centralization became rooted in the minds of the Puerto Rican late-century elite. The idea of establishing a central system across the island had quickly become a deus ex machina for those concerned with the future of Puerto Rico's agriculture. It fit with modern currents of scientificism and rationality, as it focused on the exploitation of the soil, the organization of labor, and the association of investment capital. The establishment of centrales also implied technological innovations and new management techniques. To the social, economic, and political reformers of the last decades of the nineteenth century, it represented a packaged solution to problems that had long been in existence. Conceived and designed to end internal deficiencies, the new factory system announced the coming of a new era.

3

The Formation of
Central San Vincente

Land

Central San Vicente, the northern coast sugar giant, made its forceful appearance in 1873, almost as if to assure reformers that their projects were feasible. Standing as proof of the revival of the sugar industry envisioned by progressive leaders, the achievement of Don Leonardo Igaravídez provided fuel for their fiery arguments. In the valley of Vega Baja, San Vicente promised to realize the scientific notions successfully applied in industrial nations. A modern establishment, run by a merchant/landowner marquis, the central seemed prepared to rise to the occasion.[1]

The growth of San Vicente as an enterprise parallels its owner's development of an entrepreneurial style appropriate to time and space considerations. While still a merchant, Igaravídez infiltrated Vega Baja's landowning elite through business deals, personal favors, and finally marriage. His economic interests shifted in the 1870s from the circulation of capital to the large-scale production of agricultural exports. The personal and business connections he had carefully cultivated proved not only advantageous but almost essential to the ambitious project that was the establishment of the central.

The identification of man with land and image with enterprise forces upon the historian an analysis of the trajectory leading up to landownership. Igaravídez came to represent San Vicente. The success of the enterprise was synonymous with his promotion into the ranks of Vega

Baja's landowning aristocracy. Issues of land, then, provide an appropriate perspective from which to view the growth both of the business concern and of Igaravídez as an entrepreneur.

Neither the enterprise nor its owner, however, was able to fulfill the expectations of reformers. It is almost ironic that the vast expanse of territory controlled by the enterprising landowner proved a serious liability. Land-related expenses in the context of heavy investments in machinery and other capital improvements were simply too much to handle. In the absence of immediate profits, payment of wages for agricultural labor and mortgage obligations on the land became too onerous when coupled with the necessary industrial investments. Reformers would have pointed to the failure to separate the cultivation of cane by others from the manufacture of sugar by Igaravídez himself as the weak point of the enterprise. It seems more appropriate, however, to examine Igaravídez's actions as he judged and acted upon the situation he faced with the instruments available to him at the moment. Given more time, perhaps he could have ironed out the difficulties that arose out of landownership. As it was, the ambitious project succumbed to the exigencies of a financial system unsuited for long-term investment. Both founder and establishment paid a high price for the incompatibility of their objectives with the context in which they were to operate.

The choice of Vega Baja as the site of such an experiment, however, was a wise one. By the time of its administrative creation in 1776, the *municipio* of Vega Baja and its outlying areas supported a cattle-raising economy (fig. 3.1). Fertile lands in the vicinity of the Morovis and Cibuco rivers had produced timber, some coffee, and such minor agricultural products as corn, rice, and citrus fruits since the late eighteenth century. By the middle of the nineteenth century, six sugar-producing haciendas of considerable size had emerged in the small township of 25,105 *cuerdas* (one cuerda equals .97 acre): Encarnación, Fe, Felicidad, Rosario, Santa Inés, and San Vicente. Their location in what geographers have labeled the northern coastal plain, a region that covers the northeastern half of the island, assured them of fertile clay soils and abundant rainfall. These successful estates were largely responsible for Vega Baja's substantial annual contributions to the island's general treasury. Their owners—foreigners, Spaniards, and creoles alike—controlled the best lands, those in the northeast *barrios* (sectors) known as Cabo Caribe, Ceiba, and Cibuco, which accounted for nearly 60 per-

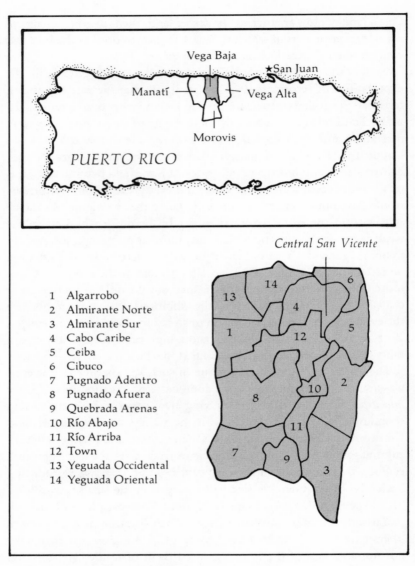

Fig. 3.1. Map of Vega Baja and its sectors

cent of the value of agricultural production in the municipality. Vega
Baja's rural population was concentrated until well into the nineteenth
century in the barrios northwest of the town, in areas relatively close to
the haciendas but not controlled by them (table 3.1).[2]

Whereas the midcentury drop in world market prices had been a
serious setback to many of Vega Baja's sugar properties, the establishment in 1873 of an efficient sugar factory offered to restore the department to its old-time glory. Having absorbed contiguous haciendas,
Central San Vicente became an 11,400-cuerda estate that occupied
45.4 percent of Vega Baja's territory, provided jobs for 38.8 percent of
its male population over 16 years of age (not counting wealthy heads-
of-household), and produced more than 50 percent of the municipality's income ($94,059.33 of $167,889.55, 56.02 percent, in 1883;
$102,104.50 of $167,936.37, 60.80 percent, in 1887). It stood proudly
in the Vega Baja lowlands, "a promise of prosperity to the county, [the

Table 3.1. Rural Population of Vega Baja by Sectors

Sector	Number of families, 1878 (%)		Number of people, 1885 (%)	
Northeast				
Cabo Caribe, Ceiba, Cibuco	158	(11.1)	604	(8.6)
Northwest				
Algarrobo, Yeguada Occidental,				
Puerto Nuevo[a]	542	(37.9)	1,849	(26.5)
Southeast				
Almirante Norte, Almirante Sur,				
Río Abajo, Río Arriba, Quebrada				
Arenas	428	(30.0)	2,890	(41.4)
Southwest				
Pugnado Adentro, Pugnado Afuera	300	(21.0)	1,644	(23.5)
Total	1,428	(100)	6,987	(100)

Sources: Delgado, Isla de Puerto-Rico, p. 140; AMVB, "Provincia de Puerto
Rico. Pueblo de la Vega. Resumen del padrón general de habitantes de este
territorio en la parte relativa a la clasificación por cabeza de familia y demás
condiciones sociales que a continuación se expresan," box 1885A, doc. 1.
[a]Yeguada Oriental apparently later became Puerto Nuevo (fig. 3.1). Late-
nineteenth- and twentieth-century sources place Puerto Nuevo to the east of
Yeguada and make no distinction between the latter's western and eastern
districts.

image] of progress replacing routinism, of talent overcoming impotence, a rebirth."[3]

San Vicente was certainly an impressive piece of property in terms of land extension. Its 3,600 cuerdas of first-class land were valued in 1880 at 900,000 pesos. Approximately another 1,400 cuerdas of arable land were worth 175,000 pesos and 6,400 of timberlands and pastures, 193,000 pesos. Sugarcane was planted on 1,500 cuerdas, coconuts and foodstuffs on 4,000. Cattle on the estate included 180 pairs of oxen, 500 cows, and 60 horses and other beasts of burden. The combined value of land, crops, and animals was 1,570,000 pesos (table 3.2).

The estate's improvements were also outstanding. A 714-square-meter wood and masonry building held sugar- and rum-making equipment. Another two-story structure contained the rooms of employees and the warehouse for agricultural goods, while a third masonry building housed the workers and served as their dining hall. In 1983 only the ruins of factory buildings, which had probably been remodeled to accommodate twentieth-century demands, remained on a clearing close to the Cibuco River. Underground channels, apparently used until recently, diverted some of the waters into the factory to run the mill that would grind the cane. There were also a stable, blacksmith's shop, carpenter's shop, and bathhouse.[4]

San Vicente's claim to fame, however, rested on its sophisticated production system. The mill ran on a 60-horsepower Cail y Cía. steam engine and five small Cornuaille boilers, which produced power for the water pumps, distillery, Derosne triple-effect evaporators, Hodeck condensers, and Rohlfs-Seyrig centrifugals.[5] This equipment made the sugar-manufacturing process a smooth operation. The juice extracted from the ground cane traveled through pipes to the top floor, where it was mixed with lime, which neutralized its acidity. The application of heat made light insoluble solids and albumin rise to the surface, while other foreign substances fell to the bottom of five 430-gallon settling tanks. In addition to the settling tanks, five filters assured the sugar technician that the hot juice that traveled to the vacuum or triple-effect evaporators was almost free of impurities. From the first to the last unit of the evaporators, the liquid was boiled at decreasing temperatures and increasing vacuums until it became a syrup containing only 35 percent water and 65 percent solid matter. It passed through one more filter onto a cooling and mixing apparatus, where the concen-

Table 3.2. Assessed Value of Central San Vicente, 1880

No. of cuerdas	Type of land	Value per cuerda	Total value ($)
3,600	First class lowlands	250	900,000
1,400	Gently sloping lands	125	175,000
800	First class pastures	50	40,000
800	Bulletwood forests in Pugnado and Cerro-Gordo	80	64,000
2,200	Pastures	25	55,000
1,600	Pastures in salt marshes	15	24,000
1,000	Pastures in salt marshes	10	10,000
11,400			1,268,000

	Type of crop		
1,000	Cane	200	200,000
500	Cane	100	50,000
4,000	Coconut palm trees	3	12,000
N/A	Minor crops	N/A	5,000
5,500			267,000

Number of head	Cattle	Value per unit	
360	Oxen	100	18,000
500	Cattle within the fence limits	—	12,500
60	Other beasts of burden	—	5,000
920			35,500

Machinery and equipment	
San Vicente's old equipment and plantation home	92,000
New machinery, equipment for bagasse, carpentry shop, balance, and distillery	88,000
Agricultural machinery and miscellaneous others	22,000
New apparatus from Cail y Cía. (mills, filters, triple effect evaporators, distillery, and other accessories)	230,000
	432,000

Railroad	
7 miles of fixed and 1.5 miles of moveable rails, wagons, and other equipment	43,000

(*continued*)

Table 3.2—*continued*

Railroad	
Rails, wheels, and other unused steel equipment	5,000
	48,000

Buildings	
Brick house and oven	2,500
New lime-making oven	500
Warehouse in Cerro-Gordo	1,500
Construction warehouse in Vega Baja	10,000
7 plantation homes	9,000
	23,500

Boats	
Two schooners and a steamboat	20,000
Dock	3,000
	23,000

Miscellaneous	
40 carts and other transportation equipment	3,000
Agricultural and industrial tools	3,000
Supply of wood	2,000
	8,000

Total value	2,105,000

Source: AMVB, "Relación de propiedad y bienes de Leonardo Igaravídez, que presenta Serapio Miticola, depositario judicial de los bienes del concurso necesario," box 1880C, doc. 72.

trated juice was crystallized. The centrifugals filtered out what syrup was left (molasses) for reboiling, and only sugar crystals remained, ready for storage and shipping in barrels.[6]

The manufacturing process was supported by a good deal of other machinery. Twelve trains, each with seven wagons, carried cane to the mill along eight-and-a-half miles of fixed and moveable railways. This capital improvement was expected to pay off handsomely once the San Juan-Arecibo railroad crossed the central and made it one of its stops,

since the finished product could be shipped out and cane from surrounding areas easily brought in. In the meantime, San Vicente relied
on its own locomotive to transport canes within the estate and on three
40- to 50-ton boats to ship its sugar from a private dock, east to Cerro
Gordo, and on to San Juan.[7]

San Vicente's labor force also became an example of efficiency and
rationality. It reportedly consisted of 1,000 workers divided into six
sections.[8] Even when few men were yet familiar with the new machinery, their diligence was the object of praise and the basis for hopeful
projections. A visitor to San Vicente claimed that as soon as they finished "healthy and economical" meals at the central's "perfectly regu-
larized" eatery, the jornaleros went straight to their work stations.[9]

This skillfull combination of natural, technological, and human resources resulted in increased production of high-quality crystallized
sugar (some of it white) ready for consumption, an achievement that
was praised throughout the island. San Vicente's sugar was reportedly
superior in grain and in color to other sugars; it did not form lumps or
leak molasses once it was placed in barrels.[10] These and other contemporary descriptions lead one to believe that San Vicente was producing
the highest grade of raw sugar, Derosne evaporator white, just as were
the most advanced ingenios in Cuba. The mill's efficiency was the ad-
miration of all; recycling all waste materials for maximum utilization,
its powerful machinery consumed 5,000 quintales of cane per day, returned 400 wagonfuls of bagasse, and produced 36 hogsheads (one
hogshead equals 13–15 quintales) of sugar. In its first harvest, San
Vicente's output reached 2,300 tons of sugar, a figure comparable to
the highest expectations of reformers and over 2.5 percent of Puerto
Rico's total production that year. Six years later, 72 percent of the juice
of 4,910 quintales of cane was extracted in one day to produce 447
quintales of sugar, a yield of over 9 percent and an indisputable
achievement. Igaravídez himself was lauded as a man of "vigorous initiative, who fearlessly ignored established tenets with as much ease as
he broke fallow land and made it produce for the public well-being."[11]

The highly publicized successes of Vega Baja's landowning entrepreneur must have filled observers with hope. It seems appropriate,
then, to follow the trajectory of San Vicente's creator from the moment
he entered the ranks of Vega Baja's well-to-do. The various channels he
used to advance his position provide a convenient vantage point from

which to view the intricate relationship between business and personal concerns in nineteenth-century Puerto Rico. As he moved freely among Vega Baja's old families, Igaravídez must have recognized the convenience of grounding his business objectives on the image of a landowner. It was advantageous, as well as inevitable, that land and man were identified. Personal image and the success of the enterprise were inextricably tied.

A man of action, Igaravídez began his career as a trendsetter in San Juan's commercial circles. Born in 1830 in neighboring Vega Alta into an apparently propertyless family, Igaravídez had moved into the import-export business in the capital by the time he was sixteen. At this early age, he acquired experience as a trader through frequent trips to St. Thomas, then a duty-free port, well known as a slave-ship stop. Once he had established a partnership with José Eustaquio Cabrera in 1866, he extended his business objectives to the town of Vega Baja.[12] Moving freely about the circles that dominated Puerto Rican society, economics, and politics and solidly established at the capital and in Vega Baja, Igaravídez carried out traditional merchant functions among the well-to-do in both locations.

Much of Igaravídez's success, at least in Vega Baja, stemmed from his effective operation of a network of personal connections to members of the town's elite families (fig. 3.2). Igaravídez's first wife, reportedly a woman of great beauty and no wealth, was Avelina Santana.[13] Her brother and sister had married into the powerful Landrón and López families, respectively. It would not be farfetched to suppose that Igaravídez met his second wife, María del Carmen Eustaquia Landrón— probably then married to Manuel Antonio López—through his first wife's family. Married a second time, he was twice related to the López family, which was in turn bound to the Landróns by at least two marriages. The Prados and Náters, two other wealthy Vega Baja landholders, also entered the family picture indirectly: members of their families married Igaravídez's siblings (fig. 3.3).

These marriages opened up avenues of influence to still other sets of extended kin. Since it is probable that any social gathering in Vega Baja would include members of these four families, the opportunity for mixing business with pleasure offered itself under the best of circumstances. Surely, Igaravídez found it useful to volunteer his services as a merchant and administrator before Vega Baja's needy landowners. By the time of his second marriage, which was more advantageous than the first in terms of both contacts with a larger network and an expanding sphere of economic activity, Igaravídez could count on his name and influence in Vega Baja households with absolute confidence.

The convenience of being able to use the intimacy provided by family ties for business transactions must not have escaped Igaravídez. It was clear that the Landróns, Prados, Náters, and Dávilas ruled Vega Baja through their monopoly of land and commerce. On numerous occasions, one or two representatives of these families got together with another member of the elite to acquire slaves, open a general store, and buy property. These informal consortiums also assured their members that personal considerations played a part in business decisions. Money was lent and returned on easy terms of credit, and fortunes were administered by capable minds and honest hands.[14]

The fast-moving world of business presented the social climber with many opportunities. Through participation as silent partner in several commercial ventures (table 3.3), Igaravídez was largely responsible for

Table 3.3. Commercial Ventures Undertaken by Igaravídez

Name of company	Dates in business	Igaravídez's investment ($)	Others' investment ($)	Igaravídez's share in profits (%)
J. E. Cabrera y Cía.	1859–67	5,000	10,000	N/A
L. Igaravídez	1871–(79)[a]	N/A	0	100
L. Vega y Cía.	1872–73	4,000	8,068	25
Girona, Guillermety y Cía.	1873–(79)[a]	5,000	3,000	N/A
Arnau, Quintana y Cía.	1876–77	25,056[b]	0	50
Igaravídez, Mariani y Cía.	1877–(79)[a]	15,500	0	33.3

Sources: AGPR, PN, Juan Ramón de Torres, box 52, 25 May 1871; box 67, 28 June 1877; Demetrio Giménez y Moreno, box 220, 11 February 1873; box 221, 23 September 1873; José Félix Lajara, box 775, 21 June 1876; box 776, 7, 16 February, 5 May 1877; box 777, 31 January 1878; Dulce María Tirado Merced, "Las raíces sociales del liberalismo criollo: El Partido Liberal Reformista (1870–1875)" (Master's thesis, University of Puerto Rico at Río Piedras, 1981), p. 74.
[a]The sources available do not indicate the date of dissolution of these companies. I would assume that they collapsed with Igaravídez's filing for bankruptcy in 1879.
[b]Igaravídez's investment in Arnau, Quintana y Cía. was really the cancellation of Arnau's debt to him. Since Arnau claimed to have debits of 25,506 pesos, I have assumed that this was the amount that Igaravídez contributed initially.

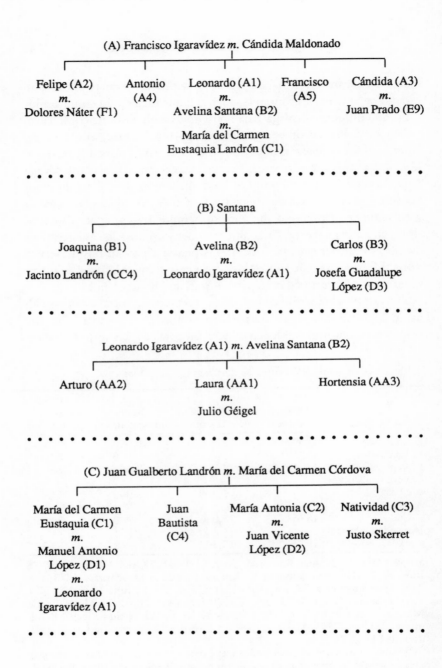

Fig. 3.2. Family trees of Vega Baja's planters as reconstructed from notarial records

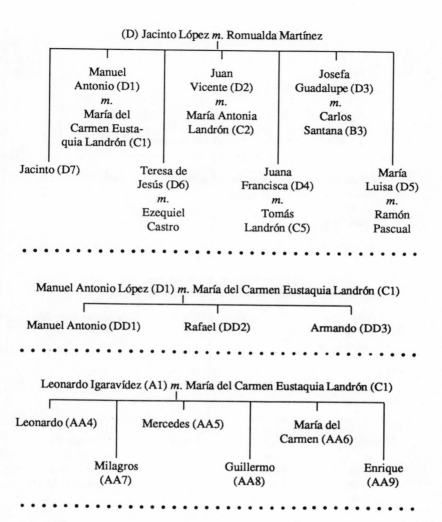

(D) Jacinto López *m.* Romualda Martínez

Manuel Antonio (D1) *m.* María del Carmen Eustaquia Landrón (C1)

Juan Vicente (D2) *m.* María Antonia Landrón (C2)

Josefa Guadalupe (D3) *m.* Carlos Santana (B3)

Jacinto (D7)

Teresa de Jesús (D6) *m.* Ezequiel Castro

Juana Francisca (D4) *m.* Tomás Landrón (C5)

María Luisa (D5) *m.* Ramón Pascual

Manuel Antonio López (D1) *m.* María del Carmen Eustaquia Landrón (C1)

Manuel Antonio (DD1)   Rafael (DD2)   Armando (DD3)

Leonardo Igaravídez (A1) *m.* María del Carmen Eustaquia Landrón (C1)

Leonardo (AA4)   Mercedes (AA5)   María del Carmen (AA6)

Milagros (AA7)   Guillermo (AA8)   Enrique (AA9)

Note: Tomás Landrón (C5) is the son of Juan Gualberto Landrón by one of two former marriages.

(*continued*)

Fig. 3.2—*continued*

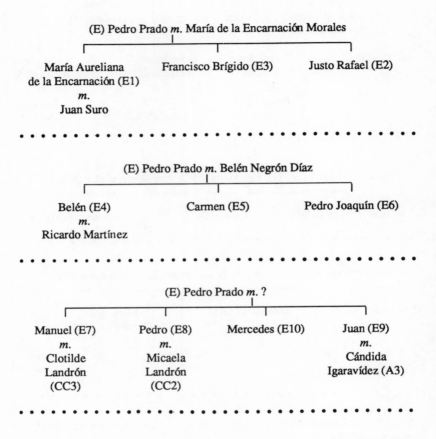

(E) Pedro Prado *m.* María de la Encarnación Morales

María Aureliana
de la Encarnación (E1)
m.
Juan Suro

Francisco Brígido (E3)

Justo Rafael (E2)

· ·

(E) Pedro Prado *m.* Belén Negrón Díaz

Belén (E4)
m.
Ricardo Martínez

Carmen (E5)

Pedro Joaquín (E6)

· ·

(E) Pedro Prado *m.* ?

Manuel (E7)
m.
Clotilde
Landrón
(CC3)

Pedro (E8)
m.
Micaela
Landrón
(CC2)

Mercedes (E10)

Juan (E9)
m.
Cándida
Igaravídez (A3)

· ·

(F) Francisco Irene Náter *m.* Felícita Marrero

- Rosa María (F3) *m.* Emilio Dávila (G1)
- Julio (F5)
- Angel Waldino (F6)
- Teresa (F2) *m.* Miguel Landrón (CC1)

- Manuel (F7)
- Francisco Celestino (F8)
- Felícita del Carmen (F4) *m.* Juan Rodríguez
- Dolores (F1) *m.* Felipe Igaravídez (A2) *m.* Manuel Fernández Juncos
- José Marcelino (F9)

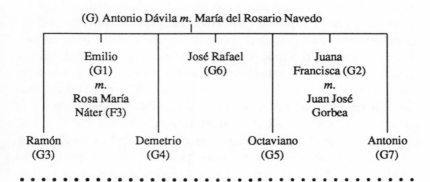

(G) Antonio Dávila *m.* María del Rosario Navedo

- Emilio (G1) *m.* Rosa María Náter (F3)
- José Rafael (G6)
- Juana Francisca (G2) *m.* Juan José Gorbea

- Ramón (G3)
- Demetrio (G4)
- Octaviano (G5)
- Antonio (G7)

(*continued*)

Fig. 3.2—*continued*

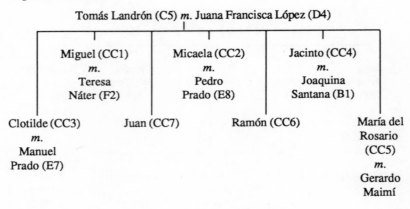

Tomás Landrón (C5) *m.* Juana Francisca López (D4)

| Miguel (CC1) *m.* Teresa Náter (F2) | Micaela (CC2) *m.* Pedro Prado (E8) | Jacinto (CC4) *m.* Joaquina Santana (B1) |

Clotilde (CC3) *m.* Manuel Prado (E7)   Juan (CC7)   Ramón (CC6)   María del Rosario (CC5) *m.* Gerardo Maimí

• •

providing financial capital to the island's landed wealthy, while his associates managed day-to-day sales of consumer goods. Having by the late 1860s entered the ranks of the most prestigious families in Vega Baja, Igaravídez purchased a nobility title in 1870 and became involved in liberal politics, further pointers to his ambitions as an influential figure in Puerto Rico's economic, social, and political life.[15]

Involvement in import houses as a silent partner, however, did not provide him with spectacular success. Initial investment costs were barely covered at the time some of the firms were dissolved. Igaravídez's association with Laureano Vega and Francisco Bugella in a regular trading company, for example, began in 1872 and ended a year later. Igaravídez had taken on the responsibility for initial capital of 4,000 pesos, and the society bought Bugella's commercial establishments "El Globo" and "El Brazo Fuerte," both of which had been appraised at 21,468 pesos a year earlier. Since their owner had declared bankruptcy in 1871, however, the new commercial association, L. Vega y Cía., acquired them and the slaves with which they operated for only 8,168 pesos. As part of the deal, the company also assumed a 4,842-peso debt associated with the establishments. Igaravídez's share in the firm's profits and losses stood at 25 percent, Bugella's and Vega's at 37.5 percent each. Each partner was to draw 1,000 pesos yearly before the calculation of profits as payment for services. By September 1873, the association was dissolved, and Igaravídez and Bugella committed

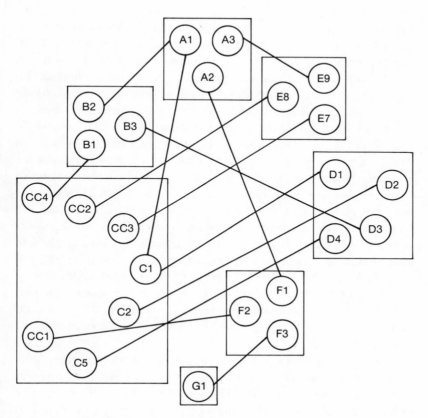

Fig. 3.3. Ties between Vega Baja's most prominent families

themselves to paying debts totaling 11,921 pesos and to receiving their share of invested capital in merchandise valued at 4,870 pesos. To further cover his loss, Igaravídez accepted "El Globo" with the intention of selling it. Vega received no money at the time of dissolution.[16]

Failure in the import business, however, did not spell defeat for a Puerto Rican nineteenth-century merchant. Igaravídez, like so many businessmen of the period, also speculated in urban and rural real estate in San Juan and Vega Baja, an activity that put him much in touch with influential citizens and that conceivably permitted the accumulation of capital outside the sphere of production. In 1869, for example, he offered 13,010 pesos for a San Juan home at the public auction of Lucas Aranzamendi's estate, only to sell it five days later to Ana Elisa

Shane de Storer, the wife of one of the estate's trustees. Subsequent payments by Igaravídez to the receivership and by Shane de Storer to Igaravídez himself make it appear as if Igaravídez was only the front that permitted Juan K. Storer to acquire the property for his own purposes.[17] Business activity, then, aimed not only at cash profits but also at participation in a network of favors and social contacts that could in the end prove even more valuable to an upwardly mobile individual.

Similarly, through separate transactions dated 1872, 1874, and 1879, Igaravídez brought three urban residential properties in Vega Baja and Arecibo from consanguine and affined kin and business associates, for no known business or personal purpose: one from Isaac Arnau (later to become his partner in a commercial company) for 5,500 pesos, another from his own mother for 2,000 pesos, and a third from Joaquina Córdova (no doubt a relative of his wife's mother) for 4,000 pesos.[18] Apparently making no gain out of these deals, Igaravídez seems to have simply rendered some people a favor. With his good will and openhanded generosity, he must have incidentally impressed his peers—including Julián E. Blanco, the other trustee at the Aranzamendi receivership, later to become Igaravídez's right-hand man. This, too, was part of the role of a man who wanted to be seen as a maker and breaker of business enterprise.

Some of Igaravídez's purchases of rural properties are more puzzling to the historian because they do not seem to have been part of a plan. In 1870, he bought for 1,550 pesos a worthless 45-cuerda piece of land that had recently been auctioned off to Bernardino Font. Two years later, he sold less than two cuerdas of prime land to Jacinto Landrón for 180 pesos. Taking advantage of Juan Bautista Landrón's declaration of bankruptcy in 1876, he purchased from the receivership a 257-cuerda estate, Hacienda Río Nuevo in Dorado, for 70,000 pesos, yet sold it two years later to Ramón Landrón for 77,000 pesos. In 1878, Igaravídez sold 105 cuerdas in Cabo Caribe for 3,008 pesos to Narciso Gonzales y Font from a larger piece he had bought some months before from Ramón Landrón.[19]

These purchases of land point either to random speculation (therefore, small profits) or to experimentation in particular situations with a view to the future, necessarily accompanied by changes in strategy. The absence of a pattern suggests that Don Leonardo was toying with the idea of enlarging his sphere of influence. The central itself, into which he had just poured enormous capital, was clearly the object of his most personal attention, economically and emotionally. Perhaps Igaravídez tried to fit these small estates into the central concept— probably as cane suppliers or plots for other crops, perhaps as added collateral for more loans, or possibly to build worker homes or a transportation network. Apparently unable to use them as intended, he must have disposed of the properties in exchange for ready cash.

Concomitant with involvement in commercial and real estate transactions, the role of the merchant in nineteenth-century Puerto Rico included financing the running expenses of hard-pressed haciendas. Strategically involved as he was in multiple money transactions, it was as a refaccionista, perhaps, that Igaravídez best advanced his position as a leading figure in the island's financial circles. As a moneylender, Igaravídez came into close contact with leading planters in the Vega Baja area and obtained a firm footing in the sphere of production. Already connected by personal and family ties to the largest landowners, he emerged as man of the hour when their agricultural operations needed financing.

The refacciones in favor of Juan Bautista Landrón, Gervasio Medina (Hacienda Media-Luna), and Manuel Fernández Juncos (Hacienda Flor del Valle) are cases in point. In the first, Igaravídez lent, at different moments and without charging interest, 4,000 pesos to Landrón, his wife's brother, who promised to return the full amount a year later (June 1871), when he was done with the *zafra* (harvest, usually from January to June). The refacción of Hacienda Media-Luna was really a 4,000-peso addition to more than 32,000 pesos that Igaravídez had lent Medina a year before (in November 1870), to be paid with close to 12,000 pesos in agricultural goods already processed and with subsequent production, depending on the market price of sugar. Fernández Juncos, who had married Igaravídez's brother's widow, borrowed more than 4,000 pesos from Igaravídez to be repaid in sugar and molasses at the end of the 1872 harvest with a guarantee of twenty-four pairs of oxen.[20] By lending a hand to already deeply troubled estates, Igaravídez won the favor and trust of Vega Baja's landowning elite.

A series of unconnected financial services rendered to a number of Vega Baja residents also offers clues to the exposure provided by a merchant's functions within a community. Igaravídez put up the 2,000-peso bond needed for the royal and municipal tax collector Juan

Plate 1. In a field near Bayamón, a child distributes sugarcane stalks to men who secure them to the ground. In the background fully grown cane sways in the breeze. Courtesy Colección fotográfica del Archivo General de Puerto Rico. Photo by Edwin Rosskam.

Plate 2. Sugar workers cultivate a cane field near Vega Baja. They secure the young plants tightly to the ground to prevent runoff water from exposing the roots. The limestone mound covered with vegetation is characteristic of the karst in the northern coastal plain. Courtesy Colección fotográfica del Archivo General de Puerto Rico. Photo by Charles Rotkin.

Antonio Roldán to be placed in the position (1871); supported the accusation of Justo Skerret, his wife's sister's husband, against the mayor of Vega Alta for electoral fraud (1872); financially backed treasury official Eduardo Andino y Vizcarrondo in negotiations to obtain his 1,000-peso pension (1876); represented Simplicio Martínez in his case before the treasury regarding late charges in the payment of taxes (1870); and served as character witness for J. C. Galbraith, a Baltimore businessman (1873). Igaravídez also served as executor of Dominga Martínez de Salgado's will and as guardian of the property inherited by the children of Miguel Landrón and Teresa Náter.[21] Treasury officials, American businessmen, and Vega Baja planters were all within the sphere of the merchant's influence.

Given his skillful blend of business and personal connections, Iga-

Plate 3. Prime cane land in Vega Baja stretches out to the coast. Courtesy Colección fotográfica del Archivo General de Puerto Rico. Photo by Jack Delano.

Plate 4. Sugar workers in a field near Yauco remove the soil to make weeding easier and secure the young cane plants. Long sleeves protect the men from the sun and from the sharp edges of the cane leaves. Courtesy Colección fotográfica del Archivo General de Puerto Rico. Photo by Jack Delano.

ravídez's move into the administration of Vega Baja lands was smooth indeed. As Avelina Santana's widower and the husband of María del Carmen Eustaquia Landrón (the widow of the largest landowner in the area), he was indirectly related to the well-bred and inbred of Vega Baja. He had been diligent in cultivating these family ties and extending his services to distant relatives and to personal friends. By the time he began to manage the largest piece of property in the area, his acceptance into the ranks of Vega Baja's landed wealthy was already a fact.

An agricultural partnership with his mother-in-law, María del Carmen Córdova, in 1867 was Igaravídez's first attempt at the administration of an estate—Hacienda Carmen—and depended entirely on

Plate 5. In a Guayanilla field a young man harvests sugarcane, the agricultural task requiring possibly the most skill and care. Once the cane is mature, it must be cut immediately. The worker must strike as close to the ground as possible without damaging the stalks that will be replanted. Courtesy Colección fotográfica del Archivo General de Puerto Rico. Photo by Jack Delano.

Plate 6. During the harvest in Guayanilla, a man removes leaves from recently cut cane before loading it onto wagons. An oxcart full of cane waits to be taken to the mill where the cane must be ground within a day. Courtesy Colección fotográfica del Archivo General de Puerto Rico. Photo by Jack Delano.

Plate 7. Newly cut cane at Central Cambalache in Arecibo. Courtesy Colección fotográfica del Archivo General de Puerto Rico. Photo by Edwin Rosskam.

Plate 8. Ruins of Central San Vicente in 1982. Photo by Jorge Irisarri.

family connections. A series of transactions meant to provide the firm with additional assets took place before its establishment. Having bought Hacienda Santa María for 6,000 pesos, Igaravídez sold it for 4,900 to Carmen Córdova, who in turn exchanged it, along with an undetermined amount of cash, for her nephew's Hacienda Candelaria. Ready to begin operations, the new company, L. Igaravídez y Cía., bought the part of Hacienda Carmen that belonged to Córdova's son and Igaravídez's brother-in-law Juan Bautista Landrón for 4,691 pesos and leased the share that was the property of María Antonia Landrón, another relative, by agreement with her husband, Juan Vicente López, the brother of Igaravídez's wife's first husband. Haciendas Candelaria, Santa María, and Carmen (except the part that belonged to Córdova's daughter Natividad) were all within the family fold. Córdova's investment consisted of incoming credits (58,139 pesos) and of what was apparently the value of her share of Hacienda Carmen as the widow of Juan Gualberto Landrón (147,939 pesos), while Igaravídez's contribution was the value of his wife's Hacienda Monterrey (22,722 pesos). He became the managing partner (*socio gestor administrador*), charging 10 percent of production, and Córdova the silent partner, receiving 100 pesos monthly. Profits were split according to the amount of capital invested by each partner.[22]

The association was apparently successful. The Landrón family was able to pay off previous obligations: a 25,000-peso loan from Storer y Cía. in three years and a 13,000-peso debt to José Ramón Fernández, the well-known conservative leader, the Marqués de la Esperanza. The company also consolidated the estate by buying outright from María Antonia Landrón her share of the property for 9,210 pesos.[23] By the time the partnership was dissolved (1873), Igaravídez's share in profits stood at 6,319 pesos and Córdova's totaled 41,144 pesos. Natividad's husband, Justo Skerret, bought the property for its original price of 189,685 pesos and assumed a 29,000-peso debt in favor of Igaravídez. In addition, the Landrón sisters were able to collect 16,000 pesos from Carlos Cabrera, who had acquired property from one of their debtors at judicial auction and was thus responsible for the individual's outstanding loans.[24] Both Igaravídez and many in his wife's family took advantage of the very positive combination of capital resources and management know-how.

Igaravídez's move from the sphere of circulation to that of production naturally involved a shift in objectives and expectations. The steps that led to the formation of Central San Vicente, however, were gradual ones, as is indicated by the fact that initially Igaravídez merely took charge of the situation he "inherited" from Manuel Antonio López, María del Carmen's late husband. In his first years as a landowner, Igaravídez continued to carry out commercial activities and committed his capital constantly in sporadic refacciones of surrounding haciendas. It was only after 1873 that he forcefully incorporated into his domain the ruined estates of Vega Baja's well-to-do and firmly established the central concept.

Igaravídez's acquisition of San Vicente lands appears almost accidental. The original estate had been divided into four parts after the death of Jacinto López and inherited in 1864 by four of his children: Teresa de Jesús, María Luisa, Josefa Guadalupe, and Manuel Antonio López. Soon after the partition, however, Manuel Antonio bought María Luisa's, Josefa Guadalupe's, and part of Teresa de Jesús's share. Two years later, Teresa de Jesús sold the remainder of her part of the inheritance to a cleric, Antonio Florencio García y Pacheco. When Manuel Antonio died, his wife María del Carmen Landrón Córdova was left in charge of the property she and her three children had legally inherited. For a brief period, the late Manuel Antonio's family made payments to Igaravídez in his role as agent for Josefa Guadalupe (married to his first wife's brother Carlos Santana) for the part of San Vicente sold by Josefa Guadalupe to her brother Manuel Antonio some years back. In his own right, Igaravídez then bought the cleric's share, which was leased to Manuel Antonio's heirs. Once Igaravídez married the widow, he came to control all the land and began making payments to all interested parties.[25]

In the meantime, Igaravídez was just as active in the affairs of other haciendas in the area. The refacción of Hacienda Rosario, run by Sucesión Dávila y Cía., the heirs of Antonio Dávila and now formal owners of the estate, is a good example of his involvement. In January 1870, administrator Ramón Dávila and Igaravídez signed a contract in which the latter committed himself to provide the former with the expenses of the hacienda not only during the ongoing harvest (at 100–125 pesos per week) but also during the low season (at 80–100 pesos per week). Included were also the costs of hiring twelve slaves at 100 pesos per month and of supplying ingredients for their meals, such as jerked beef, codfish, and oil. As was usual in such a contract, Igaravídez charged 1.5 percent interest monthly and a 2.5 percent commission for the sale of the product through his San Juan merchant house. Dávila placed as collateral the hacienda itself and the goods produced. The contract expired in late August.

Sucesión Dávila was not able to honor the agreement, although it did pay off a 7,250-peso debt to one Manuel Quintero of Morovis. In December 1870, it still owed Igaravídez 1,725 pesos and asked him to further supply up to 700 pesos monthly as requested by Dávila through order forms. All other conditions remained the same and Igaravídez renewed the contract until August 1871. By 1875, however, the agricultural partnership formed by the Dávila descendants was dissolved and the refaccionista acquired the property.[26]

The refacción of Hacienda Rosario points to many of the typical problems of the sugar industry in the nineteenth century. Sucesión Dávila was obviously in dire financial straits; it was borrowing money just as the zafra was getting started and required financing even into *tiempo muerto* (low season). Exceptional in its explicit reference to the practice of renting slaves, the case of Hacienda Rosario confirms the difficulty of planters in obtaining a reliable work force in zafra months. It is probable that these twelve bondsmen were used for factory work, for their high rental fee suggests that they performed skilled work.

The hacienda's loss since 1850 of a number of its slaves and its replacement of them with day laborers, usually employed in agricultural tasks, also indicates a lack of workers precisely in the industrial aspects of production.[27] That Sucesión Dávila was not able to fulfill the conditions of the contract is also characteristic; many hacendados continued borrowing money and eventually were forced to sell their property to the refaccionista or to auction it after court intervention.

Igaravídez's involvement in Hacienda Fe followed a similar pattern. Having been indirectly involved in previous refacciones of the estate by Látimer y Cía., Igaravídez only became a direct participant in the business concerns of the agricultural partnership formed by Carlos Santana (his first wife's brother) and owner Jacinto Landrón (surely related to his second wife) when he agreed in 1870 to lend them 150 pesos weekly and to pay municipal and royal taxes on the property.[28] Offering to provide the business with foodstuffs and agricultural equipment, the refaccionista would charge 18 percent annual interest on the loan and a 2.5 percent commission for the sale of agricultural goods. Two years later, in 1872, Hacienda Fe received another loan from Igaravídez—both in his own right and as administrator of his daughters' assets—for 25,000 pesos, to be paid in two years at 12 percent interest. Financed again in 1873 through a separate transaction with Látimer y Cía., Hacienda Fe failed to pay its creditors in 1874 more than 48,000 pesos, over half of which was owed Igaravídez himself. Purchased in its entirety by Carlos Santana in 1875, the property was immediately bought by Igaravídez, who simply assumed all outstanding debts.[29]

Hacienda Encarnación, the third estate to which Igaravídez committed his resources, was not so much financed by the merchant/landowner as defended against encroachment by claimants to the property. The plantation consisted of 853 cuerdas and had passed from one owner to another from 1867 to 1871: the heirs of Pedro Prado and María de la Encarnación Morales (María Aureliana de la Encarnación, Francisco Brígido, and Justo Rafael), who owned two-thirds of the estate, sold their share to Pablo Soliveras, who in turn sold it to Pascual Lorenzo. Látimer y Cía. bought this part of Hacienda Encarnación from Lorenzo in 1871 and sold it soon afterward to Pedro Prado (Junior), one of the Prado descendants from another marriage. Belén Negrón Díaz, the widow of Pedro Prado, who apparently owned the remaining third, promised to sell this share to Manuel, another Prado, and to Pedro. Yet she not only retained her part of the estate, but tried to take possession of the remainder of it in payment of 3,400 pesos owed to Marcelina Díaz, Vda. de (widow of) Negrón (her mother?) by Prado's heirs. Although Negrón Díaz managed to have the court order the seizure and sale of the property in 1875, Igaravídez—who in 1872 had helped finance the estate in a simple and informal refacción— intervened as guarantor in favor of Carlos Francisco Pierret, who apparently leased Hacienda Encarnación and cultivated plantains and sugarcane for Igaravídez's use. By 1877, Igaravídez had bought from Belén Negrón Díaz this part of the property, thus preventing further attacks on Hacienda Encarnación.[30]

Igaravídez's interest in Hacienda Felicidad differs in that he showed from the start his intention of buying the land. Beginning in 1869, he financed the hacienda's operations and bought some parts of it. By 1871, he owned half of it and became the administrator of the property for Náter Hnos., the agricultural society formed on the premises by the descendants of Manuel Náter and Felícita Marrero. At the time, property taxes and the debts contracted by Náter Hnos. were pending payment, including 15,000 pesos to both Manuel Náter (Junior) and Igaravídez. In order to pay its creditors the required 12,000-peso installment yearly, Náter Hnos. contracted Igaravídez's services as administrator, in return for 10 percent of production until all debts were canceled. From 1871 to 1876, Igaravídez continued making payments, providing refacciones, and coordinating agricultural activities, until Manuel Náter (Junior) sold Igaravídez his three-eighths participation in the partnership.[31]

It is as Igaravídez began effectively to control land in this period that his split functions as merchant, financier, administrator, and landowner dovetailed into a new role: industrial entrepreneur. Although involvement in the refacciones related above and in the administration of others' land has been interpreted as the actions of a good neighbor at a critical moment (and there is no reason to doubt Don Leonardo's good intentions),[32] it is also true that at some point during these years, the Marqués de Cabo-Caribe made a concerted effort to acquire land, perhaps thinking he could make it more productive. He abandoned altogether his commercial activities and dedicated all his efforts to buying land and equipment for what was to be the most modern sugar-making establishment on the island. Backed by the seemingly endless resources provided by business contacts and previous accumulations of capital and with a daring strategy in hand, Igaravídez ventured into terrain never explored before.

Igaravídez's bold initiative brings to mind a number of conventions regarding entrepreneurial activity and style. His actions fit definitions developed in the 1950s and 1960s by scholars in the field: "innovation upon a solid operational base achieved through the medium of business decisions" or "a purposeful activity . . . undertaken to initiate, maintain or aggrandize a profit-oriented business unit." Also applicable are the functions usually identified with good business management: (1) identification and change of business objectives of the enterprise; (2) development and maintenance of an organization, including effective relations with subordinates and employees; (3) securing and retaining adequate financial resources and nurturing good relations with existing and potential investors; (4) acquisition of efficient technological equipment and its revision as new machinery appears; (5) development of a market for products, devising of new products to meet or anticipate market demands; and (6) maintenance of good relations with public authorities and society at large.[33]

But it would be difficult, and probably gratuitous, to select a moment in which Igaravídez started thinking and acting differently. This would imply looking for a change in personality, almost as if he had modified attitudes and behavior overnight to conform to a predetermined pattern. A more appropriate line of inquiry would embrace both the requirements of the project and Igaravídez's use of the resources available in Puerto Rico at the time.[34] This approach would give full credit to the ambitious goals to which the entrepreneur committed himself and place in proper perspective the risks of the context in which he planned to operate. Igaravídez's trajectory, then, would be correctly appraised as a continuation of, and not a break from, previous activities.

It is imperative, then, to include Igaravídez's early moves toward landownership as part of the trajectory he followed to become an industrial entrepreneur. Becoming more and more involved in land-related businesses as merchant-financier, feeling at home among Vega Baja's seigneurial families as a result of personal ties, realizing perhaps that the prestige of landowning opened a number of doors closed to merchants, Igaravídez must have gathered momentum for his new industrial role. Once the central concept came into existence—in Igaravídez's mind, at least—he forcefully brought together all available resources to make it work. Old patterns of action served new objectives as successful landowner turned industrial entrepreneur.

The identification of new business objectives was undoubtedly present in Igaravídez's hurried accumulation of land from 1871 to 1875. Don Leonardo's initial involvement in the affairs of other haciendas appeared to pay off handsomely: once the properties defaulted on their loans, the entrepreneur proceeded to buy them for next to nothing, assuming their obligations on the terms originally stipulated. From 1869 to 1876, he purchased piecemeal all of Hacienda Felicidad except for Dolores Náter's share. He acquired Hacienda Santa Inés at judicial auction in 1871, and in 1875 became the sole owner of Hacienda Fe and of Hacienda Rosario, after the dissolution of the agricultural partnership formed by the Dávila descendants. Finally, parts of Hacienda Encarnación were sold or leased to Igaravídez in 1877 by Belén Negrón Díaz, Pedro Prado's widow. Other transactions during this period eventually made him the owner of 11,400 cuerdas of Vega Baja land.[35]

A shift in Igaravídez's long-term plans is also evident in his first attempts to control the area's sugar-manufacturing operations. A contract signed in 1871 with José Pablo Morales (Hacienda Hornos in Toa Alta) is unique in its inflexible separation of cane cultivation from sugar processing: supported by a 4,000-peso loan from Igaravídez, Morales was to plant cane in eighty cuerdas at two specified moments; Igaravídez would set up milling equipment on four cuerdas provided free of charge by Morales. The landowner was responsible for all cane-cutting costs during the eight zafras the contract would be in effect; the new industrialist committed himself to giving preference to Morales's cane, although he was free to grind that of other landowners. Taxes on the property would be split in half and Don Leonardo was given the option of keeping his machinery on the premises for a land rent of 100 pesos yearly, in case the agreeement did not work out as planned. If Igaravídez decided to sell the equipment, however, Morales would have first option to acquire it. Interest on the loan stood at an unusually low 12 percent and commission for the sale of half of the sugar was 1.5 percent, instead of the more common 2.5 percent.[36]

Something must not have worked out as expected. The cancellation of an agreement made between Morales and Igaravídez in 1874 indicates that Igaravídez was leasing all of the property (250 cuerdas) and growing cane on some of it. At the 1876 expiration of the contract, both land and machinery reverted to Morales, who agreed to pay Igaravídez 8,500 pesos for the transaction.[37] The first central experiment seemed to have failed, or rather, was shunned by Igaravídez to make way for Central San Vicente, a much more ambitious plan that made its appearance in 1873.

Igaravídez's innovative development and maintenance of what he hoped would be an efficient organization—as suggested by the exaggerated application of division of labor principles—could have revealed to observers where he was heading. San Vicente's labor force was divided into discrete units of operation, with the most specific and seemingly unimportant tasks detailed in workers' lists (table 3.4). Management priorities channeled workers into the occupations as needed at different times during the year. During zafra months, the ratio of agricultural to industrial laborers was three to one or less, while throughout tiempo muerto (July to December) that proportion almost always exceeded ten to one (table 3.5). Igaravídez was careful to use more or less the same men for similar tasks year-round. He also made sure provisions for meals were handled by the central. As he secured a steady supply of laborers through these policies, Don Leonardo moved closer to the ideal of an effective and reliable wage labor force.

Securing adequate financial sources, a complicated procedure for most nineteenth-century landowners, proved relatively simple for Igaravídez, at least initially. In order to obtain the funds needed to finance operations, he borrowed money freely from local and international circles (table 3.6). In the absence of banks, island commercial companies and foreign financiers offered generous credit in these early years. Igaravídez borrowed large amounts of capital, offering as collateral the sugar to be produced or the central itself and its dependencies. It was only after 1879 that his overcommitments were discovered. The financial downfall of San Vicente, however, must be examined in the context of conditions external to the enterprise and deserves treatment in a separate chapter.

Moving at a fast pace, the man of business turned his attention to appropriate technology. Not satisfied with the obsolete equipment in-

Table 3.4. Workers' Occupations According to San Vicente's Ledgers

Agricultural

Unskilled	Skilled	Services
*Chapodo (clearing land with hoes and machetes)	*Corte de espeques/corte de caña y desyervo (harvesting cane; saving stalks to be replanted)	*Mudadores (replacing pairs of oxen on carts; moving oxen to grazing grounds)
*Limpieza en Blandito (clearing almost swampy lands)	*Semilla (preparing new cane by cutting grown stalks at the knot)	*Fosforeros (placing phosphorus as poison for crabs on young cane)
*Escombro (clearing arable or pasture land of extraneous objects)	*Resiembro de sepas/siembra de caña (replanting stalks not firmly planted)	*Racioneros (taking lunch to field workers)
*Malojillo/arrancando y botando (removing weeds from arable land)	*Arados/y cultivos (plowing)	*Ratoneros (placing poison for mice on growing cane)
*Desyervos (weeding cane after planting)	*Zanjeros/y deshorillado de caña (digging ditches for runoff water; clearing walkways)	*Linea (transporting movable railway from back to front as carts move forward)
*Aporcadores (gathering soil around young cane stalks)	*Siembra/bombeo de tierro y desyervo (planting new cane stalks)	*Carreteros/carretillas (driving oxen carts loaded with cane or wastes)
*Zanque y aticrro (straightening plant and securing roots by pushing downward on soil; plowing uncultivated soil)		*Ceniceros (depositing ashes from factory chimney on soil as fertilizer)
*Desmache (removing leaves from cane stalks)		*Sirvientes (running errands)
*Cortando pomarrosas (collecting roscapples)		
*Peones mano (hiring hands from other haciendas to help in particular tasks)		

Industrial

Machinery	Services
*Toneleros (weighing incoming cane)	*Guardias (taking care of property)
*Fogoneros (tending fires to keep steam pressure up)	*Pesebreros (taking care of animals; washing horses in river daily)
*Máquinas (running industrial equipment)	*Cercado (securing fences)
*Centrífugas (supervising centrifugals)	*Conducción leña (feeding wood to fire)
	*Trabajo noche/llegada de trenes de noche (night work, especially after arrival of wagonloads of cane)

* Destilación (making rum)
* Conductor de frutos (transporting cane through moving platform)
* Wagoneros (directing movement of cars inside factory)
* Bagazo seco (collecting dry bagasse)
* Peones al Malazó (loading sugar into wagons going to centrifugals)
* Limpieza (maintaining factory machinery)
* Zanjeros (building underground ditches; channeling waste material into them)
* Limpeza caños (cleaning underground ditches of waste material)
* Escombro (removing extraneous objects and materials from factory)
* Desembarque caldera (unloading machinery just arrived at river dock)
* Sirvientes (helping sugar technicians)
* Material/almacén (storing agricultural products or construction materials in warehouse)

Other

* Ajustados y otros gastos (payments for particular tasks and for materials)

Artisans

* Freneros (making brakes and bridles)
* Herreros (making horseshoes; repairing iron machinery)
* Albañiles (repairing rollers)
* Carpinteros (fixing ox carts and other wooden equipment)
* Corte maderas (preparing wood for future use)

Maintenance

* Casa Rosario (guarding overseer's house)
* Viajeros/y cuido de caballos (carrying messages from overseer's house)
* Guardias (keeping cattle on grazing grounds and away from plantation)
* Cortadores de leña (cutting timber two months before zafra in inland forests and swamps)
* Cojido paja (collecting coconut leaves for thatch)
* Camino de carril/camino de hierro/puente (maintaining railways and bridge for heavy machinery)

Sources: AGPR, AT, SC, Jornales, box 71, docs. 963, 964, 965; Documentos relacionados a la quiebra, box 31, doc. 451; Manuel Moreno Fraginals, *El ingenio. Complejo económico social cubano del azúcar*, vol. 3 (Havana: Editorial de Ciencias Sociales, 1978), glossary; Mintz, *Worker in the Cane*, glossary; Carlos Peñaranda, *Cartas puertorriqueñas, 1878–1880* (1885; rpt. San Juan: Editorial "El Cemí," 1967), p. 87; interview of Félix Pizarro Santos, 78-year-old former sugar worker in Vega Baja, 1983.

Table 3.5. Workers by Occupation, by Seasons

Number of workers[a]	Unskilled, skilled, and service agricultural	Industrial, artisan, and night	Maintenance and other	Total	Agricultural to industrial ratio
Tiempo muerto					
August 1885					
16–22	144	15	12	171	10:1
23–29	147	11	11	169	13:1
September 1885					
(Aug.) 30–6	141	14	8	173	10:1
7–13	151	10	6	167	15:1
October 1879					
5–11	75	—	4	79	—
12–18	79	—	5	84	—
19–25	59	—	5	64	—
November 1883					
18–24	56	9	12	77	6:1
December 1883					
(Nov.) 25–1	145	15	21	181	10:1
2–8	32	10	4	46	3:1
Zafra					
January 1880					
25–31	65	—	8	73	—
February 1880					
1–7	71	—	5	76	—
8–14	54	—	11	65	—
15–21	53	16	7	76	3:1
22–28	42	37	16	95	1:1
March 1880					
(Feb.) 29–6	54	23	5	82	2:1

Sources: AGPR, AT, SC, Jornales, box 71, docs. 963, 964; Documentos relacionados a la quiebra, box 31, doc. 451.
[a] These figures are drawn from a random sample of workers from San Vicente's ledgers for the years 1879–80, 1883, and 1885 and combined to create an artificial composite 16-week period spanning both *zafra* and *tiempo muerto*.

herited from ruined haciendas (most of it unusable, as is clear from the sale contracts), Igaravídez bought all of San Vicente's manufacturing equipment in 1873 from Cail y Cía. through Emilio Louhet, the French firm's agent in Puerto Rico. Although I could not determine the cost of the machinery, it is known that Igaravídez owed Cail y Cía. 120,805 pesos in 1878. At that time, the equipment was still considered the property of the French house, which had the right to seize all of Igaravídez's assets in case of default.[38]

Table 3.6. Loans Obtained from Local and International Firms

Date	Company	Amount[a] ($)
1869	Látimer y Cía.	42,556.62
1869	Sturges Co., New York	100,000
1873	Látimer y Cía.	40,500
1873	Daniel Ancel et Fils, Paris	19,300
1876	Félix Simplicio Alfonzo	40,000
1876	Ephrussi, Imperial Bank of London	90,000
1878	James Barber Son Co.	31,500
1878	Sociedad Anónima de Crédito Mercantil	45,000
1879	Sociedad Anónima de Crédito Mercantil	50,000

Sources: AGPR, PN, Demetrio Giménez y Moreno, box 213, 10 August 1869; box 221, 27 November, 23 December 1873; box 227, 19 April 1876; box 229, 11 September 1876; box 234, 24 August 1878; box 238, 2 August 1879; Juan Ramón de Torres, box 49, 8 October 1869.
[a] Included here are only the very large amounts provided as a line of credit by established firms. Igaravídez also contracted a variety of obligations with individuals and especially with the Caja de Ahorros, covered subsequently. Additional loans (whose origin I have not been able to trace) are included in table 1 of Andrés Ramos Mattei, *La hacienda azucarera. Su crecimiento y crisis en Puerto Rico (Siglo XIX)* (Río Piedras: Centro de Estudios de la Realidad Puertorriqueña, 1981), p. 30. Particularly important are two 1874 obligations to Moitessier Neveu and Darthes Bros. for 40,000 and 137,610 pesos, respectively. I believe other discrepancies between Ramos Mattei's table and mine are the result of the common practice by scribes of including previous pending obligations in subsequent agreements to pay.

In characteristic fashion, Don Leonardo also acquired and maintained the right to use the water from the Cibuco river, an element essential to the smooth operation of the recently purchased equipment. Whereas the previous owner of San Vicente had obtained permission to build a dam by agreement with his neighbors and had even taken on the responsibility of repairing the town bridge when necessary, Igaravídez limited his effort to confirming this authorization in 1868 and then proceeded to use the water for heavy industrial purposes. An 1886 legal battle with municipal authorities over the rising water level caused by the dam at San Vicente, a problem for the town in the absence of a safe bridge, was surprisingly resolved in favor of Igaravídez.[39]

As a successful entrepreneur, Igaravídez made more contacts with other members of the island's elite by participating in business ventures and in political forums to further his objectives. The establishment of good relations with the Vega Baja landowning community facilitated by his personal ties to the most prestigious families was a stepping-stone in this process. His title of nobility also provided him with special considerations and made him an important personage in the island's high society. Once connected to the most influential and wealthiest individuals, he became involved in more ambitious business projects, such as the Banco de Puerto Rico, an issuing and discount institution whose primary function was to regulate credit. As a member of Puerto Rico's Partido Conservador Templado (which in its short life supported the assimilation of Puerto Rico into Spain's administrative machinery as a province and social and economic reform, but refused to be identified with any ideological current), he associated with many of the influential men who later formed the Partido Liberal Reformista. Don Leonardo also aspired to be heard in the metropolis: he was reportedly a close associate of leading Republican figures and was elected as a delegate to and president of the highly influential Provincial Deputation in 1871 and 1879, respectively.[40]

Having removed himself from commercial activities, which were the exclusive sphere of the merchant/exporters who provided planters with funds, and dependent now on others to place his sugar on the market, Igaravídez made use of these social and political contacts to advertise his product. He sent samples of the high-quality sugar obtained in his mill to the Provincial Deputation in 1873 for exhibition to the public.[41] In 1878, he planned to present his sugar (some of it white) before the Universal Exposition in Paris and asked experts to certify that both the process and the system described in accounts of the processing of the product were the ones used.[42] Circumventing the obstacles posed by existing economic structures, Don Leonardo relied on personal, business, and political relations to obtain exposure in local and international markets concerned with high quality and innovative processes.

Igaravídez's attitudes and behavior during the early 1870s were highly effective. He mobilized resources, ran risks, took a personal interest, applied pressure—conforming almost to the letter to later conceptualizations of entrepreneurial personalities. But to place Igaravídez into the mold cast by the literature on entrepreneurship would be misleading. Igaravídez's decision-making style, in fact, reveals that he was a man of his times. What distinguished him was the scope of his activities, and not necessarily his goals or his methods. As any other successful businessman, Don Leonardo took his image as the lord of vast properties very seriously. It enhanced his social prestige, which he must have especially treasured as a self-made man. It also placed him in a convenient position within the island's economic elite. Business behavior went hand in hand with social aspirations in nineteenth-century Puerto Rico. Igaravídez used both to define his role as a producer of change. He behaved no differently than others in his position and with his resources.

An early thirst for land promoted Igaravídez's image as an enterprising landlord. Don Leonardo hurriedly acquired surrounding haciendas at a time when the estates had exhausted their possibilities as profit-making enterprises. He may have been forced to buy them as the only way to make them produce cane for the central.[43] He could also have calculated that they would eventually serve as added collateral for loans on machinery. Or perhaps he simply took advantage of their precarious financial situation to promote his social position as the most prestigious landowner in the area. The alternatives are not exclusive. Yet the simultaneous purchase of small tracts of land from poorer neighbors suggests a desire to consolidate his dominion.[44] His understanding—shared by others at the time—that landholding brought prestige and influence was undoubtedly a consideration that entered Igaravídez's business decisions.

Besides providing absolute control over certain resources, amassing land made the seigneurial lifestyle a reality. Contemporary accounts portray Igaravídez as an authoritarian patriarch. A bold organizer, he apparently refused to delegate responsibility and got personally involved with the most insignificant details, from forming construction brigades for worker homes to correcting visitors on misconceptions of the factory's operations. On his regular surveys of the estate, he reportedly wore white and was accompanied by a groom, much like a traveling gentleman. A solid member of the local community, he donated the altar that adorned the simple Vega Baja church.[45] Fully participating in activities that promoted his image as an influential figure, Igaravídez advanced his position among the rich and powerful.

The vast expanse of available land promoted the creative use of resources. San Vicente, a producer of export crops, also grew foodstuffs for internal consumption. Jerked beef, codfish, and oil complemented the staple meal of sweet potatoes and plantains prepared at the central's eatery daily. The practice of permitting workers to settle on the premises and cultivate small plots of land served both to tie the labor force to the enterprise and to allow it some access to the means of production.[46] Igaravídez tried to make the novel project work, using all the instruments at his disposal.

But from a strictly profit-making point of view, the possession of such vast amounts of land for no specific purpose was irrational. Simultaneously consolidating the five dependencies while applying innovative factorylike techniques apparently rendered impossible the coordination of the cultivation and the manufacturing processes. Moreover, if San Vicente had contracted with neighboring haciendas for supplies of cane, as it did briefly with haciendas Hornos, Encarnación, and others, it would have paid its suppliers only 5 percent of the weight of the cane in sugar at the current market price.[47] The landowners would have borne the risk for market fluctuations, while the manufacturer's profit would have been secured. By acting as a landowner himself, Igaravídez became vulnerable to the same difficulties they faced.

The mistake was fatal. The few remaining ledgers of the central show that more than half of its expenses were on agricultural activities at San Vicente, Rosario, Fe, and Felicidad lands (table 3.7). Other expenses in 1881 included industrial repairs and labor, maintenance for the court-appointed trustees of the failed estate, and payments to the government and to creditors. If one were to exclude receivership-related expenses altogether, placing taxes under land-related expenses, the agricultural/industrial ratio would be much higher.

The problem of high agricultural costs was exacerbated by the fact that the central's demand for labor did not significantly decrease at any particular time during the year (fig. 3.4). Forced as it was to depend on income from the zafra to pay for operations throughout the year, the sugar factory faced problems not found in other manufacturing enterprises. As is clear from table 3.8, these revenues barely covered expenses during tiempo muerto, and San Vicente resorted to refacciones, just as did ordinary haciendas during those months. The steady weekly expenses of the complex that resulted from the need to pay constant attention to the soil presented the landowner/manufacturer with a truly unresolvable difficulty.

San Vicente stood as the symbol on which the hopes of Puerto Rican reformers and Vega Baja's landowners were pinned. The installa-

Table 3.7. Monthly Expenses at San Vicente, December 1880–May 1881 (in pesos)

	12–31 Dec. 1880	Jan. 1881	Feb. 1881	Mar. 1881	Apr. 1881	May 1881
Agricultural						
San Vicente fields	1,190	1,948	1,948	2,048	1,993	1,808
Rosario and Fe fields	870	1,500	1,501	1,466	1,505	1,410
Felicidad fields	870	1,508	1,508	1,473	1,528	1,433
Sharecroppers	70	—	—	—	—	—
Labor force meals	80	925	850	1,000	800	900
Leasing of land	—	—	—	—	180	90
Subtotal	3,080	5,881	5,807	5,987	6,006	5,641
Industrial						
Factory maintenance	300	1,875	1,050	1,300	800	1,400
Boat crew salary	90	—	360	315	315	315
Employee salaries	331	461	523	563	563	563
Worker wages	—	1,050	1,000	800	541	800
Subtotal	721	3,386	2,933	2,978	2,219	3,078
Other						
Trustees' meals	105	204	184	204	197	203
Pending obligations	1,634	—	1,000	—	—	—
Taxes	116	—	—	—	3,059	3,059
Unforeseen	342	175	75	130	—	—
Subtotal	2,197	379	1,259	334	3,256	3,262
Total	5,998	9,646	9,999	9,299	11,481	11,981
Agricultural expenses as a percentage of total expenses	51.4%	60.9%	58.1%	64.4%	52.3%	47.1%

Sources: AGPR, AT, SC, Documentos relacionados a la quiebra, box 31, doc. 447, 22 December 1880, 1, 12 January, 7 February, 2 March, 8 April, 1 May 1881.

tion of sophisticated equipment, the introduction of division of labor, and the adoption of innovative methods of production and administration seemed to mark the arrival of change to the northern coast. But Igaravídez, enterprising as he was, was also a man of his time. Central San Vicente, then, was a fair reflection of its owner's understanding of his role as social and economic leader. Its use of land remained a statement regarding the overlapping of business and social objectives in nineteenth-century Puerto Rico. The climate, however, was not favorable, given the dimensions of the experiment.

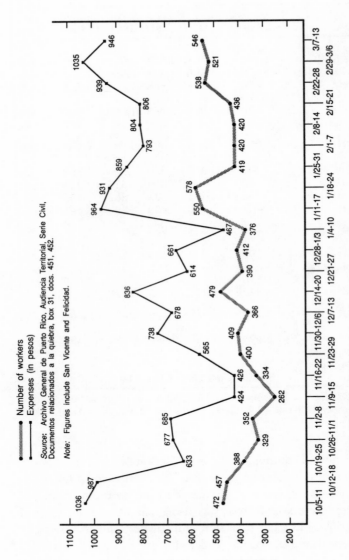

Fig. 3.4. Number of workers and total expenses (1879–80)

Source: Archivo General de Puerto Rico, Audiencia Territorial, Serie Civil, Documentos relacionados a la quiebra, box 31, docs. 451, 452.

Note: Figures include San Vicente and Felicidad.

Table 3.8. Seasonal Income and Expenses, 1883–1886 (in pesos)

Season	Expenses	Income	Gain/loss	Balance
Tiempo muerto, 1883				
October	3,000	17,872[a]	14,872	14,872
November	20,518	12,701[a]	−7,817	7,055
December	7,450	1,108	−6,342	713
Zafra, 1884				
January	3,900	4,637	737	1,450
February	4,700	4,000	−700	750
March	5,000	6,000	1,000	1,750
April	4,000	24,000	20,000	21,750
May	4,700	—	−4,700	17,050
June	11,434	14,000	2,566	19,616
Tiempo muerto, 1884				
July	8,000	9,000	1,000	20,616
August	10,600	3,000	−7,600	13,016
September	—	—	—	—
October	9,935	—	−9,935	3,081
November	—	7,919	7,919	11,000
December	7,800	—	−7,800	3,200
Zafra, 1885				
January	2,500	—	−2,500	700
February	—	—	—	—
March	2,500	10,000	7,500	8,200
April	3,300	10,000	6,700	14,900
May	2,500	8,500	6,000	20,900
June	—	6,100	6,100	27,000
Tiempo muerto, 1885				
July	850	11,000	10,150	37,150
August	4,000	7,000[a]	3,000	40,150
September	6,000	5,000	−1,000	39,150
October	11,000	—	−11,000	28,150
November	9,300	—	−9,300	18,850
December	8,732	—	−8,732	10,118
Zafra, 1886				
January	5,700	—	−5,700	4,418
February	3,500	3,000	−500	3,918
March	6,300	12,000	5,700	9,618
April	2,000	5,500	3,500	13,118
May	2,000	12,000	10,000	23,118
June	2,200	8,000	5,800	28,918

Source: AGPR, AT, SC, Caja de caudales, box 30, doc. 424.
[a]These figures represent income from sources other than sales of sugar. Other fluctuations in San Vicente's accounts can be explained by the fact that only during the zafra and the months immediately following did the complex obtain income from the sale of its products. Well into tiempo muerto every year the central's cash flow was low.

4

The Decline of Central
San Vicente

Capital

Igaravídez resorted to the means available not only to promote his position in influential economic and social circles, as is clear from the last chapter, but also to give life to his business decisions by capitalizing the enterprise. Because of the context in which he operated, though, borrowing money turned out to be the immediate source of San Vicente's disappearance. Puerto Rico's short experience with credit-granting mechanisms translated into an informality that worked well when loans were small and repayment periods short. But the ambitious goals to which Igaravídez was committed necessitated unusually large investments. In an attempt to transcend the confines of existing credit channels, Igaravídez overextended himself, convinced of his ability to repay his obligations with forthcoming profits. Once he declared insolvency and faced the accusation of embezzlement, arguments regarding the economic soundness of the project went unheard. The strict application of the Commercial Code responded to a rigid bureaucratic line advanced by some of his creditors, more interested in receiving a small but immediate return on their loans than in participating in a promised flow of income at a later date. Even as the central recuperated, those who still believed in the venture succumbed to a series of personal attacks. Like the haciendas before it, San Vicente ultimately fell victim to external forces that had little to do with its internal organization.

Igaravídez's obligations included small loans, large investments, and running expenses. The absence of banks forced the average nineteenth-century businessman to rely on highly personalized credit mechanisms for day-to-day commercial transactions in Puerto Rico. Exchanges took place through individuals or private firms in the form of vouchers, draft bills, or promissory notes.[1] Personal connections, name, and birth were important considerations in determining creditworthiness. These methods extended even to paying with notes for items for personal use and of little worth, almost as if cash itself were involved. It was not uncommon, then, for a note to change hands as many as five times, its ultimate holder legally empowered to require the money from the underwriter, the guarantor, the endorser, or any previous beneficiaries.[2] Sometimes individuals defaulted on the payment of a voucher; the law, however, encouraged creditors to demand payment through a formal protest and permitted the obligation to continue to circulate as usual.[3]

Igaravídez's use of the short-term instruments available to obtain capital was creative, to say the least, and, for a long time, effective. The most straightforward of three methods he used to secure credit almost automatically was to undersign a draft (table 4.1). Igaravídez would issue a voucher in an individual's or commercial firm's favor, committing himself to paying the full amount in one to three months to whoever legally held the obligation at the time it was due. This procedure either made money immediately available to Igaravídez (as if he had borrowed money from a bank) or, if he was incurring an obligation with the beneficiary, permitted him to postpone payments of principal. Among Igaravídez's most generous creditors were Gil Gordils and the commercial companies Carreras e hijos and Barreras y Castillo, for whom he personally signed 71,550 pesos' worth of vouchers. It was clear that Igaravídez himself had issued the obligations originally and was responsible for repaying the loans.

As the guarantor of a loan, however, he shared this task with the underwriter. For example, Arturo McCormick issued the notes Igaravídez was required to pay in September 1873 (table 4.2). They were drawn in favor of various people, and by law Igaravídez was liable for providing the money at the required time just as was McCormick, the underwriter. Igaravídez must have struck a deal with McCormick and assumed full responsibility for future payments to the note holders, as

Table 4.1. Vouchers Undersigned by Igaravídez

Date	In favor of	Holder	Amount ($)
7/78	Caja de Ahorros	Caja de Ahorros	10,000
8/78	Caja de Ahorros	Caja de Ahorros	10,000
6/79	Gil Gordils	José Pérez Moris	3,150
6/79	Carreras e hijos	Crédito Mercantil	2,000
6/79	Gil Gordils	Crédito Mercantil	3,000
7/79	Carreras e hijos	Crédito Mercantil	1,000
7/79	Orcasitas y Cía.	José Orcasitas y Ortiz	1,575
7/79	Orcasitas y Cía.	Orcasitas y Cía.	1,575
7/79	Carreras e hijos	Crédito Mercantil	2,000
7/79	Gil Gordils	Crédito Mercantil	2,000
7/79	Gil Gordils	Crédito Mercantil	2,400
7/79	Carreras e hijos	Crédito Mercantil	2,400
7/79	Gil Gordils	Crédito Mercantil	2,000
7/79	Barreras y Castillo	Crédito Mercantil	1,500
7/79	Barreras y Castillo	Crédito Mercantil	2,500
7/79	Gil Gordils	Crédito Mercantil	3,000
7/79	Carreras e hijos	Crédito Mercantil	2,000
7/79	Silvestre Iglesias	Miguel Saralegui Taca	1,050
7/79	Carreras e hijos	Crédito Mercantil	1,400
7/79	Caja de Ahorros	Caja de Ahorros	21,000
8/79	Carreras e hijos	Crédito Mercantil	2,000
8/79	Mariano Vasallo	Caja de Ahorros	6,000[a]
8/79	Gil Gordils	Caja de Ahorros	6,000[a]
9/79	Federico Aguayo y González	Federico Aguayo y González	2,100
9/79	Gil Gordils	Crédito Mercantil	2,700
9/79	Gil Gordils	Crédito Mercantil	2,400
9/79	Ricardo Mendizábal	Chavarri, Mendizábal y Cía.	10,500
9/79	Gil Gordils	Eduardo Trujillo Piza	1,000
10/79	Gil Gordils	Caja de Ahorros	6,000
10/79	Gil Gordils	Caja de Ahorros	6,000
10/79	Gil Gordils	Caja de Ahorros	9,100
10/79	Caja de Ahorros	Caja de Ahorros	10,500
10/79	Igaravídez, Mariani y Cía.	Caja de Ahorros	6,000
10/79	Gil Gordils	Caja de Ahorros	6,000
	Bartolomé Simonet Morrill[b]	Bartolomé Simonet Morrill	3,360
	Federico Aguayo y González[b]	Federico Aguayo y González	661
	Total		155,771

Sources: AGPR, PN, Demetrio Giménez y Moreno, box 239, 28 October, 6 November 1879; box 240, 11, 17, 21, 25, 26 November, 1, 11, 22, 26, 31 December 1879; box 242, 7, 12, 21, 26 January, 19, 27 February, 4, 11, 27, 28 September 1880; Juan Ramón de Torres, box 77, 21 November 1879.
[a] Indicates voucher undersigned by Igaravídez, Mariani y Cía.
[b] Indicates several vouchers at different dates.

Table 4.2. Vouchers Guaranteed by Igaravídez

Date	Undersigned by	Holder	Amount ($)
7/3/73[a]	Ledesma y Cía.	Vda. de Vías	1,000
7/3/73[a]	Arturo McCormick	Pedro de Menchaca	1,000
7/3/73[a]	Arturo McCormick	Sobrinos de Ezquiaga	1,274
7/3/73[a]	Arturo McCormick	Juan y Capetillo	563
7/3/73[a]	Arturo McCormick	Juan y Capetillo	500
7/3/73[a]	Arturo McCormick	Venancio Luina	500
7/4/73[a]	Ledesma y Cía.	Sobrinos de Ezquiaga	476
7/4/73[a]	Ledesma y Cía.	Francisco Brunet	1,523
7/5/73[a]	Ledesma y Cía.	Schion, Willink y Cía.	1,164
7/5/73[a]	Arturo McCormick	B. Boras y Hnos.	150
7/8/73[a]	Arturo McCormick	Látimer y Cía.	2,000
7/10/73[a]	Arturo McCormick	Lavandera y Cía.	551
7/10/73[a]	Arturo McCormick	Vilaseca y Cía.	1,130
7/10/73[a]	Arturo McCormick	C. Audifredd y Cía.	700
7/18/73[a]	Arturo McCormick	Látimer y Cía.	700
7/2/79	Justo Skerret	Crédito Mercantil	1,000
8/9/79	Gil Gordils	Quírico Masjuan Mundo	500
11/10/79	Gil Gordils	Quírico Masjuan Mundo	500
	Total		15,231

Sources: AGPR, PN, Demetrio Giménez y Moreno, box 220, 3, 4, 5, 8, 10, 18 July 1873; box 242, 3 February 1880; Juan Ramón de Torres, box 77, 10, 18 November, 10 December 1879.
[a] Indicates date lack of payment was protested before the authorities.

McCormick made the same amounts available to him at the time of issue. Although he temporarily avoided appearing as underwriter of even more obligations, Igaravídez was nevertheless required to pay as guarantor a total of 15,231 pesos to different note holders in 1873. McCormick, who was also legally responsible for the obligations, simply pointed an accusatory finger at Igaravídez, for whom, he claimed, he was only doing a favor.

A third way in which Igaravídez obtained cash was by having a voucher drawn in his favor (table 4.3). This method required the undersigner—a friend—to "commit himself to paying" Igaravídez a certain amount by a fixed date, as if Igaravídez had rendered the underwriter a service for which he owed Igaravídez that amount. It appears that the exchange of money for services was purely fictitious, and that Igaravídez agreed never to require payment from the underwriter. To obtain ready cash or to cover previous obligations, Igaraví-

Table 4.3. Vouchers in Favor of Igaravídez

Date	Undersigned by	Holder	Amount ($)
6/25/79	Igaravídez, Mariani y Cía.	Crédito Mercantil	5,000
6/28/79	Gil Gordils	Crédito Mercantil	4,000
7/19/79	Lope Córdova	Crédito Mercantil	2,500
8/11/79	Barreras y Castillo	Crédito Mercantil	940
8/11/79	Igaravídez, Mariani y Cía.	Crédito Mercantil	2,000
8/25/79	Barreras y Castillo	Crédito Mercantil	862
8/25/79	Barreras y Castillo	Antonio Moreno y Santi	863
8/30/79	Carlos Santana	Crédito Mercantil	2,400
9/2/79	Carlos Santana	Crédito Mercantil	2,000
9/2/79	Igaravídez, Mariani y Cía.	Crédito Mercantil	2,700
9/19/79	Eduardo López Cepero	Pablo Rodríguez Arnau	1,000
9/20/79	Gil Gordils	Crédito Mercantil	4,000
9/26/79	Sainz y Cía.	Pablo Rodríguez Arnau	1,000
9/26/79	Rabell Bos.	Crédito Mercantil	2,000
9/26/79	Barreras y Castillo	Crédito Mercantil	1,170
9/30/79	Igaravídez, Mariani y Cía.	Crédito Mercantil	1,700
9/30/79	Carreras e hijos	Pedro Vidal Amadeo	800
10/6/79	Carreras e hijos	Pedro Matanzo Rodríguez	1,000
10/6/79	Carlos Santana	Crédito Mercantil	2,000
10/10/79	Bartolomé Simonet	Balmes y Hno.	1,000
10/10/79	Carlos de Choudens	Crosas y Finlay	8,400
	Total		47,335

Sources: AGPR, PN, Demetrio Giménez y Moreno, box 239, 27 October 1879; box 240, 12, 21, 26 November, 11, 12, 16, 26, 31 December 1879; box 242, 7, 11, 12, 21, 22, 29 January, 4 February 1880.

dez presumably endorsed the vouchers promptly in favor of another individual or firm. By doing this, however, he assumed responsibility for payment to the holder of the obligation in the future. He avoided, nevertheless, appearing as the underwriter of the note. Using this procedure, Igaravídez obtained more than 33,000 pesos from the Sociedad Anónima de Crédito Mercantil.

The purpose to which these monies were put is not known. Because such large amounts were obtained by means of a reputation based on social prestige and in countless small transactions (most under 10,000 pesos), it appears that they were personal loans, perhaps to be used for the payment of mortgages on the recently acquired properties. This interpretation is plausible given that the dates of issue point precisely to the months just prior to Igaravídez's formal default on all his obligations, well into tiempo muerto. As payments for the five haciendas became due, one suspects that Igaravídez found himself barely able to cover the regular refacciones into which he had previously entered and so borrowed money desperately in order not to default on the mortgages. This situation eventually became untenable, and his insolvency was made public.

The ownership of vast amounts of land once more looked problematic. As stated earlier, several likely explanations exist for Igaravídez's strategy with respect to the neighboring haciendas. The social prestige that went with landownership may have seduced Igaravídez into following in the footsteps of Vega Baja's elite families. The attractions of a seigneurial life-style were irresistible. A second alternative is that Igaravídez acquired the land around San Vicente so as to control the cultivation of cane in the region. The financial debacle faced by Vega Baja planters suggests that they would be hard-pressed to produce the large amounts of raw material required by the central. A third explanation is that Igaravídez sought to control available land as a means to obtain a reliable labor force. As will be argued in the next chapter, he could not only dispossess peasants of their means of subsistence (and so force them to sell their labor force at the central) but also offer workers as a fringe benefit a piece of land on which to settle (in this way creating an artificially resident labor force). Finally, he could have estimated the collateral value of the land and figured it would serve as a means of obtaining loans to establish the factory.

Any of these reasons, and very probably all of them together, are plausible. Igaravídez's entrepreneurial style was one in which sound business decisions and the image of prosperity were equally important components of the formula for success. The land acquired, then, served the dual purpose of launching Igaravídez into the ranks of Vega Baja's well to do and of providing the project with the necessary funds. The financial mechanisms available in nineteenth-century Puerto Rico, in fact, calculated the worth of an individual not just on the basis of the property he owned and could place as collateral but on the promise he showed as a community and business leader. Business decisions went hand in hand with social prestige. Landownership was almost a prerequisite for the industrial entrepreneur.

Large-scale improvements to haciendas, such as extending the amount of land under cultivation or buying machinery, required funds from well-known European and U.S. investors who demanded as collateral the enterprise itself. Since a project such as Central San Vicente required immense capital investments immediately upon its establishment, Igaravídez—whose credit rating and personal connections with other merchants were outstanding in the early seventies—assumed obligations with the most prestigious lending institutions under the strictest of conditions. Commonly found in the contracts he signed were a *claúsula de guarentigio*, which permitted creditors to require payment directly, without first obtaining a court sentence to the same effect; a commitment to pay *mancomunada y solidariamente*, so that a creditor could demand full payment proportionally from all the debtors or from Igaravídez only; and a refusal to appeal in case of default to the provisions of *quita y espera*, whereby creditors could be legally requested to lower the amount of an outstanding debt and extend the period of time in which to pay it.

In an 1869 $100,000 loan from Sturges & Co. of New York, for example, Igaravídez and his wife agreed to have their property seized and foreclosed immediately should they fail to meet the conditions of the contract. In similar fashion, Igaravídez bought San Vicente's manufacturing equipment in 1873 from Cail y Cía. of Paris by mortgaging all his properties, still owing the company 120,805 pesos in 1878 and committing himself to pay immediately should he happen to declare bankruptcy. Daniel Ancel et fils of Le Havre advanced 100,000 francs to Igaravídez in 1873 and accepted as security a 29,000-peso note from his brother-in-law Justo Skerret. By 1877, Igaravídez had borrowed close to 10,000 pesos from Fernando Vázquez Ramos and 40,000 pesos from Félix Simplicio Alfonzo, mortgaging part of his and his wife's properties and empowering his creditor to dispose of them should Igaravídez fail to pay interest in any given month.[4] As opposed to the small and complicated transactions discussed above, these long-term loans for more substantial amounts were undoubtedly channeled into the sugar complex directly.

The strategy Igaravídez followed to promote his project backfired, although ironically it saved the project from total disaster. The haciendas served as collateral for the sizable loans needed, yet forced Igaravídez to divert capital into paying for the land and making it produce. By not concentrating solely on the industrial tasks as the advocates of centralization urged, he continued to lay out money for the most expensive and remained vulnerable to the most risky aspects of production. But, as I will argue later, the failure to centralize was a blessing in disguise. If Central San Vicente had produced sugar according to the stipulations in reformers' plans, perhaps it would not have been able to place it successfully on the market. As it was, the complex produced efficiently enough and could have solved its internal deficiencies, had it not been for the limitations that available financial mechanisms imposed on a project of such dimensions.

Finally, the manufacture of sugar—an activity that required constant inputs but generated income only seasonally—depended on intermediate credit for its continuous operations. For day-to-day expenses, local refaccionistas—merchant/exporters with connections in international markets—either opened lines of credit through their own firms for hacendados or underwrote their clients' risky agricultural investments through time drafts issued in the merchant's name and arranged with overseas or local lending companies.[5] Látimer y Cía. of San Juan, for example, in three loans committed nearly 40,000, 20,000 and 40,500 pesos to be used during specific time periods in 1869 and 1873, with the understanding that Igaravídez would pay the firm with manufactured sugar after each zafra. Ephrussi y Cía. in France, James Barber Son & Co. in Great Britain, and Sociedad Anónima de Crédito Mercantil in Puerto Rico opened lines of credit for 40,000, 31,500, and 95,000 pesos respectively, in 1876, 1878, and 1879; Igaravídez pledged all his properties and future assets as security.[6] But because the price of sugar fluctuated so violently during this period, it was common for a loan not to be fully repaid at the time agreed, usually after the zafra. A planter could easily enter into an obligation based on market conditions at the time of issue, only to discover that income from sugar sales fell short of his expectations.

Both the intricate arrangements behind the scenes that became the rule in Igaravídez's small personal loans and the stringent conditions of repayment on large loans and intermediate lines of credit appear to have been extreme methods for obtaining cash. Yet, Igaravídez's use of his wife's and his company's assets for his own business concerns—based, if not on coercion of his wife or an incomplete disclosure of facts to his creditors, surely on a show of power and authority—was not outside the bounds of ordinary practice. His personal friends' and business associates' negation of responsibility in Igaravídez's money matters was also foreseeable given his assurances of responsibility for settling particular debts. That he flaunted his acquiescence to strict repayment conditions was natural in a system in which appearances of financial security had such importance. All were common practices in a male-dominated, highly personalized, and prestige-conscious society.

Exceptional, no doubt, is the ease with which the ambitious entrepreneur mobilized such large amounts without real guarantees. Forced to borrow small amounts in the form of refacciones through local companies with limited financial capital, Igaravídez resorted to overcommitment as the only way to obtain the funds needed to launch the enterprise. One suspects he was convinced of San Vicente's ultimate success; if the central failed, his creditors would inevitably discover that the property he had placed as security over and over again would not cover the loans. Taking advantage of the good will and mutual trust on which business transactions rested, Igaravídez obtained the money needed, expecting to repay it as profits poured in. His ungraceful fate followed logically.

That Igaravídez proceeded the way that he did is not particularly surprising, given the unfavorable business climate promoted by the absence of local banks. The operations of financial intermediaries in Puerto Rico suffered from several limitations: they were not based on savings, as are loans by a bank backed by deposits; they were not investment oriented but served merely to keep the productive and distributive apparatus in motion; they often depended on transactions with outside credit institutions whose deposits were necessarily in foreign currency and had to be replaced according to currency exchange fluctuations. Credit instruments generated no new savings, concentrated only on the circulation of available monies, and facilitated the flight abroad of profits from most of these exchanges.[7] Since island refaccionistas were perfectly satisfied with the immediate gains resulting from their monopoly of trade and foreign exchange (through control over the circulation of goods and capital), they were not likely to become the agents for change. Puerto Rican planters were forced to borrow under the terms dictated by local merchants or, if that option seemed inadequate, to make creative use of the mechanisms available.

That the personal element remained paramount in business transactions is evident not only in the means of obtaining credit but in the use of legal instruments for collecting the money owed.[8] In October

1879, Igaravídez officially defaulted on the payment of some of his obligations and subjected himself to the decisions of a *concurso voluntario de acreedores*.[9] He expected to use some clauses in the Civil Code to his advantage. Filing for a concurso, for example, automatically stopped interest from accruing because all obligations were legally due. Igaravídez also hoped to negotiate a flexible payment plan with his creditors, as the enterprise recuperated under more austere management.[10] Instead, he encountered the opposition of one of his largest creditors, Darthes Hnos., who insisted on a formal declaration of bankruptcy as stipulated in the Commercial Code (and consequently, judicial intervention), given Igaravídez's status as a merchant and the commercial nature of his obligations. Igaravídez, however, managed to have his application for *concurso necesario* approved in December 1879, a Pyrrhic victory in that it all but acknowledged the gravity of the situation. The court immediately named a custodian to look after the interests of the creditors, as Igaravídez tried to avert the impending threat of full bankruptcy hearings. He spent most of 1880 fighting Darthes Hnos. and Chavarri, Mendizábal y Cía., who were quite intent on forcing a full declaration of bankruptcy, using as evidence the documents Igaravídez himself had presented at court as the law required.[11] How much personal influence different parties were able to exert became a crucial issue for the duration of the case.

It must have been during the initial examination period—clearly a deviation from Igaravídez' plans when he filed for a concurso voluntario—that the extent of his indebtedness was discovered. In order to borrow such large quantities, he had knowingly overextended his credit; his assets could never have properly covered his liabilities. This circumstance placed him in the third-class bankruptcy category (*quiebra culpable*), designed for those whose financial difficulties were not temporary and fortuitous but were expected to continue over the long term because they resulted from irresponsible administration. More careful analysis, however, suggests that Igaravídez could easily have been placed in fourth-class bankruptcy (*quiebra fraudulenta*), reserved for fraudulent actions. Not only had he placed as security his and his wife's properties over and over again, he had also contracted an enormous amount of debt shortly before he declared insolvency, used funds that rightfully belonged to his creditors after forming the concurso, and disposed of goods (a thousand barrels of sugar) he had placed as guarantee for his obligations, all considered serious offenses in the Commercial Code.[12] Even more damaging were his transactions with the Caja de Ahorros, then also facing bankruptcy hearings; since no individual was supposed to withdraw more than 1,000 pesos from the savings institution, Igaravídez's business with the Caja—loans totaling 195,000 pesos—stood out as a glaring irregularity.[13]

Igaravídez must never have forgiven himself for having allowed the case to reach the courts. Hoping to limit somewhat the extent of the tribunal's findings, he insisted that his assets were more than his liabilities and that there was no proof he had made use of funds after he called the concurso. He asked the court to dismiss Darthes Hnos. and Chavarri, Mendizábal y Cía. as plaintiffs and demanded that his creditors return his books to the authorities.[14] Darthes Hnos. and Chavarri, Mendizábal y Cía. insisted that all aspects of the case should be tried jointly, as it bounced from court to court in 1880 and as more and more creditors attempted to be legally recognized. Igaravídez's personal influence no longer resulted in preferential treatment, as powerful creditors began to have their say.

Much of the anxiety, excruciating to defendant and plaintiffs alike, could have been avoided if both parties' efforts had been more carefully directed. Don Leonardo, on the one hand, had only to prove to his creditors that his project had good chances for success: San Vicente's productivity was high by any standards (nearly 3,100 pounds of sugar per acre); its sugar yield, record breaking (over 9 percent); its income from sales, impressive (2.79 pesos per quintal). My rough estimate of annual profits, allowing for the most adverse circumstances, is more than $40,000.[15] Igaravídez's creditors, on the other hand, had simply to agree on a method and schedule of payment that would make it possible for the central to continue operations as it paid off its debts. A solution advantageous to all—one that permitted the complex to develop its potential and to meet its obligations—was clearly within the reach of the parties involved.

But human reactions are unpredictable, and dissension and infighting prevailed over rational evaluations and sound judgments. In July 1881, several well-known personalities in commercial and legal circles were named to a commission that would mediate the interests of debtor and creditors. A group of creditors, however, refused to reach any agreement unless all obligations with the powerful (and dangerous)

Darthes Hnos. and the Caja de Ahorros were settled. These dissidents, and the French consul who represented Cail y Cía., were against the declaration of bankruptcy requested by Darthes Hnos. and promoted the gradual payment of obligations. The dissidents believed, rightly, that San Vicente could overcome existing difficulties, especially the most recent ones caused by the careless administration of Serapio Miticola, the trustee appointed by the court after a good friend of Igaravídez was dismissed on the grounds of conflicting interests.[16] Their inflexible stance, however, only complicated things.

To make matters worse, the appearance of new creditors increased the number of people that had to be dealt with and the time needed for decisions. In August 1881, the Caja de Ahorros was recognized as a legal plaintiff in the case over the opposition of Igaravídez's counsel, who argued that only the debtor and the administrator who represented the rights and assets of the creditors should be heard in the proceedings.[17] Shortly thereafter, a Vega Baja merchant, Francisco de Diego, sued for lack of payment on a 3,782-peso credit line opened at his establishment for San Vicente's workers by Serapio Miticola, the controversial administrator who had since died. By March 1882, five other creditors were demanding acknowledgment as coplaintiffs in the original suit.[18]

Igaravídez's renown in island society—a factor that should have accelerated the dispensation of justice—only delayed the procedures at hand. For a time, a number of lawyers, court clerks, and consultants dismissed themselves from the case, as they considered their involvement in it to be based on personal interest. No judge could be found to try the case, an even greater problem when it passed to a lay judge in a municipal court from the court of first instance in San Juan. The president of the Real Audiencia itself was formally required to step down because he was a friend of several parties in the case. Igaravídez must have become impatient with the unnecessarily long procedure and expected a more expedient treatment than he was afforded, for he was accused of showing no respect for and threatening the court.[19]

Much of what delayed the case was the result of human folly. Serapio Miticola's two-year period of crooked management soon after the concurso was formed resulted in the embezzlement of funds everyone thought had been disbursed to Francisco de Diego's general store. The Vega Baja merchant's demand for payment from the concurso, moreover, appears to have been the logical conclusion of an out-of-court agreement between Igaravídez's creditors and de Diego, who shared the same lawyer. Intentional dilatory practices among the counsel of both parties, in fact, prevented the case from being examined on its merits and reduced all discussion to irrelevant technicalities contained in the Commercial Code's small print. Only in late 1883 was an unequivocal verdict reached—bankruptcy with all its consequences. Igaravídez was sentenced to prison for fraud and embezzlement, and his properties were placed in the hands of the court.[20]

That Igaravídez was responsible for his own misfortune is not to be doubted. Given his previous experience as a merchant and lender, he must have entered obligations understanding the risks involved and the elements at stake. He nevertheless fatally misjudged the impact of his actions in a context of limited time and resources. The financial needs of the project went well beyond the capacity of existing structures, and the time needed for tangible returns was much more than credit institutions were willing to wait.[21] More importantly, the human element seemed to win out over practical concerns: the courts permitted the most irrational conduct to prevail. As interested parties struggled to defend their own positions, the justice that might have been achieved by a quick resolution based on the central's chances for rehabilitation was lost.

The reaction of local newspapers to San Vicente's troubles confirms the passions that the case aroused in Puerto Rican society. For a couple of months after the declaration of bankruptcy in October 1879, *El Boletín Mercantil* (the organ of the unconditionally pro-Spanish conservatives) and *El Agente* (the well-known liberal newspaper) debated the bankruptcy case of the Caja de Ahorros, which was intimately related to Igaravídez's embarrassing fate. *El Boletín* condemned the Caja for acting irresponsibly, especially during the time it functioned as "the base of operations for Igaravídez's speculations." Ignoring its role as the protector of its members' savings, the articles argued, the Caja de Ahorros had not renewed its charter since 1875, had effectively changed its lending policies without informing its members, had made no effort to collect outstanding obligations, and was not keeping its account books up-to-date. *El Boletín* explained this behavior by accusing the Caja's board of directors, all good friends and business associates of Leonardo Igaravídez, of abandoning safe and honest business practices in favor of risky capitalistic investment.[22]

A cursory glance at the articles in *El Boletín* reveals a number of factors that were to acquire significance in San Vicente's bankruptcy case. Igaravídez had stepped on the toes of the powerful, many of whom shared the opinion of the conservative businessmen who constituted *El Boletín*'s readership. Because the newspaper had lost $32,000 as a result of the Caja's loans to Igaravídez, its attacks against "speculating with hard-earned savings" were frontal. More dangerous, however, was *El Boletín*'s merchant sponsors' perception of Igaravídez as a maverick planter who threatened their monopoly on credit. If successfully linked to the conservative-liberal political split on the island, these economic considerations could add extraneous elements to Igaravídez's case before the courts. Fortunately for Igaravídez, politics itself became a more interesting topic to the local press. After the initial uproar, his name came up only once more in *El Boletín*. Removed from the public eye, the heated debate became a more rational affair.

But for other reasons, the receivership period (1883–87) was as catastrophic a time as the original court intervention in 1880. The price of sugar, relatively stable in the 1860s and 1870s, went down precipitously in 1884. Few creditors were understanding with respect to the central's now habitual delay in paying its obligations. When the trustees named by the court in 1884 failed to pay taxes, as happened often, the central was prosecuted by the municipality. At least twice the town council refused to make exceptions for San Vicente, claiming that they had already lowered the amount to be disbursed and could not wait any longer for the payment. The municipality made such an issue of it, that even San Vicente's workers were formally prosecuted for the payment of taxes when their debt amounted to only 48 *centavos* each.[23]

Why the municipality lost patience with its biggest employer and former highest contributor to the town's fiscal well-being is a mystery. One possibility is that the town council's composition changed from a predominance of landowners, who would be sympathetic to Igaravídez's troubles, to an overrepresentation by merchants, more willing to punish Igaravídez's daring. Another explanation could be that the town council, once made up of Igaravídez's friends or other people who owed him favors, came to be dominated by his enemies. The limited information that is available shows that neither of these alternatives is completely true. While the town council was full of Igaravídez's cronies and leading landowners in the early 1870s, its composition seems mixed by the end of the decade. The names of town councillors in the late 1870s are not reminiscent of any important merchant or demanding creditor.[24] What is undeniable is that the situation had become less favorable. Nothing could outdo the combination of old business associates and friendly landowners of the early days.

The widespread distrust of the central's capabilities surely had to do with its administration by outsiders. San Vicente seemed plagued by careless court-appointed administrators who relied on excessive borrowing to keep the complex barely afloat.[25] The vision of even the most farsighted creditors—those who understood that it was most expedient to allow the central to recuperate as it slowly paid its debts—must have been clouded by these events. Those who wanted to cash in on the profits immediately were shocked by the sloppy management of the complex and remained highly suspicious of the central's ability to pay under the circumstances.

It is not surprising that Igaravídez's return from jail in March 1887 would dissipate these attitudes. An agreement approved in February of that year by the central's creditors indicates that they had an enormous degree of confidence in the resolution of issues now in Igaravídez's hands. The *convenio* stated that the administration of the complex by Igaravídez himself was enough of a guarantee for the faithful fulfillment of the agreement. An appointed referee commission, nevertheless, would be called on to intercede in favor of the creditors in case of default on the periodic payment of installments on obligations (liquidation dividends) and to take over the property should an emergency arise. Igaravídez would then work with the commission to settle all outstanding debts in order of importance, deal with all legal suits, establish satisfactory accounting procedures (based on expenses of 11,000 pesos a month), and meet all extraordinary obligations. Almost as if to confirm his autonomy, the agreement stipulated that Igaravídez was free to act according to his judgment and that he should be responsible for setting up and covering the expenses incurred in relation to the necessary meetings with the creditors.[26]

Although he returned from jail a sick man, Igaravídez was indeed prepared to confront the situation caused by the lack of vision of previous administrators. He called a meeting in March 1887, by which time the receivership had run out of money with which to pay his creditors, and committed himself to the following guidelines: (1) by the third of each month, all monies received from the sale of products would be deposited in the safe of a commercial company; (2) all creditors would meet once more to establish their claims and agree on a method of payment; and (3) 4,800 pesos would purchase an urgently needed locomotive, but in the meantime ten to twelve pairs of oxen would transport canes to the mill.[27]

The degree of confidence generated by Igaravídez's return was well founded. The centralista was able to have the creditor agreement approved, after disbursing 20,000 pesos to Francisco de Armas, who had refused to submit to the terms of the convenio and demanded immediate payment, and to José Esteban Ramos, who attempted to seize some lands at Hacienda Encarnación. Even though the agreement set the liquidation dividend to be distributed among his creditors at only 64,000 pesos because of a drop in the price of sugar, he paid 100,000 pesos to his creditors, having originally at his disposition only 9,000 pesos from the receivership account. Deficits resulting from partial repayment of crop loans were, in fact, smaller during his administration (table 4.4). After Igaravídez died in March 1888, the temporary administrator was able to further these successes, especially as empty coffers dictated the implementation of austerity policies.[28] That in one year the central was back on its feet, if not operating at full capacity, indicates that, in fact, time and good management were essential factors for success.

Igaravídez's identification with San Vicente, however, was eventually counterproductive. His vigorous presence forestalled further attacks on the property; his death opened the way for demands of money from old and new creditors alike. The municipality, for example, accused the central of not paying taxes for the third quarter of 1887 and seized enough sugar and rum to satisfy the debt until it was paid. More importantly, Igaravídez had apparently not put all available money toward paying the dividends due his creditors according to the agreement reached in February 1887. Following the pattern of earlier years, the authorities accused the central of embezzlement in December 1888.[29]

Table 4.4. Income and Expenses at Central San Vicente during Igaravídez's Administration (in pesos)

15 March–30 November 1887	
Expenses	
Operating expenses	93,500
Taxes	6,659
Locomotive	5,092
Oxen	800
Total	106,053
Income	91,723
Deficit	14,329
1 December 1887–23 March 1888	
Expenses	
Operating expenses and previous deficit	41,250
State taxes	4,061
Municipal taxes	5,331
Total	64,972
Income	59,344
Deficit	5,628

Source: *Memoria leída en la reunión de acreedores de Don Leonardo Igaravídez que tuvo efecto en 17 de julio de 1888, presidida por el Señor Don Augusto de Cottes, Presidente de la Comisión elegida por aquéllos al celebrar el convenio que puso fin a la quiebra del Señor Igaravídez, para vigilar su observancia e intervenir en su cumplimiento* (Puerto-Rico: Imprenta y Librería de Acosta, 1888), 17 July 1888, p. 7.

Upon Igaravídez's death in March 1888, the court called upon a commission of referees/auditors. Under the powerful leadership of Julián Blanco y Sosa, its primary task was to avoid judicial intervention until Igaravídez's successors could be placed in legal possession of the property.[30] As overseer of the interests of the creditors, it also had to deal effectively with recent threats to the property by privileged creditors who had not subjected their claims to the agreements of the collective of creditors.[31] The commission reduced the dividend to be distributed at the time to 32,000 pesos, given decreases in the price of sugar and in the amount of production, and made plans to cut down expenses even more drastically.

Once more the central proved to be a viable project when managed ably. Faced with a broken mill and axis soon after it began to administer the central, the commission ordered a new one from Cail y Cía., attempted to repair the old one as well as it could, and proceeded to grind cane in a nearby hacienda. A number of workers were fired, had their wages reduced, or both as a way of concentrating labor on 930 cuerdas of cane in good condition (down from 1,500 in 1880). Expenses for the period between 24 March and 31 October 1888 were reduced by close to 30,000 pesos; a deficit of only 7,500 pesos was the resulting balance between income and expenses, and even this was covered by revenues from other sources.[32]

Like its predecessors, however, the commission did not take the payment of taxes as seriously as the municipality wanted it to. During the few months the commission remained at the head of the central, administrators Julián Blanco and Julio Pérez had the usual conflicts with the town council. They requested lower tax rates and an extension of the deadline and protested the seizure of land or products as guarantees of payment. The town council was not inclined to make any concessions for San Vicente; in fact, it accused the enterprise of untruthful declarations of production figures and refused to be moved by the alleged internal disorders of the property.[33] Very few sympathized with San Vicente's troubles in the late 1880s.

The supremacy of Julián Blanco as actual head of the central, however, was never disputed. Even though the referee commission was forced to intervene in February 1889 in order to avoid judicial intervention and as stipulated in the convenio of 1887 for cases of default, Blanco's impressive record as administrator was not forgotten, and he was elected representative of the commission. From March 1888 to February 1889, he had achieved savings of more than 40,000 pesos. In addition, Blanco advised Igaravídez's heirs to request a postponement of liquidation dividend payments for May and September 1890, so that only net profits would be distributed in that time. Expenses through crop loans were limited to 10,000 pesos monthly. Mortgaged property could be disposed of to meet outstanding obligations. In addition, production increases to 3,000 tons of sugar and 600 hogsheads of rum were to be established as the rule. In their meeting of 28 May 1889, the creditors collectively agreed to give Blanco's administration a vote of confidence in an open letter to the island government requesting leniency with respect to the central's tax obligations.[34]

Blanco was only a good manager, however, and the context of personal enmity, narrow self-seeking, and shortsightedness in which he operated required much more than proof of the central's sound administration. The achievement of near-prebankruptcy levels of production was soon forgotten before the personal attacks of the López Landrón brothers (Igaravídez's wife's sons by Manuel Antonio López) and of José Gallart y Forgas (a creditor who abstained from voicing an opinion or abiding by the decisions of the collective). Just as the creditors feared, the status as privileged creditors of those who had not agreed to the convenio threatened the existence of the central as a productive unit. When the López Landrón brothers and Gallart y Forgas tried to foreclose the property, only Igaravídez himself would have been able to counter every legal instrument and personal connection they used.

Events soon moved beyond Blanco's control; they had nothing to do with business management and everything to do with the vagaries of the legal system. For little under a year, José Gallart y Forgas had been plotting to take over the property using an obligation for close to 80,000 pesos issued by Igaravídez and bought with Igaravídez's consent by Gallart's now deceased uncle Juan Forgas from Sturges & Co., the original lender. In January 1884, the collective of creditors had acknowledged the obligation; by 1888, they recognized the threat that its existence posed given that its holder had not subjected it to the agreement. Gallart y Forgas, the original holder's nephew, waited as was required by law for the bankruptcy proceedings to end before attacking the central. Although both low and high courts found his title defective in 1888, he was able to obtain a writ of foreclosure from the San Juan court in January 1889. The court order to seize the property could not be carried out, however, because the López Landrón brothers had filed a third-party claim to ownership in the Vega Baja court.[35]

The intervention of the López Landrón brothers in Vega Baja did not rest on even the pretense of legality. The legal claims through both mother and father of Manuel, Armando, and Rafael López Landrón—the sons of María del Carmen Eustaquia Landrón (Igaravídez's second wife) by Manuel Antonio López—to the old Hacienda San Vicente had been recognized at the creditors' meetings. Since such recognition constituted a promise of payment, their many attempts to acquire the central as legal heirs to the property had been repeatedly denied by the courts. In April 1888, however, they entered the plantation accompanied by the minor Igaravídez orphans, took possession of the central by force, and stripped the property of furniture, animals, agricultural goods, and warehouse materials. In the same devious way, they col-luded in December with the notary public who had prepared María del Carmen Eustaquia Landrón's will. They altered the deed so as to include the central, which—if it had ever been considered theirs—was clearly the property of the collective of creditors even before their mother's death. Faced as they were with the possibility of Gallart fore-closing on the property, they invaded once more in March 1889, us-ing as a front their aunt's children. The plan involved a fictitious suit in which the heirs of María Luisa López demanded payment from the heirs of Manuel Antonio López for that part of San Vicente that Manuel Antonio had bought from his sister María Luisa. Supposedly, then, the López Landrón brothers would not be able to pay the re-quired amount and the children of María Luisa López would be en-titled to take possession of the central to settle the debt.[36]

The resentment and envy of many years surfaced in these attacks. Despite Igaravídez's efforts throughout his lifetime to bring his step-sons into the family fold, it is said, they only demanded more and more from the family fortune, perhaps because they considered Iga-ravídez had usurped their position as the rightful heirs of San Vicente. In 1887, for example, their cousin Miguel López Landrón required from the ayuntamiento a listing of all ex-slaves claimed by Igaravídez as his property before 1873 and the names of the estates they came from, apparently trying to determine which ones belonged to the old Ha-cienda San Vicente. The desire to head the enterprise must have influ-enced Manuel López Landrón to take advantage of Igaravídez's good will: he appears as the administrator of the central at the time the town council seized its goods in 1888, shortly before Igaravídez's death. As co-owners and privileged creditors of the hacienda, then, the López Landrón brothers were quite interested in keeping it within the family fold; they had much to lose if outsiders were permitted to control the future of the property.[37]

This attack was not as much on the central as on Julián Blanco him-self. As the property was being invaded, for example, its administrator was kept in San Juan by a false summons to a nonexistent law suit. When he was able to set out toward Vega Baja, a roadblock outside the capital delayed him for hours. Municipal officials discriminated against his interests: Blanco's men were refused a copy of the foreclo-sure order and were even imprisoned. By the time the Vega Baja court tried the case, the judge was forced to disqualify himself from the proceedings because of his close association with the López Landrón brothers.[38]

The case was, in fact, suspect from the beginning, and the proceedings were highly criticized. What was owed María Luisa López de Pascual was only 8,000, not 56,000, pesos, Igaravídez and his wife having made most payments before they died. The central could not be foreclosed for such a small debt, let alone when its maturity date was ten years old. What was worse, those accused in the foreclosure order (the López Landrón brothers), not the plaintiffs (María Luisa's children or their representatives), were placed in charge at the scene by municipal officials.[39] Three months after the seizure of the property, the court judged the López Landrón brothers to be illegally in control of the central and declared that they had no part in Gallart's attempt at foreclosure.[40]

Once Gallart was free to attack the central, he requested an appraisal of San Vicente's lands and equipment. Because the inheritances owing to the López Landrón heirs and to the Igaravídez Landrón heirs and the machinery claimed by Cail y Cía. were excluded from this appraisal, the total for agricultural goods and machinery was only 66,289 and 166,628 pesos, respectively. Igaravídez's descendants requested that the core of the central be left intact, given its commitments to other haciendas for the grinding of cane and its high contributions to the municipal treasury. The court ignored these pleas and auctioned the property, after it informed interested parties—Ephrussi y Cía., Félix S. Alfonso, Sociedad Anónima de Crédito Mercantil, James Barber Son & Co., and Cail y Cía.—of the turn of events.[41] By 1895, the central had been dismembered and distributed to the López Landrón brothers, to José Gallart y Forgas, and to other creditors.

San Vicente's disappearance as a major producer of sugar was the result of the absence of a financial and legal apparatus that could sustain the dimensions and scope of such an ambitious project. Although controlling vast amounts of land caused the enterprise a number of difficulties, land-related expenses did not pose insurmountable obstacles to financial success and noncentralization did not cause the project to fail. (On the contrary, the failure to centralize may have actually saved San Vicente from producing nonmarketable sugar.) With hindsight, one can safely identify San Vicente as the victim of forces external to the organization of the enterprise.

The comparative perspective offered by a parallel case in turn-of-the-century Peru is instructive. The Aspíllagas, a landowning family with entrepreneurial pretensions, based their sugar-making business from 1875 to 1920 on control of land, labor, and capital in the north coast. The two brothers responsible for the project relied on personal connections and political allegiances to advance the economic interests of the enterprise. Hacienda Cayatlí, as did its Puerto Rican counterpart, invested large amounts of capital in machinery that required the reorganization of labor, although it never centralized. It weathered market crises by manipulating the work force as it continued to invest in equipment so as to produce more efficiently. But in contrast to San Vicente, the Aspíllaga estate survived the threat of bankruptcy and public auction because its owners had access to capital. Faced with a situation objectively similar to Igaravídez's, the Aspíllagas could count on the support of peers in acquiring credit.[42]

Puerto Rico was simply not prepared to support the ambitious plans Igaravídez had in mind. Local investment capital in large amounts was nonexistent. Unwilling to give up the advantage created by Spanish protectionism, merchants objected to the establishment of banks for credit, leaving Igaravídez dependent on available instruments to make capital improvements on his operations. Forced to use these borrowing mechanisms creatively, he promoted his project through traditional social and economic linkages. As he ventured outside the limits imposed by the island's rigid financial and legal infrastructure, San Vicente stood to lose. Igaravídez was punished by shortsighted contemporaries in an almost personal vendetta with political undertones under the guise of Spanish law. The central, then, suffered not principally from internal deficiencies—the preoccupation of nineteenth-century thinkers and an aspect of production constantly being worked over at San Vicente—but from external forces over which it had little control.

5

The Failure of Central
San Vicente

Labor

Central San Vicente failed also in perhaps a more important way. Despite its almost absolute control of Vega Baja's economic apparatus, the complex was unable to establish labor relations based strictly on wages as envisioned by agricultural reformers. The skills of experienced industrial laborers affected management decisions regarding where the labor effort was to be channeled. In addition, paternalistic carryovers from slavery battled modern impersonal incentives, preventing management from putting into place production methods based solely on the sale of labor power for a wage. Because San Vicente's laborers adapted to the transformations they encountered, residential patterns and daily life for Vega Baja's population were preserved.[1]

The failure to establish a system of wage labor must be explained alongside the thwarted attempt to turn laborers into a proletariat. Sidney W. Mintz's description of the "new" workers in the twentieth-century sugar industry is applicable here: (1) landless and propertyless, (2) wage earners, (3) store-buying, and (4) employed by a corporation (as opposed to a family-run business).[2] Although San Vicente had every intention of following these steps to subjugate the rural population to the needs of the enterprise, the access of laborers to the means of production preserved their independence of spirit and prevented their ruthless exploitation. Most jornaleros balanced the amount of time they spent at the complex with time dedicated to other economic and personal activities. In spite of the central's plans for a steady and reliable work force, the inflexible work discipline that economic motivation nurtures and that is characteristic of industrial capitalism did not materialize.

As a consequence, class conflict failed to develop. Along with nineteenth-century reformers, I hold that the massive investment of capital in technology that took place at San Vicente required a more efficient application of labor. Motivated as it always had been by the search for profits, management must have felt compelled to organize labor along more regular and formal patterns and to abandon personal practices. The rise of overt conflict between capital and labor was inevitable, once their relationship was revealed as based solely on the exchange of labor power for wages. But because San Vicente's capital investment plans were not entirely realized, the extraction of labor surpluses continued to be disguised not as a free and equal exchange (as would be the case in mature capitalism), but as a *favorable* arrangement for the worker. Social classes—managers and workers—never had the opportunity to define their interests vis-à-vis one another, and so class conflict never arose.[3]

An analysis of the relationship between the workers and the workplace is central to determining the nature of exchanges between the rural population of Vega Baja and Central San Vicente. It is apparent that the ties that bound central and jornaleros, if not as relaxed as those among equals, were relatively flexible and, in certain respects, mutually beneficial. Both workers and enterprise experimented with the transformations at hand; neither had defined a position or formulated clear objectives to confront the changes encountered. Although the complex did its best to encompass all aspects of the workers' lives, the workers apparently had some degree of independence in their exchanges with the factory. Ultimately, central and jornalero worked out a series of compromises that impeded the imposition of industrial demands on the work force.

The element that defines most basically how exchanges take place between a labor force and an enterprise is how often workers go to work. The more powerful the influence of the employer, the stronger its chances of obtaining the labor it needs when it wants it. The more alternatives open to the worker, the stronger his or her autonomy and bargaining position. Central San Vicente could manipulate its labor force through the offer of employment, control of available land, and (conceivably) influence peddling at the local government level, if necessary. But its workers could also withhold their services if better conditions or pay were available elsewhere, if they had access to the means of production, and (possibly) if they were willing to risk getting in trouble with the authorities.[4]

One would expect patterns of work attendance to develop somewhat differently for Vega Baja's nonwhite population, if only because of the circumstances under which the give-and-take between management and labor would occur. Former slaves would be most vulnerable to the plantation's demands, as the power of the law and the influence of their employer with town officials made their apprenticeship contracts more than legally binding.[5] Further, the experience of formally asserting their rights and seeking alternative options was relatively new to them, as well as to other free blacks and mulattoes. Their strengths lay primarily in their numbers and in their skills.

From the perspective of management the 593 men who form the sample of this study constituted a reliable labor force appropriate to the needs of the complex.[6] The operation of the enterprise required their skills in sundry tasks related to both the agricultural and the manufacturing phases of production. During the three years for which there are records (1879, 1883, and 1885), the jornaleros of San Vicente performed fifty-nine different tasks at the central. A substantial portion of the individuals who appear in the account books of any given year worked either of the other two years, if not both.[7] An approximately equal number of weeks worked and weeks not worked is also characteristic for the period. It seems, then, that the same workers appeared at the central every year and worked there at least as often as they did elsewhere. Since the number of workers that the complex attracted in any given week (fig. 5.1) was never a cause for complaint on the part of administrators, one supposes that the labor situation did not particularly trouble management at San Vicente.

Persons of color also made their labor available to the estate on a regular basis. General data on the racial characteristics of the central's workers indicate that San Vicente's labor force was composed of a large number of blacks and mulattoes.[8] All evidence indicates that a good proportion of the nonwhites who filled the ranks of the laboring class during the life of the complex were either "free colored" or

Number of workers (divided by 10)
Number of days worked per week

Sources: Archivo General de Puerto Rico, Audiencia Territorial, Serie Civil, Jornales, box 71, docs. 963, 964, 965; Documentos relacionados a la quiebra, box 31, docs. 451, 452.

Note: Figures refer to selected weeks in 1879–80, 1883, and 1885. Worker figures for 1879–80 include San Vicente and Felicidad; figures for 1883 and 1885 refer only to San Vicente.

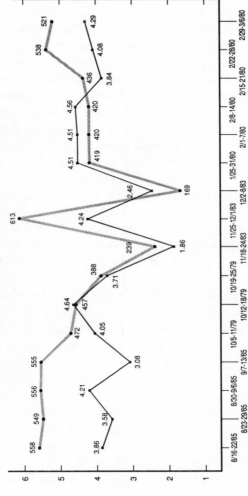

Fig. 5.1. Number of workers and of days worked

Source: Archivo General de Puerto Rico, Audiencia Territorial, Serie Civil, Jornales, box 71, docs. 963, 964, 965; Documentos relacionados a la quiebra, box 31, docs. 451, 452.

Note: Figures refer to selected weeks in 1879–80, 1883, and 1885. Worker figures for 1879–80 include San Vicente and Felicidad; figures for 1883 and 1885 refer only to San Vicente.

former slaves with no previous ties to San Vicente. Only 65 men in the sample (less than 34 percent of all nonwhites) appeared as slaves in the period from 1860 to 1873, and only 19 of these had belonged to Igaravídez before abolition in 1873. Yet more than 70 percent of the recently freed slaves had signed contracts with San Vicente and its five dependencies (38 out of 54 contracts signed by the workers from the sample) in 1873. The central seemed to have no trouble in obtaining its share of the nonwhite and non-San Vicente former slave population as part of its labor force immediately after abolition.

The regularity of San Vicente's labor force, which stands in sharp contrast to contemporary accounts about the unreliability of rural workers, may cast a shadow of doubt on the representativeness of the sample of workers chosen for this study. Although by definition the most stable group among the universe of jornaleros (those men that appeared in at least one other source of information), the diverse patterns recorded for different variables indicate that the sample is in no way biased to favor the inclusion of only the most reliable and steady workers. In fact, the existence of disparities between variables whose patterns of behavior were expected to be related (such as the number of weeks worked, access to land, and residential distribution) indicates that the tendencies recorded can be considered representative for the area's population.

Whereas San Vicente's administrators must have been satisfied with the number of men who came to work each week at the complex, the central was never able to monopolize employment opportunities for Vega Baja's population. Working exclusively for wages was not an attractive alternative either for former slaves who now were masters of their own destiny or for small landholders who naturally felt a primary attachment to their own land. Close to 15 percent of the jornaleros owned either cattle or land in 1883 (table 5.1), a high proportion if one considers the amount of land occupied by the central and takes into account that other records that pertain to the workers' access to the means of production might have been lost. Another option was settling within San Vicente's perimeter itself, on some of the 52 percent of its land not under cultivation, and raising minor crops there. That the percentage of workers with recorded residences in Vega Baja is very low in the three periods available (less than 50 percent in 1860–73 and 1883–85 and close to 30 percent in 1887–91) leads one

Table 5.1. Property Holders and Workers, 1883–1885

Occupation	Number of workers (%)	
Property holders	45	(14.6)
Artisans or domestic workers	7	(2.3)
Agricultural or industrial workers	256	(83.1)
Total	308	(100)

Source: Processed data from AMVB, various.

to believe that many decided to squat on their employer's land. Although most jornaleros at San Vicente appeared in official records precisely as wage earners, a substantial number of them relied on other means for their daily subsistence.

Massive unemployment during tiempo muerto and ceaseless exploitation during the zafra were unknown to San Vicente's work force for another reason. Since the plans of reformers regarding the separation of the agricultural from the manufacturing aspects of production were never put into practice, San Vicente was forced to employ men in field tasks. But the agricultural laborsaving devices that became commonplace in the early twentieth century had not formed a part of San Vicente's technological overhaul. Ploughing, for example, was not mechanized, so that in the best of cases the oxen that pulled the heavy equipment required the guidance of several men.[9] Agricultural functions—precisely that part of the production effort that had not undergone substantial reorganization—continued to be performed as part of the operations of the enterprise, and employment patterns remained more or less constant throughout the year. The number of workers at the central did not increase progressively as the harvest approached in January nor did it decline precipitously in July. As the central satisfied its demands for labor throughout the year, its jornaleros experimented in developing a work cycle consonant with their other economic and personal pursuits.

The accounts kept by a Vega Baja merchant contain a powerful statement of the workers' autonomy and testify to their relative independence. Apparently running into cash-flow difficulties at the close of the harvest, the central resorted to the convenient method of remunerating workers through a line of credit at a local business. But San Vicente's workers were reluctant to accept as a substitute for cash payments the merchandise of Francisco de Diego's store, with which the enterprise contracted in 1881.[10] Neither the value of goods received by the workers nor the number of workers choosing this method of payment remotely approaches the figures on wages and jornaleros of other years. It is clear that few workers decided to accept this offer; the majority preferred to wait for cash payments, a decision that indicates that they had other ways to supplement their daily existence.

The same appears to have been true for former slaves immediately after abolition. The appearance of only a minority of the former slaves of Igaravídez, one of the largest slaveholders in the island, in San Vicente's work force between 1879 and 1885 points to a heavy population movement away from the central and to a certain independence of spirit in the early apprenticeship period.[11] What is even more telling, only 69 of Vega Baja's *libertos* signed apprenticeship contracts with San Vicente in 1873. If those who signed agreements with its five dependencies are included, the number rises to only 126 out of a total 307 contracts recorded in Vega Baja. Although more than half of those who initially contracted with San Vicente remained there, the reduced number of local former slaves who signed contracts points to their employment in other occupations elsewhere and by extension to their decision to remove themselves from the operations of the central soon after abolition.

In the face of worker autonomy, planters had to devise ways to attract the number of workers necessary for the daily operation of their enterprises. Wage policies appear to have been directed at attracting workers, especially skilled ones. San Vicente started paying wages on time and in cash, not issuing internal tokens or providing credit as did coffee haciendas and as became common for sugar plantations later in this period.[12] This policy should have impressed on the workers the notion that San Vicente was a financially solid enterprise that adhered to sound business practices, foremost among which was the fair exchange of wages for labor.

San Vicente also paid nonwhites a bit more than it did whites (43 centavos and 40 centavos, respectively, as a daily average for the years 1879, 1883, and 1885), apparently in another attempt to attract local reliable workers. Nonwhites outnumbered whites two to one in higher wage categories (table 5.2). Colored people were evenly distributed in all wage categories as opposed to whites, who were concentrated in

Table 5.2. Daily Wage Distribution by Race

Centavos	Whites	Nonwhites	Total
12–43	57	68	125
43–150	37	83	120
Total	94	151	245

Source: Processed data from AMVB, various.

the lower wage categories (over 60 percent of whites worked in the lowest two categories). Possibly because they were former slaves and had industrial skills or were more familiar with factory operations after many years' experience, nonwhites found themselves favored by an enterprise hungry for steady laborers.[13]

The central could also offer conditions of work that appealed to laborers. The contracts that San Vicente signed with former slaves demonstrate that management considered their presence essential to the smooth operation of the enterprise and strove to attract them. The agreements signed between Igaravídez's representative and slave "protectors" appointed by law provided the jornaleros of San Vicente with more benefits than those offered by other landowners or administrators. Among the incentives to work at San Vicente were four cuerdas of land for cultivation and/or construction purposes or a room, and a cow for milk. Workers in other estates received a room, if anything. San Vicente's new jornaleros were also better paid; most of them received four to five *reales* (one real was equal to 12.5 centavos) per day, as compared to three to four reales for those of other haciendas.[14] San Vicente was ready to pay the price of keeping its labor force.

Another way in which the central attempted to make the complex attractive to its workers was to offer meals on its premises. San Vicente purchased sweet potatoes from two independent suppliers and plantains from Hacienda Encarnación, probably supplementing this basic diet with codfish or jerked beef bought from a local merchant. The complex also hired a man to prepare employee and worker rations of first, second, and third class.[15] Although the number of meals provided fluctuated considerably, it was consistently at least three times the number of workers (fig. 5.2). Considering that each laborer worked about three days per week, these figures indicate that most workers

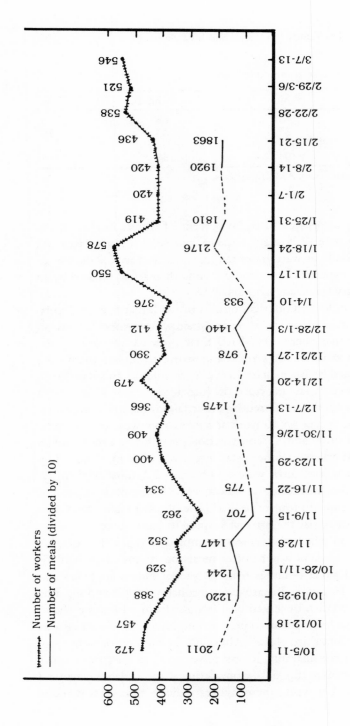

Fig. 5.2. Number of workers and of meals (1879–80)

Source: Archivo General de Puerto Rico, Audiencia Territorial, Serie Civil, Documentos relacionados a la quiebra, box 31, doc. 451, 452.
Note: Figures include San Vicente and Felicidad.

took advantage of the convenience of having their lunch prepared and served in the workplace.

These seemingly calculated policies, however, were mixed with a number of time-tested practices that gave San Vicente's administrators the flexibility they needed to experiment. When it was convenient, they did not think twice before returning to familiar patterns rather than insisting on a new course whose initial implementation was difficult and whose final outcome was uncertain. Below the surface, the absence of a consistent policy regarding remuneration is obvious. Cash payments, the dismissal of jornaleros, and the reduction of their wages at different moments during the life of the complex suggest an attempt to establish impersonal exchanges between laborers and enterprise.[16] But unexplained delays in wage payments and the credit line for workers mentioned above point to the ease with which the administration returned to more traditional practices.

The inconsistencies reflected by maximum and minimum wages for each occupation and wage patterns for the various age groups, for example, indicate that the central based its wage policy on more than the services rendered. The difference between the highest and the lowest amounts disbursed was so great (table 5.3) and the fluctuations in wage for the same person so small that skill does not seem to have determined remuneration scales. Men in productive ages appear in the lower and higher wage categories in just about the same proportion as men of less productive ages (table 5.4). The differences in average daily wage between age groups, moreover, are minimal (table 5.5) and contribute little to explaining San Vicente's remuneration practices. It seems that the central responded to individual characteristics, such as personal contacts or duration of employment, that cannot be determined from available sources.

Just as naturally as San Vicente clung to personalized wage payment practices, the central resorted to other methods characteristic of traditional labor-management relations to assure itself of workers. Two attempts to establish worker colonies near San Vicente illustrate the enterprise's resourcefulness in the face of potential labor shortages. A local Junta de Colonias was formed in Vega Baja in 1886 to organize the establishment of settlements in Pugnado Afuera for the most hardworking laborers, who would cultivate adjacent lands. The minutes of its meetings made continuous reference to a Junta de Beneficencia

Table 5.3. Lowest, Highest, and Average Daily Wage per Task (in pesos)

Task[a]	Lowest	Highest	Average
Clearing land with hoes and machetes	.36	.50	.46
Plowing	.13	.64	.39
Removing weeds before planting	.12	.62	.34
Digging ditches for run-off water	.36	.63	.48
Planting new cane stalks	.15	.79	.41
Weeding cane fields	.23	1.00	.42
Removing leaves from cane stalks	.25	.75	.44
Harvesting cane	.31	.62	.43
Maintaining railways	.31	.50	.46
Replacing oxen in carts	.25	.52	.41
Directing wagons	.19	.74	.38
Collecting palm tree leaves for thatch	.19	.47	.37

Sources: AGPR, AT, SC, Jornales, box 71, docs. 963, 964; Documentos relacionados a la quiebra, box 31, doc. 451.
[a]Only the tasks at which more than 10 people worked in the sample weeks of 1879, 1883, and 1885 have been included.

that, formed in 1867 with the same purpose, had succeeded only in buying the necessary land. The 1886 *junta* tried to complete the task begun in 1867 by recovering almost 800 pesos from Isaac Arnau, the trustee in charge when the Junta de Beneficencia was dissolved.[17]

If Igaravídez participated in the early efforts to establish worker settlements, it seems important to recognize two possible reasons for his involvement. The 1867 and 1886 attempts at establishing agricultural colonies could have been intended as a charitable act for the benefit of the poor of Vega Baja. An 1880 account of similar efforts by Don Leonardo refers to his organization of construction crews for the building of homes as directed to the "improvement of the proletariat," and no doubt Igaravídez himself believed this. But his altruism did not rule out the practical use of these residences as a means of tying a potential labor force to areas close to the central. Newspapers of the period expressed this view unequivocally. Available for work in the rapidly growing sugar complex, these laborers would have been expected to provide San Vicente with a steady work force. That the colonies were to be a reward for the most diligent assured the central that its laborers would also be efficient. Interestingly enough, the land had been seized from a very poor group of residents who held no title but cultivated surrounding tracts.[18]

Table 5.4. Daily Wage Distribution by Age

Centavos	10–19, 50–79	20–49	Total
12–43	22	75	97
43–150	18	83	101
Total	40	158	198

Source: Processed data from AMVB, various.

Table 5.5. Average Wage by Age (in pesos)

Age	Average wage
10–19	.435
20–29	.424
30–39	.402
40–49	.423
50–59	.410
60–69	.441
70–79	.353

Source: Processed data from AMVB, various.

Both enterprise and labor force tacitly advanced their economic interests. Even though its jornaleros' work alternatives could have been a source of irritation for the San Vicente administration, the central did not suffer from a scarcity of hands as a result of the workers' lack of interest. Cash-flow problems for the daily expenses of the complex, in fact, may have been the cause of decreases in the number of workers employed each week. Violent fluctuations in the number of workers in November 1883 (a phenomenon not recorded in other years), for example, resulted from the scarcity of cash to pay wages and not from the unavailability of manpower. Only in this way can it be said that the enterprise controlled employment opportunities for the neighboring population.

Similar work arrangements sprang up after the abolition of slavery in other parts of the Caribbean. Apprenticeship, importation of workers, and sharecropping—proposed and adopted, either separately or combined, as solutions to the "labor problem" in several of the British possessions—served to satisfy the demands of plantations as well as the needs of laborers. The literature on the English-speaking Carib-

bean sugar industry has, in fact, been mostly responsible for setting
the parameters within which to study labor relations in this period.
The access of former slaves and wage workers to the means of production and the mechanisms for labor coercion available to planters became the essential instruments for negotiation in the nineteenth century
and the elements for relevant comparisons with other islands in the
twentieth century. For the Caribbean generally, how much control
planters had over workers' access to the economic, political, and social
means of protecting their interests largely determined the success of
each group's efforts.[19]

The persistence of noncapitalist relations of production within capitalist structures among Latin American rural populations is a frequent
phenomenon. Although scholars seek to classify patterns of labor relations as more or less feudal or more or less capitalist in an effort to
determine movement toward a predominant mode of production, the
more common occurrence in peripheral areas has been the emergence
of labor systems and relations of production that are both capitalist
and noncapitalist. These systems borrow creatively from existing political, economic, and social structures that neither are consonant with
each other nor have parallel developments. Their evolution is nonlin-
ear and their interaction unpredictable. This model, as its originator
James L. Dietz has explained, permits examining complex structures
and the changes they undergo.[20] It is particularly useful to the study of
nineteenth-century Puerto Rico in that it embraces the elements of exploitation, resistance, manipulation, material advantage, collective well-
being, and other nontangibles without necessarily considering them
self-exclusive.

Another element that defines the pattern of exchanges between factory and worker is the direction in which the labor effort is channeled.
Although Central San Vicente's laborers were able to defend their autonomy with respect to the frequency and length of their daily stints at
the workplace, the enterprise could place its workers in different occupations throughout the year. From tiempo muerto to zafra, for example, the number of workers performing agricultural tasks declined
by 58 percent as the number of industrial workers increased by 46
percent.[21] Loading cane onto wagons in the factory was a job carried
out only during the grinding months, just as planting cane required
substantial increases in the agricultural labor force during tiempo

muerto. That the number of men performing a particular job throughout the year was small when compared to the number of times that
task was peformed (table 5.6) indicates that the central shifted workers
from one task to another when priorities changed, perhaps to develop
a variety of skills within a system based on division of labor.

But the managers at San Vicente did not always match the nature of
a task and the age of a worker. Given that high numbers accentuate
tendencies, I have grouped tasks that usually employ a small number
of workers into four large functions: (1) agricultural unskilled and
services, (2) agricultural skilled, (3) industrial and artisan, (4) maintenance and other. Because most workers were engaged in any given
chore only one of the sample weeks, the frequency of employment appears under two broad categories: worked once and worked more than
once.

Young men, not surprisingly, were more numerous in all occupations. Also as expected, men in productive ages carried out maintenance and industrial functions, which require stamina and alertness, in
notably larger numbers than did older men, who also worked less frequently at these tasks (table 5.7). But men presumed less productive
filled skilled and unskilled agricultural occupations, in which tasks

Table 5.6. Workers and Frequency per Task

Task[a]	Workers	Times task performed
Clearing land with hoes and machetes	16	38
Plowing	38	102
Removing weeds before planting	87	182
Digging ditches for run-off water	67	211
Planting new cane stalks	129	247
Weeding cane fields	159	319
Removing leaves from cane stalks	51	85
Harvesting cane	45	61
Maintaining railways	12	18
Replacing oxen in carts	11	31
Directing wagons	45	54
Collecting palm tree leaves for thatch	13	13

Sources: AGPR, AT, SC, Jornales, box 71, docs. 963, 964; Documentos relacionados a la quiebra, box 31, doc. 451.
[a] Only the tasks at which more than 10 people worked in the sample weeks of
1879, 1883, and 1885 have been included.

Table 5.7. Industrial and Maintenance Tasks by Age

	Age		
	10–19, 50–59	20–49	Total
Industrial and artisan			
Worked once	4	17	21
Worked more than once	2	14	16
Total	6	31	37
Maintenance and other			
Worked once	1	9	10
Worked more than once	2	12	14
Total	3	21	24

Source: Processed data from AMVB, various.

must be performed quickly and efficiently, more than once in roughly the same proportions as did younger men (table 5.8). It seems that the central did not discriminate on the basis of age when assigning men to tasks regularly. Either age was not taken into account as a practice or management responded to day-to-day circumstances that are now unknown. The impression is of an enterprise in which traditional practices, nonbusiness concerns, and exceptional cases were more important than the policies contemporaries would have defined as modern, rational, and consistent.

Occupational distribution by race presents itself largely as a carryover from the days of slavery. Compared to whites, other groups were more heavily represented in industrial and maintenance occupations: the number of whites in industrial functions is quite reduced, and nonwhites outnumbered their white counterparts almost five to one in maintenance functions (table 5.9). Slaves carried out precisely these tasks before abolition because they were a resident labor force that complemented the work of free men in the fields during the zafra, and because whites refused to work late and in the factory.[22] Similarly, agricultural tasks were performed by the various racial groups in numbers that closely resemble those for San Vicente's working population as a whole. Just as in the days of slavery, no marked differences appear in the frequency with which the various racial groups filled agricultural tasks (table 5.10). That in postabolition San Vicente nonwhites performed functions that required careful attention or constant at-

Table 5.8. Agricultural Skilled and Unskilled Tasks by Age

	Age		
	10–19, 50–79	20–49	Total
Skilled			
Worked once	10	35	45
Worked more than once	13	45	58
Total	23	80	103
Unskilled and services			
Worked once	14	58	72
Worked more than once	11	53	64
Total	25	111	136

Source: Processed data from AMVB, various.

tendance and other tasks were filled equally by both racial groups points to the persistence of work cycles characteristic of slave haciendas.

Age distribution by race also indicates the repetition of patterns commonly associated with slavery. Whites and nonwhites were fairly evenly distributed among the various age groups, but there were eight former slaves between the ages of ten and nineteen (table 5.11). This racial imbalance among children suggests that whites were more likely than were nonwhites to find means other than collective work at the central to support their families and could avoid San Vicente altogether by moving elsewhere. Nonwhites, on the other hand, depended on wage labor, remained tied to the sugar complex, and served its needs, much as they had done as slaves.

Table 5.9. Industrial and Maintenance Tasks by Race

	Whites	Nonwhites	Total
Industrial and artisan			
Worked once	9	28	37
Worked more than once	5	21	26
Total	14	49	63
Maintenance and other			
Worked once	4	13	17
Worked more than once	2	15	17
Total	6	28	34

Source: Processed data from AMVB, various.

Table 5.10. Agricultural Skilled and Unskilled Tasks by Race

	Whites	Nonwhites	Total
Skilled			
Worked once	19	38	57
Worked more than once	25	48	73
Total	44	86	130
Unskilled and services			
Worked once	34	49	83
Worked more than once	32	58	90
Total	66	107	173

Source: Processed data from AMVB, various.

San Vicente, then, strove to operate under general principles of division of labor at the same time that it left intact numerous past patterns of labor relations. In some instances, such as the channeling of the labor effort by age, management decisions do not follow any obvious pattern. The tendency of San Vicente's nonwhites to perform the same functions slaves used to carry out on haciendas and under the same demanding conditions, on the other hand, is both quite compatible with economic rationality and reminiscent of times past. Similarly, the fact that Igaravídez both bought and sold slaves just prior to abolition points to ad hoc decisions that took into consideration progressive practices and time-sanctioned policies.[23]

One would expect the central's influence on the daily life of the workers to extend beyond the premises. Remarkably, patterns of residence in the municipality were not affected by San Vicente's control of land and capacity for employment. For the nonwhite population, in fact, the presence of the industrial giant seems to have simply confirmed the patterns of residential segregation commonly associated with slavery. Evidence also suggests that Vega Baja's rural population did not succumb to the demands that the complex imposed on it in 1873, even as it continued to be the enterprise's obvious target for the following two decades. The continuity that marked patterns of geographical and socioeconomic mobility was reflected in the absence of exceptionally complicated cases in the court records of these years.

When it came to choosing a place to live, San Vicente's workers seemingly ignored the presence of the central and its continuous de-

Table 5.11. Age Distribution by Race, 1880

		Nonwhites			
Age	Whites (%)	Former slaves (%)	Other (%)	Total (%)	Total (%)
10–19	—	8 (12.9)	—	8 (6.3)	8 (3.2)
20–29	51 (41.8)	20 (32.3)	33 (51.6)	53 (42.1)	104 (41.9)
30–39	31 (25.4)	10 (16.1)	12 (18.7)	22 (17.5)	53 (21.4)
40–49	24 (19.7)	12 (19.4)	11 (17.2)	23 (18.3)	47 (19.0)
50–59	4 (3.3)	9 (14.5)	5 (7.8)	14 (11.1)	18 (7.3)
60–69	6 (4.9)	3 (4.8)	2 (3.1)	5 (3.9)	11 (4.4)
70–79	6 (4.9)	—	1 (1.6)	1 (0.8)	7 (2.8)
Total	122 (100)	62 (100)	64 (100)	126 (100)	248 (100)

Source: Processed data from AMVB, various.

mands for an accessible labor force. Table 5.12 presents the number of workers with established residences in Vega Baja by area (fig. 2.1). The residential patterns of San Vicente's work force in 1883–85, the shortest time span with the largest number of cases, show an even distribution among the areas of the municipality. The greatest number of the 287 workers whose residence is known lived in the area west of the central. A high concentration of people in the area immediately surrounding the workplace was made especially significant by its proximity to the town itself. The distribution across the municipality is nevertheless quite even, as 43 percent of the workers at the central lived in areas that can be considered well outside the perimeter of the sugar complex.

The central did not seem to attract Vega Baja's workers. Whereas a quick look at the percentages in table 5.12 suggests population movement toward the complex after 1887, the more remarkable phenomenon is a loss of population in all four sectors precisely in the years San Vicente began to recuperate. Laborers simply removed themselves from municipal boundaries and worked at San Vicente only intermittently. The percentage distribution for those fifty-two workers who remained in Vega Baja throughout the three time periods, moreover, remained more or less the same. The only movement that can safely be appreciated in terms of distance from the complex, in fact, took place from areas close to the central to those further away in 1883–85. Contrary

Table 5.12. Number of Workers by Sector (%)

Sector	1860–73	1883–85	1887–91
Northeast			
Cabo Caribe, Ceiba, Cibuco, Town	78 (26.4)	80 (27.9)	57 (32.8)
Northwest			
Algarrobo, Yeguada Occidental,			
Puerto Nuevo	91 (30.8)	83 (28.9)	62 (35.6)
Southeast			
Almirante Norte, Almirante Sur,			
Río Abajo, Río Arriba, Quebrada			
Arenas	73 (24.7)	69 (24.0)	22 (12.6)
Southwest			
Pugnado Adentro, Pugnado Afuera	53 (18.0)	55 (19.2)	33 (19.0)
Total	295 (100)	287 (100)	174 (100)

Source: Processed data from AMVB, various.

to expectations, San Vicente did not attract individuals who had established residences in Vega Baja before 1873 to the areas it controlled and influenced as it grew.

Similarly, the residential patterns of San Vicente's nonwhites resembled those associated with slavery. Whereas figures for the working population as a whole show an even distribution across the municipality (table 5.12), data for the three time periods on those individuals whose race is known indicate not only that close to 70 percent of the nonwhites lived in the two divisions closest to the central but also that the nonwhite was twice the white population in those areas. The opposite is also true: whites concentrated in the two areas farthest from the complex and outnumbered nonwhites easily, especially in the areas close to the river (table 5.13).

This distribution is significant on two counts. In the first place, that proximity to the workplace appears as a function of race confirms the suspicion that nonwhites were more dependent on their income from wages than were whites and were thus forced to live near, if not in, the complex itself. (Nonwhites, in fact, worked an average of 3.9 days per week compared to 3.2 days for whites.) Secondly, these postabolition patterns of segregation appear to have been simply a carryover from the days of slavery: nonwhites (slaves) lived in the coastal areas, where they worked in the sugar plantations; whites (free men) lived further

Table 5.13. White and Nonwhite Population by Sector

Sector	1860–73		1883–85		1887–91	
	White	Nonwhite	White	Nonwhite	White	Nonwhite
Northeast						
Cabo Caribe, Ceiba, Cibuco, Town	18	40	6	22	6	14
Northwest						
Algarrobo, Yeguada Occidental, Puerto Nuevo	27	50	10	25	10	22
Southeast						
Almirante Norte, Almirante Sur, Río Abajo, Río Arriba, Quebrada Arenas	52	17	21	11	10	4
Southwest						
Pugnado Adentro, Pugnado Afuera	25	22	13	14	13	10
Total	122	129	50	72	39	50

Source: Processed data from AMVB, various.

inland in the mountains, where they were able to cultivate plots of land not appropriated by haciendas and to keep a distance from them.

The extent to which San Vicente's workers were able to control their economic future outside the central is indicated further by analyzing an occupational sample that shows movement from jornalero status through industrial or artisan tasks into some sort of proprietor status, be it as a landholder or a cattle owner, from 1870–73 through 1883–85 to 1887–91. Of the 45 men for whom occupational information exists in all three time periods, more than a quarter attained proprietor status by 1883–85, and close to half by 1887–91. Whereas one would expect a sudden proletarianization of Vega Baja's population in terms of loss of access to the means of production and subjection to the demands of the enterprise, nearly the opposite seems to be true.[24]

The permanence of social and economic patterns in Vega Baja despite the emergence of San Vicente as a gigantic employer is noteworthy. My expectation, of course, was not that San Vicente's laborers would have started to behave like industrial workers in ten years. Mintz's work on Santa Isabel has convincingly shown that proletarianization is a gradual process.[25] But the absence of any measurable impact on the conduct and practices of San Vicente's workers both outside and inside the workplace is telling. The central made every effort to implement a wage labor system that would proletarianize its workers as reformers described and as understood today. Although its life was short and its opportunities for success limited as a consequence, it established a number of practices that could have changed the life-styles of Vega Baja's population. San Vicente's laborers, though, proved to have the means to resist both the element of coercion and of lure that the existence of the complex represented.

That the presence of the sugar complex seems to have caused no significant disruptions in the daily life of Vega Baja's population is also suggested by the nature of the social disorders described in *juicios verbales* or local court hearings. Conceivably, workers who begin to lose "territory," however defined, over which they previously had control will attempt to regain their losses through what may not appear at first sight to be the right channels or in ways not obviously effective. One would not be surprised to discover, in response, a retrenchment on the part of officials in the face of what they are bound to consider challenges to their authority. The way in which workers choose to make a statement, of course, varies case by case, as does what authorities perceive to be a questioning of their own right to define and establish order.[26]

All of the minor (and some major) infractions of the law as recorded in the local court hearings would indicate that the workers of San Vicente easily adapted to (if they did not ignore) the sudden appearance of the business giant in their living space. Because only 37 of the jornaleros in the sample got into any kind of trouble with the law in the period 1879–91, I have drawn on the court records of other San Vicente workers to paint a picture of worker relations within the town itself. Overt social unrest and increased political activism do not seem to have occurred, a finding that is consistent with the workers' other actions and reactions. Rather, a wide range of human behavior is manifest in juicios verbales: indebtedness and physical violence were common charges before the law; a mixture of misunderstanding and support, envious resentment and common sense colors the cases examined. Under these circumstances, officials reacted with leniency when deemed necesary, with full force when respect for authority was at stake. Ultimately, Vega Baja and its workers come across as a stable yet problematic population, a small town not particularly preoccupied with the economic, social, and political world that surrounded it but concerned with its own stability and cohesiveness. The official response was more an adaptation to local conditions than a strict application of the law.

Indebtedness was common for the workers of San Vicente. Most often, the authorities or the damaged party pressed charges. In the *apremios* (demands for money) carried out by the municipal government to secure the payment of back taxes, treasury officials followed a standard procedure: they pressed formal charges before the town magistrate, visited the house of the debtor to request the money owed, threatened to seize property until payments were made, and—once convinced that the person was truly insolvent—apparently dropped charges. Only in the 1881 case of the massive accusation of the "*jornaleros de la jurisdicción*," in which overseers were charged with the task of retaining part of each worker's wage to cover the 48-centavo tax on income, was the municipality able to recover 80.63 pesos, as much as they could have expected from 167 dutiful taxpayers. Vega Baja's public officials seem not particularly concerned with workers' tax payments and apparently adopted a realistic attitude with respect to its revenue collection devices.

Stricter, however, were the accusations of town merchants whose establishments customarily ran a line of credit through which regular clients could purchase personal articles. José Manuel Portela, Ramón B. Portela, and Manuel Otero figure prominently among the merchants with whom San Vicente's jornaleros opened accounts. They and others pressed charges against twenty-three workers for amounts ranging from 50 centavos to nearly 10 pesos. Igaravídez, Mariani y Cía. accused two jornaleros of owing close to 20 and 40 pesos; the company apparently sold construction materials that the debtors bought as supplies for other types of work. Debtors were permitted to schedule payment according to their needs, and plaintiffs in these cases invariably recovered the amounts owed.

Many of the elements that characterize the situation of indebtedness for San Vicente's workers are present in the juicio verbal of Vicente Portalatín, a free black (in 1860) who planted cane at San Vicente for only one week in 1885. He was married to Severa Santana, who owned a house near the cemetery, which he offered in 1879 as guarantee for 10 pesos he had borrowed from merchant José Urgal. He also promised José M. Rolan weekly payments on a 2-peso debt in 1883. In an 1885 agreement with José M. Portela, Portalatín apparently again offered as collateral the house near the cemetery. His wife, however, considered this to be her exclusive property; she sued Portalatín and Portela and obtained third-party claim to ownership, although a higher court revoked this sentence. Relations between Portalatín and his creditor Portela were not cordial two months after the incident; Portalatín was accused of libel, after having "offended all Galicians" and referring to Portela specifically as a "*pícaro y ladrón*" (scoundrel and thief). He was fined 125 pesos, which he could not pay. Declaring insolvency, he spent eleven days in jail.

Vicente Portalatín's case is exceptional in that it can be reconstructed with some detail. This wealth of information, however, raises more questions than it answers. How tied Portalatín (or any other worker, for that matter) was to the town merchants is something to be investigated once many more juicios verbales are examined across the island. The independence of action evident in his wife's defense of her property and the court's initial show of approval should also be studied in other instances. Determining the frequency of outbursts like Portalatín's against Galicians, which point to a feeling of helplessness before a powerful minority, will help explain how *peninsulares* were perceived on the island and on what grounds. Portalatín's case, nevertheless, promotes an understanding of the typical approaches used and agreements reached in juicios verbales: almost never did the case get out of hand; contending parties usually reached a compromise that was fair to both and asked the judge to see it through.

More serious crimes required the application of more stringent principles as outlined in the Penal Code. In six cases of theft examined, particular attention was paid to (1) the seriousness of the crime, determined by value categories (most objects stolen had a value of 25–250 *pesetas*) and by aggravating circumstances (such as darkness, vagrancy, false pretenses); and (2) restitution of the amount involved. Prison terms, however, varied considerably: two months and a day was the sentence for thefts for less than 25 pesetas, but also for more than 25 but less than 250 pesetas. Some people served more than three years for theft of an amount not specified in the proceedings; one person was in jail for only nine days after having beaten up two people (one of them his fellow worker at San Vicente) because they refused to give him money.

These cases point to a flexibility in local proceedings that had apparently become customary in the face-to-face application of the law. In all cases, the accused—men between the ages of eighteen and twenty-six—pleaded guilty, some even offering the reasons for having committed the crime: hunger, friendship ties with the principal perpetrators, or lack of work. As the young men must have suspected, these voluntary confessions usually resulted in lighter sentences, a practice that indicates a move toward the institutionalization of local rules for socially accepted behavior and sanctions.

Other crimes involved one-sided or mutual physical assault, usually the product of some sort of misunderstanding and, at other times, the result of uncontrolled emotions of anger or vengeance. Five jornaleros appeared in police records as having broken the peace or caused disturbances in public places. Two of them threw rocks and cursed each other; one was the victim of a friend's anger and machete when he took too long in delivering some money he set out to get; another's response to an acquaintance's greeting was interpreted as an insult and caused physical retaliation; the fifth was responsible for disrupting a private dance during a drinking spree. Even for crimes that appear to have been humorous, jail sentences were quite harsh (5–30 days) and fines varied considerably (15–125 pesetas). No pattern seems to emerge from these attempts at administering justice.

Most crimes in which the authorities themselves were the accusers had to do with attempts at making everyday life in Vega Baja a smooth process. Four of San Vicente's workers, for example, owned horses, mares, and cows that were found roaming about unclaimed on a neighbor's property. The penal code stipulated a fine of 25 pesetas and the payment of damages to the owner of the property. In all cases, payments were made without protest and things returned to normal with no further disturbances. The tables turned in at least one case: two jornaleros sued a *guardia civil* (law enforcement officer) who had seized their fighting cocks in the public plaza; they received the cocks' fair price as a result. Apparently, the interruption of the popular Puerto Rican pastime was a more serious crime than disturbing the peace.

A most peculiar case, exceptional in that it involved many of San Vicente's jornaleros, refers to the excesses of another guardian of the peace in the carrying out of his duty. The accuser, Juan Sánchez—alias *"Títere"* (mischievous and streetwise)—picked a fight with another *"muchacho moreno"* (dark or black boy) who also worked at San Vicente. This unimportant incident was complicated by the persecution of Sánchez by a man who carried a horse bridle. Sánchez naturally fled the scene of the crime, as his pursuer, guardia civil Antonio Joven, followed him. Sánchez found refuge in the home of various townsfolk, including *"el ciego* (the blindman) Cosme Galíndez,"* a co-worker at San Vicente. After a lengthy chase, Joven caught up with Sánchez, took him to the police station, and beat him up in the presence of various townspeople. Witnesses to the street affair and eventual beating testified in favor of Sánchez. The judge, however, was more impressed by Joven's description of Sánchez's disrespectful behavior and irreverent gesticulations. He dropped charges against the guardia civil, alleging that no crime except a mild beating had been committed.

Several details make this account especially valuable to the understanding of Vega Baja life. References to people's "street" names—"el ciego," "Títere," "muchacho moreno"—point to a familiarity in day-to-day operations not found in other sources. That Sánchez had a well-deserved reputation as the disorderly town clown with much support from his neighbors indicates a healthy tolerance, and even incorporation, of deviant behavior within local patterns of social expectations. If they did not condone Sanchez's activities, official authorities apparently also looked the other way. Whereas the judge could have pressed charges for disorderly conduct, Sánchez's case against Joven was merely dropped.

By far the most revealing type of accusation has to do with the private lives of Vega Baja's residents. Ricardo Torres pressed charges against a woman who publicly referred to him as a worthless drunkard and thief. Paulino Miranda demanded justice regarding co-worker José María López's abduction of his daughter under the promise of marriage. Eugenio Dávila was accused of aggression by his mistress Eulalia. Julián Rodríguez accused co-worker Francisco Ortega's wife of verbal abuse regarding his and his wife's moral conduct.

These cases, along with breaches of informal contracts regarding land, animals, or crops, were usually resolved to the satisfaction of both parties in the most simple manner. Torres, for example, explained that because this woman's boyfriend misinterpreted some of the information Torres offered about her (namely, that she had a son in another part of the island), he was now caught up in a lovers' quarrel, the result of which had been personal insults directed against him by the woman. José María López reiterated his promise of marriage, provided he was given a four-month extension, to Miranda's daughter. Dávila confirmed that he had had a "slight disagreement" with his mistress as a result of her jealous outburst over another woman. Rodríguez and Ortega agreed that their wives' calling each other "whore" was clearly the product of "*chismes de familia*" (family gossip). Their attempt at not complicating things resulted in a healthy balance between what was perceived as reasonable and practical and what was understood as fair, moral, and honorable.

Vega Baja's juicios verbales place San Vicente's laborers in a context that, like the workplace itself, could have been transformed by the establishment of an industrial routine unfamiliar to those it most closely touched. The existence of the sugar complex, however, did not change life-styles, suggest new rules of behavior, or dictate new sanctions. Vega Baja's population seemed to proceed with business as usual, more often than not quietly adapting to the new situations.[27]

Labor relations at Central San Vicente preserved the quality that had characterized hacienda life and did not evolve into strictly business transactions. Incentives in the form of wages reflected the new organization of production, but rewards for efficient laborers remained paternalistic concessions, such as permission to use land or the show of support in time of need. Workers seem to have successfully dealt with deviations from previously accepted patterns, maintaining their independence of action through alternative employment. San Vicente failed to proletarianize its workers and class conflict did not develop.

My findings are consistent with Mintz's observations on Hacienda Vieja for the 1880s. Labor relations in postemancipation sugar plantations (what he calls the "family type hacienda") remained more or less the same as those in "slave and *agregado* plantations." One important similarity between Hacienda Vieja and Central San Vicente is the face-to-face contact workers had with members of the landowning family. A crucial difference, however, is worth noting. Hacienda Vieja was not capitalized, while San Vicente was—and heavily. This element makes San Vicente a likely candidate for Mintz's "corporate land and factory combine" category, where contacts between capital and labor are impersonal, wage-based, and negotiated through paid managers. Yet labor relations remained as described by Mintz for the previous stage of development, the family type hacienda. Clearly, then, capital investment alone did not determine the character of labor relations. Rather, the combination of the reorganization of labor that goes along with capital investment and the opportunity for workers to resist it defined the parameters of proletarianization and class conflict.[28]

6

Conclusions

New Perspectives on Land, Labor, and Capital in a Caribbean Context

The nature of socioeconomic change in its myriad manifestations has forever fascinated historians. We have attempted to give meaning to the clouded testimony of participants in and observers of moments we consider significant. In the case of Central San Vicente, I chose to study the chimerical aims of a group of reformers, the mixed attitudes of its founder, the obstacles posed by the financial infrastructure, and the resistance of its workers. In the final analysis, both management and workers acted and reacted to trace a course convenient to them, as profound adaptation marked their lives.

The concerns of reformers during Puerto Rico's chronic agricultural crisis are a convenient starting point for understanding the historical moment under study. Their doomsday analysis of the sugar industry was laden with misconceptions. To be alarmed about the drop in the price of sugar was natural. But one had only to remember how planters had increased their production in the face of falling prices during the 1850s to be reassured. Similarly, the decrease in the number of mills must have been disturbing, but the figure only indicated that obsolete haciendas were being replaced by larger, more efficient units.

It is noteworthy that the quite erroneous arguments of nineteenth-century agricultural analysts have endured well into the present. Several historians have described the 1870s as a period of crisis during which the sugar industry faced the choice of reorganizing structurally or perishing. Andrés A. Ramos Mattei, the foremost exponent of this view, argues that Puerto Rican planters either produced better-grade sugar under a revised system of production or they dropped out of the market. The hacienda system as it was known could not continue producing sugar at high costs to sell it at falling prices. The example of Cuba reinforces this assumption; having re-organized (centralized), it reentered the market on a more competitive basis. By extension, Puerto Rico's sugar economy, which generally failed to centralize, should have failed.[1]

Indeed, the facts pointed to the necessity of restructuring the sugar industry to make it more competitive and consequently less vulnerable to the market. But reformers aspired to produce high-quality sugar, which could very well not find appropriate outlets. The market, in fact, was unpredictable, and export producers would always be at its mercy. Moreover, reformers would have needed Spain's support in the form of infrastructure and international trade negotiation. Clearly, reformers adopted goals unsuitable to circumstances and based their outcome on false expectations.

The solutions proposed were removed from reality. The low quality of Puerto Rican sugar and the high costs of producing it should not have concerned planters.[2] Improvements in sugar quality would only have alienated importers from the United States—Puerto Rico's principal market at the time—who were interested only in refining low-grade sugars from their Caribbean suppliers. Even with falling prices and high production costs, sugar manufacturing remained profitable.

As they offered solutions for existing difficulties, the reformers failed to identify the distinguishing feature of monoculture for export. The impact of the appearance on the market of beet sugar—greater quantities of a better quality product at falling prices—should have brought the message home. Planters and reformers expected that modernizing their operations would exempt them from shrinking the profits accrued in earlier decades. That a more competitive position was no safeguard against the fluctuations of the international market was a point they chose to ignore. They discounted the influence of the market, an autonomous, uncontrollable entity that determined profits for agricultural exporters.

Reformers misjudged the situation in yet another way. Many of their plans depended on Spain's good will. Banks were an essential element if large amounts of capital were to be invested. A reliable transportation and communications network would be needed to support projects to revive the sugar industry. Finally, the active role of the mother country in negotiating better terms of trade was a necessary ingredient in the blueprint for economic success. Satisfied neither with the monetary system nor with existing provisions for agricultural credit and land tenure, the reformers sought to establish more liberal economic and financial structures. It should have been clear that Spain was much too busy with domestic wrangles to dedicate the time and energy required to the projects proposed.

But it was natural for agricultural analysts to adopt the rational ideal of centralization as their goal. The routinism with which agricultural tasks were carried out and the absence of technological improvements became the focus of their attack. The establishment of a cadastre, a public record for taxation purposes of district landholdings, corresponded to a new insistence on systematization. Inspired by the spirit of science in a period of positivist thought, reformers found the progressive notions of division of labor attractive. Impressed with advanced technology, they equated centralization with the installation of sophisticated equipment, such as that used in the beet sugar industry. Entry into world markets through a competitive system of exchange was a logical corollary. Their goal was to compete in the international market, and centralization meant improving the quality of the product to meet more demanding external conditions.[3]

The reformers' appraisal of the Puerto Rican worker is much in line with these philosophical tenets. The rural population's attitudes ran quite contrary to ideals of constant, and therefore productive, work. Women and gambling were distractions from a disciplined life and strict ethical codes. Judging all activity from a utilitarian and self-serving standpoint, these men envisioned the transformation of the rural population into armies of workers who would labor enthusiastically because of the benefits the capitalist system offered them.[4]

The ideal of centralization, then, symbolized the collective aspirations of island leaders intent on establishing in Puerto Rico the social and economic patterns associated with capitalist production: wage labor, free markets, industrialization, and large investments. It became the cure-all for Puerto Rico's sugar industry—and, by extension, for that of other islands. The reformers' insistence on centralization closely paralleled the positivists' obsession with progress and order. It was almost impossible for these men to consider that the most important element of the equation was outside their control.

The careful articulation of what agricultural analysts treated as generic problems and solutions obscures the fact that different sets of circumstances promoted the establishment of centrales in other islands. With hindsight, the scarcity of labor and the abundance of capital have been identified as contributing factors to their success in Cuba, in addition to a well-developed transportation network, a more stable trading situation, and the not insignificant detail that the sugar industry was rebuilt from its foundation after insurgents burned hundreds of ingenios to the ground during the Ten Years' War. Trinidad established centrales encouraged by the steady stream of Asian immigrants, the existence of suitable uncultivated clayland, and the availability of capital. But Barbados did not follow suit, even though production expanded as cane cultivation successfully extended into just about every available acre of land. Jamaica relied at the end of the century on a "discredited, decapitalised and outmoded production pattern" that could not have led to centralization. The complex factors at play make generalizations impossible.[5]

As are those of the other Caribbean islands, the case of Puerto Rico is unique. One could explore the connections between centralization in the northern coast and the presence of dense peasant populations in surrounding areas.[6] But Central San Vicente's isolation is easier to explain. Its demise and the course of similar enterprises for the rest of the century resulted from the lack of financial mechanisms to support projects of such magnitude and from Spain's apathy toward economic development. The sugarcane industry, centralized or not, faced an unpromising future.

Central San Vicente, in the same way it filled reformers with hope in its early days, must have sobered their expectations of radical transformations as it slowly collapsed. The combination of an innovative owner/manager, a skilled labor force, fertile land, and sophisticated machinery working together to put out a high-quality product was enthusiastically received. But as an ongoing business activity, San Vicente also relied on well-established patterns for obtaining capital and for dealing with workers. Igaravídez acquired the necessary funds using the social connections landownership brought. In the face of an uncooperative financial system and a hostile social climate, the enterprise was likely to disappear. Likewise, Don Leonardo invested in technology that required the reorganization of labor but was unable to establish labor relations based strictly on wages. Central San Vicente, an experiment in capitalism, failed.

The conflicting forces that shaped the actual operations of a particular sugar factory, however, render impossible the task of placing the central within any of the typologies that attempt to clarify issues of land extension, labor arrangements, management attitudes, control mechanisms, and orientation of production. San Vicente, like any socioeconomic unit of production, was a hybrid in the ways that it used its vast territory, in its treatment of the work force, in its connections to markets. Extending over vast amounts of land, the complex assured its owner not only control over labor and cane supplies but also supremacy within the landowning elite. Mixing modern business objectives with old-time social considerations, San Vicente produced not only sugar for the commodities markets but also minor crops for internal consumption. Management policies oscillated from the callousness characteristic of businesslike attitudes to the paternalism associated with traditional notions of social responsibility. A blend of the semifeudal, internally oriented, and status-promoting hacienda with a resident labor force characteristic of northern Mexico and the proto-capitalistic, commodities-oriented, and profit-making plantation associated with the Caribbean slave societies, San Vicente approached the reality these ideal types aim to identify and explain.

Because centralization entailed a continuous redefinition of the hacendado's role in society, San Vicente's founder cannot be fit into a mold either. Doubtless Don Leonardo's activities as a merchant-turning-entrepreneur conform to the processes of innovation, management, and adjustment to external conditions outlined in entrepreneurial studies. The nature of decisions made at the risk of not being able to make the same or similar ones again also points to projections for an indefinite future, to expectations of continuous development. Owning vast amounts of land, then, could or could not have been a source of pride; it certainly became a business decision. The same is true for other seemingly contradictory policies at San Vicente. It is Igaravídez's role within a changing social and economic context that makes the case at hand exceptional.[7]

Borrowing the best of both worlds, however, did not automatically lead to success. Whereas San Vicente could have resolved its internal problems (those associated with land use, for example), it was destined to fall prey to the financial and legal infrastructure of the colony. In the final analysis, the central disappeared because its requirements for capital could not be satisfied by existing credit mechanisms. Igaravídez was forced to overextend his credit in order to launch his ambitious project. His creditors, interested in immediate and easy returns on their investment, demanded the strict application of the Commercial Code to Igaravídez's shady transactions. In this context, the legal infrastructure that regulated money exchanges merely promoted immediate gain and remained unresponsive to the promise of future profits.

The reactions of San Vicente's labor force followed the patterns and pace of the changes described above. The immediate effect of abolition was not a dislocation of existing structures followed by a slow recovery, as occurred in other parts of the Caribbean. The sugar giant's lack of longevity resulted in limited impact on Vega Baja's rural population. Perhaps because the desired reorganization of the labor effort took place under the auspices of the old hacendado himself, or because traditional ways of work and play were deeply rooted in the rural population, the establishment of capitalist relations of production with their concomitant class conflict and proletarianization did not materialize. The master's laws were fought not on their own terms, but through the moral norms understood by the workers.[8] The jornaleros of San Vicente, in fact, operated within a gray area between traditional values and new rules. Ultimately, it was they who adapted best under the circumstances, changing few of their conceptions of daily life at work and home.

Suggestive but not representative of the changes between 1870 and 1900, the story of San Vicente remains enigmatic in the face of developments in the twentieth-century sugar industry. Industrial capitalism made its appearance on the island in the last three decades of the nineteenth century in at least one locality, Vega Baja. Central San Vicente followed the prescription for capitalism that reformers wrote: scientific land use, sophisticated machinery, and wage labor. In its effort to invest capital in technology that would require a redefinition of labor relations, it also sought to establish what are generally understood today as capitalist relations of production. I have argued that it failed *as a capitalist enterprise* precisely because it never followed through on the reorganization of labor that heavy capital investment required. Paradoxically, Central San Vicente should not have disappeared *as a sugarmaking operation* under the conditions described in the preceding pages. The fate of capitalism in Central San Vicente or anywhere else, in fact, has little to do with the business aspects of the enterprise.

The twentieth-century sugar industry, in contrast, witnessed the profound social and economic transformations associated with full-fledged capitalism. Beginning in 1900 and with tacit support from the new metropolitan government, U.S. corporations appropriated the best lowlands from Puerto Rican peasants, thus controlling the supply of cane and labor in fields and factories. U.S. firms also enjoyed control of the market through political connections and of credit through highly developed structures of capital investment. Soon enough, however, the decline of nonsugar agriculture, violent seasonal fluctuations in employment, dependence on U.S. subsidies, and preferential market treatment became major foci of attention for economists and politicians alike. The capitalistic sugar industry did not launch Puerto Rico into the ranks of developed nations as had been hoped. Neither did it succeed from the strictly business point of view. A new formula for success—based on manufacturing companies attracted to the island by tax breaks, which would provide next to full employment, and which would eventually operate in the absence of incentives—replaced the equally chimerical rhetoric of nineteenth-century reformers.[9] To this day, Puerto Rico's sugar industry is still trying to reconcile its capitalist aspirations with a history of economic failures.

Notes

Abbreviations

AGPR	Archivo General de Puerto Rico
AMVB	Archivo Municipal de Vega Baja
AT	(Fondo) Audiencia Territorial
SC	(Serie) Civil
SCr	(Serie) Criminal
DP	(Fondo) Diputación Provincial
OP	(Fondo) Obras Públicas
PN	(Fondo) Protocolos Notariales
SG	(Serie) Sala de Gobierno

Chapter 1

1. Two contrasting views of politics, economy, and society in the Caribbean possessions of European powers can be identified. Franklin W. Knight, *The Caribbean. The Genesis of a Fragmented Nationalism*, and James L. Dietz, *Economic History of Puerto Rico. Institutional Change and Capitalist Development*, emphasize metropolitan considerations as a dominant influence in the colony's life. Fernando Picó, *Historia general de Puerto Rico*, gives credit to local efforts in carving out societies specifically adapted to existing conditions at the micro level. John Lynch, *The Spanish American Revolutions 1808–1826*, refers to the Bourbon reforms as "the new imperialism" that marked the last decades of the eighteenth century.

2. Francisco A. Scarano, *Sugar and Slavery in Puerto Rico. The Plantation Economy of Ponce, 1800–1850*, pp. 18–24, is in large part a reaction to the view presented in Luis González Vales, "Towards a Plantation Society (1860–1866)," pp. 79–107.

3. Lidio Cruz Monclova, *Historia de Puerto Rico (Siglo XIX)*, contains the most detailed account of Puerto Rico's nineteenth-century political history. Jesus Lalinde Abadía, *La administración española en el siglo XIX puertorriqueño (Pervivencia de la variante indiana del decisionismo castellano en Puerto Rico)*, pp. 8–9, discusses Spanish policy in the island at different periods. For a panorama of arguments regarding Spain's political life during the nineteenth century, see Miguel Artola, *La burguesía revolucionaria (1808–1869)*; José Luis Comellas, *Los moderados en el poder, 1844–1854*; V. G. Kiernan, *The Revolution of 1854 in Spanish History*; Manuel Tuñón de Lara, "El problema del poder en el sexenio 1868–1874," pp. 138–82; C. A. M. Hennessy, *The Federal Republic in Spain. Pi y Margall and the Federal Republican Movement, 1868–1874*; Miguel Martínez Cuadrado, *La burguesía conservadora (1874–1931)*.

4. Josep Fradera, "Aproximación al colonialismo liberal español, 1833–1868."

5. Various aspects of the rise and fall of the nineteenth-century sugar industry are discussed in: Guillermo A. Baralt, *Esclavos rebeldes. Conspiraciones y sublevaciones de esclavos en Puerto Rico (1795–1873)*, pp. 81–83; Laird W. Bergad, "Agrarian History of Puerto Rico, 1870–1930," pp. 63–67; Eugenio Fernández Méndez, *Historia cultural de Puerto Rico*, pp. 243–46, 256–58, 268–70; Gervasio L. García Rodríguez, *Primeros fermentos de organización obrera en Puerto Rico, 1873–1898*, pp. 1–5; González Vales, "Towards a Plantation Society (1860–1866)" and "The Challenge to Colonialism (1866–1897)," pp. 92–95; Andrés Ramos Mattei, *La hacienda azucarera. Su crecimiento y crisis en Puerto Rico (Siglo XIX)*, pp. 17–39; Francisco Scarano, "Slavery and Free Labor in the Puerto Rican Sugar Economy: 1815–1873," pp. 553–55. Roland T. Ely, *Cuando reinaba su majestad el azúcar. Estudio histórico-sociológico de una tragedia latinoamericana: el monocultivo en Cuba. Origen y evolución del proceso*, pp. 419–21, offers a good description of the situation in the international market. Peter L. Eisenberg, *The Sugar Industry in Pernambuco. Modernization Without Change, 1840–1910*, p. 22, shows the disastrous effects of the introduction of beet sugar for Brazil. The reaction to these circumstances in Puerto Rico is covered in Ramos Mattei, *Hacienda azucarera*, p. 23, and Manuel Moreno Fraginals, "Plantations in the Caribbean: Cuba, Puerto Rico, and the Dominican Republic in the Late Nineteenth Century," pp. 14, 16.

6. For contrasting views, see Scarano, *Sugar and Slavery*, pp. 22–24 and Dietz, *Economic History*, pp. 21–24.

7. The relationship between colonial/regional elites and their metropoli-

tan/national centers can be examined in different contexts. See Pierre Vilar, *Crecimiento y desarrollo. Economía e historia. Reflexiones sobre el caso español*; João Manuel Cardoso de Mello, *O Capitalismo Tardio. Contribuição à revisão crítica da formação e do desenvolvimento da economia brasileira*; Aldo Ferrer, *La economía argentina. Las etapas de su desarrollo y problemas actuales*; Alonso Aguilar Monteverde, *Dialéctica de la economía mexicana. Del colonialismo al imperialismo.*

8. Whites (300,406) made up 51.5 percent of the population (583,181) in 1860, while slaves (41,738) and free blacks (241,037) constituted 7.2 percent and 41.3 percent, respectively. Instituto Geográfico y Estadístico, *Censo de la población de España según el empadronamiento hecho el 31 de diciembre de 1860 por la Dirección General del Instituto Geográfico y Estadístico*, pp. 774–97. Fernando Picó, *Libertad y servidumbre en el Puerto Rico del siglo XIX (Los jornaleros utuadeños en vísperas del auge del café)*, pp. 82, 164, speaks of "peonización" and "clase en formación" to refer to the beginnings of proletarianization and the development of class consciousness in the coffee areas in particular. The concept of "class in the making" is developed in E. P. Thompson, *The Making of the English Working Class.*

9. María Asunción García Ochoa, *La política española en Puerto Rico durante el siglo XIX*; María Isabel Bonnín Orozco, "Las fortunas vulnerables: Comerciantes y agricultores en los contratos de refacción de Ponce, 1865–1875"; Pedro San Miguel, *El mundo que creó el azúcar. Las haciendas en Vega Baja, 1800–1873*; Laird W. Bergad, "Towards Puerto Rico's Grito de Lares: Coffee, Social Stratification, and Class Conflicts, 1828–1868."

10. Astrid T. Cubano Iguina, "Trade and Politics in Nineteenth-Century Puerto Rico," and Cruz M. Ortiz Cuadra, "Crédito y azúcar: Los hacendados de Humacao ante la crisis del dulce, 1865–1900," suggest that the elite was one: the propertied class.

11. I borrow this conceptualization from Knight, *The Caribbean*, pp. 65, 123.

12. Scarano, *Sugar and Slavery*, pp. 3–35, offers an excellent overview of these changes. For a collection of sugar statistics throughout the nineteenth century, see Salvador Brau, *Ensayos. Disquisiciones sociológicas*; Cayetano Coll y Toste, ed., *Boletín Histórico de Puerto Rico*, vols. 2, 4, and 5; E. D. Colón, *Datos sobre la agricultura en Puerto Rico antes de 1898*; Pedro Tomás de Córdova, *Memorias geográficas, históricas, económicas adísticas de la Isla de Puerto Rico*, vols. 3 and 5; and *Estadística general del comercio exterior de la provincia de Puerto Rico.*

13. Pure competition is defined by Wyllis R. Knight, "Agriculture," p. 4. Loida Figueroa Mercado, *History of Puerto Rico. From the beginning to the [sic] 1892*, p. 148, argues that incentives in the 1940s had the same effect as nineteenth-century legislation: after the initial boom, the economy could not support previous levels of growth.

14. Cubano, "Trade and Politics," pp. 153–57, and Fernández Méndez, *Historia cultural*, pp. 221–22, 239–41 offer different views of social differences in nineteenth-century Puerto Rico. Labor Gómez Acevedo, *Organización y reglamentación del trabajo en el Puerto Rico del siglo XIX (Propietarios y jornaleros)* focuses on the relationship between planter and worker in particular.

15. I use the words *hacienda* and *plantation* interchangeably to mean generally the socioeconomic units of agricultural production common in nineteenth-century Puerto Rico. Use of these terms to refer to Puerto Rican estates, then, should not be construed as a statement on the size of the property, its market orientation, predominant mode of production, or status of the labor force. The applicability of these theoretical models is still to be tested empirically by Puerto Rican historians; they are discussed fully in Eric R. Wolf and Sidney W. Mintz, "Haciendas and Plantations in Middle America and the Antilles," pp. 380–412; James Lockhart, "Encomienda and Hacienda: The Evolution of the Great Estate in the Spanish Indies," pp. 411–29; Robert Keith, "Encomienda, Hacienda and Corregimiento in Spanish America: A Structural Analysis," pp. 431–46; Magnus Mörner, "The Spanish American Hacienda: A Survey of Recent Research and Debate," pp. 183–216; Enrique Florescano, ed., *Haciendas, latifundios y plantaciones en América Latina*; Robert G. Keith, ed., *Haciendas and Plantations in Latin American History*; Eric Van Young, "Mexican Rural History since Chevalier: The Historiography of the Colonial Hacienda," pp. 5–62. Similar works appeared for the study of plantations: Lloyd A. Best, "Outlines of a Model of Pure Plantation Economy," pp. 283–327; George L. Beckford, *Persistent Poverty. Underdevelopment in Plantation Economies of the Third World.* For the Puerto Rican case, see Fernández Méndez, *Historia cultural*, pp. 207–321; Sidney W. Mintz, "Labor and Sugar in Puerto Rico and in Jamaica, 1800–1850," pp. 273–80; and José Curet, *De la esclavitud a la abolición: Transiciones económicas en las haciendas azucareras de Ponce, 1845–1873.*

16. Planters form an elusive group. Ramos Mattei, *Hacienda azucarera*, p. 39, refers to them as "standardbearers for retrogression and stagnation." To Fernández Méndez, *Historia cultural*, p. 218, they appear as business-oriented sugar lords. A. G. Quintero Rivera, in *Historia de unas clases sin historia (Comentarios críticos al* País de cuatro pisos), p. 7, and in "Background to the Emergence of Imperialist Capitalism in Puerto Rico," pp. 87–117, however, portrays hacendados (correctly so, I would argue) as limited in their actions by the colonial context in which they operated.

17. As will be evident later, I refer to capitalism broadly as that mode of production in which capital investment in technology requires the reorganization of labor under a wage system. This presupposes, of course, that workers have lost access to the means of production and sell their force of labor because of economic necessity. Discussions of various applications of this definition can

be found in: Eugene D. Genovese, *The World the Slaveholders Made. Two Essays in Interpretation*, p. 16; Paul A. Baran and Paul M. Sweezy, *Monopoly Capital: An Essay in the American Economic and Social Order*, p. 324; Caio Prado, Junior, *Esbôço dos fundamentos da teoria econômica*, pp. 47–48.

Chapter 2

1. The major critics of the situation in the rural/agricultural areas and the exponents of a need for change in this period were Federico Asenjo y Arteaga, José Ballesteros Muñoz, Salvador Brau, Enrique Delgado, Manuel Fernández Umpierre, Fernando López Tuero, Santiago MacCormick, M. y J. Rosich, and Francisco del Valle Atiles. Short biographies of some of them can be found in Adolfo de Hostos, *Diccionario histórico bibliográfico comentado de Puerto Rico*; F. E. Jackson, ed. *The Representative Men of Porto Rico*; Javier Figueroa, *Diccionario histórico-biográfico*.

2. This semicoerced wage labor system has been fully discussed in Gómez Acevedo, *Organización y reglamentación*.

3. Ramos Mattei, *Hacienda azucarera*, pp. 17–24; Ortiz Cuadra, "Crédito y azúcar," pp. 48–64.

4. *Agricultural Resources and Capabilities of Porto Rico*, p. 15; Ramos Mattei, *Hacienda azucarera*, p. 20.

5. *Report of Brig. Gen. Geo. W. Davis, U.S.V., on Civil Affairs of Puerto Rico, 1899*, p. 37; Santiago MacCormick, *Factorías centrales en Puerto-Rico*, vi–vii. Noel Deerr, *The History of Sugar*, vol. 1, p. 126, however, gives a 76,411-ton figure for 1879.

6. On active haciendas, see Ramos Mattei, *Hacienda azucarera*, pp. 19, 20; *Agricultural Resources*, p. 13; Cayetano Coll y Toste, *Reseña del estado social, económico e industrial de la Isla de Puerto-Rico al tomar posesión de ella los Estados-Unidos*, pp. 9, 10; MacCormick, *Factorías centrales*, vi. On sucrose yield, see Ramos Mattei, *Hacienda azucarera*, pp. 21, 22–23.

7. Muscovado is considered a low-grade sugar because of its high molasses content. Other raw sugars include "clayed," which is a grade above muscovado, and "centrifugal," the highest grade of raw sugar, equal to 96° on the Polariscope test scale. Both of these fall below No. 12 D.S. (Dutch Standard), the dividing line between the raw and the refined products. Cf. Paul L. Vogt, *The Sugar Refining Industry in the United States. Its Development and Present Condition*, pp. 26–27, and Manuel Moreno Fraginals, *El ingenio. Complejo económico social cubano del azúcar*, vol. 1, p. 236. The prices of sugar are from Moreno Fraginals, *El ingenio*, vol. 1, p. 254. For a complete listing of the London price of raw sugar throughout the nineteenth century, see Deerr, *History of Sugar*, vol. 2, pp. 530–31. For tonnage of Cuban sugar, see Deerr, *History of Sugar*, vol. 1, p. 131.

8. Ely, *Cuando reinaba*, p. 603, states there were 1,365 ingenios in 1860, 1,189 in 1879, and 450 in 1894. That cultivated land increased as the number of economic units dropped, however, indicates that it was the larger and mechanized mills that survived, incorporating probably the lands of failed estates. Cf. Ramos Mattei, *Hacienda azucarera*, pp. 20, 24; and Moreno Fraginals, "Plantations in the Caribbean," p. 5.

9. Ely, *Cuando reinaba*, p. 539; Moreno Fraginals, *Ingenio*, vol. 1, pp. 246–47, 254; Santiago MacCormick, *Artículos publicados en el periódico "El Asimilista," debidos a la pluma del Sr. D. Santiago MacCormick con motivo de otros propios del Sr. D. Manuel Fernández Umpierre, dados a la luz en el "Boletín Mercantil,"* p. 32; *Almanaque de la Isla de Puerto-Rico 1891*, pp. 102–3.

10. Ramos Mattei, *Hacienda azucarera*, pp. 19–20; Federico Asenjo y Arteaga, *El catastro de Puerto-Rico. Necesidad de su formación y posibilidad de llevarlo a cabo*, p. 10; Ely, *Cuando reinaba*, pp. 320, 325.

11. For good synopses of positivist philosophy in Europe, see Ernst Cassirer, "El positivismo y su ideal de conocimiento histórico. Hipólito Taine," pp. 295–308; Auguste Comte, "Los tres estados de la inteligencia humana," pp. 653–58; and Nicola Abbagnano, "Positivism." Richard Graham, *Britain and the Onset of Modernization in Brazil, 1850–1914*, pp. 35, 36, 39, 232–34, and Leopoldo Zea, *Positivism in Mexico*, offer valuable suggestions with respect to the application of these attitudes in developing areas. The influence of positivism in Puerto Rico, however, has only been traced to the person of Eugenio María de Hostos, a well-known educator and politician of the period. See Ralph Lee Woodward, Jr., ed., *Positivism in Latin America, 1850–1900. Are Order and Progress Reconcilable?*

12. *Boletín Mercantil de Puerto-Rico*, 15, 17, 26 April 1875; Asenjo y Arteaga, *Catastro*, p. 9.

13. For the "axis" quote, MacCormick, *Factorías centrales*, v. On the yield, MacCormick, *Artículos*, p. 14. On farmers' isolation, MacCormick, *Factorías centrales*, p. 33. On wasteful practices, Francisco del Valle Atiles, *El campesino puertorriqueño. Sus condiciones físicas, intelectuales y morales, causas que las determinan y medios para mejorarlas*, p. 97.

14. I use *jíbaro* only to mean the small self-sufficient landowner whose margin of profits protected him from having to sell his labor. *Agregados, medianeros*, or *arrendatarios* were usually people who cultivated a piece of land controlled by a large landowner under an infinite variety of arrangements regarding rent payments, products grown, share in profits, and length of stay. The *jornalero* worked for a *jornal*, or daily wage, although his access to and/or proprietorship of land could vary in each individual case. *Jornalero* and *peón*, however, are terms frequently used interchangeably with the understanding that both have been alienated from the means of production. Cf. del Valle Atiles, *Campesino*

puertorriqueño; Rafael Romeu, *Leyes de arrendamiento y desahucio de la Península, Cuba y Puerto-Rico, con notas para su mejor inteligencia y un formulario para su exacto cumplimiento de los juzgados municipales y de paz*; Salvador Brau, *Las clases jornaleras de Puerto-Rico. Su estado actual, causas que lo sostienen y medios de propender al adelante moral y material de dichas clases. Memoria premiada en el Certamen del Ateneo Puerto-riqueño.* Dietz, *Economic History*, pp. 40–53, and Lydia Milagros González and A. G. Quintero Rivera, *La otra cara de la historia. La historia de Puerto Rico desde su cara obrera*, vol. 1, pp. 39–57, contain very helpful explanations of the different types of arrangements that existed between landowners and landholders.

15. Del Valle Atiles, *Campesino puertorriqueño*, p. 120; Fernando López Tuero, *Isla de Puerto Rico. Estudios de economía rural*, p. 52; Asenjo y Arteaga, *Catastro*, p. 13.

16. MacCormick, *Factorías centrales*, p. 21.

17. The most useful reference for the island's geography is Rafael Picó, *Nueva geografía de Puerto Rico. Física, económica, social.* Figueroa Mercado, *History of Puerto Rico*, pp. 30–32, summarizes its most salient points. Bergad, "Agrarian History," p. 63, offers nineteenth-century figures.

18. José Ballesteros Muñoz, *Descripción y cultivo de la caña de azúcar, formada con notas adquiridas sobre el terreno en diez y ocho años de práctica*, p. 28; López Tuero, *Economía rural*, p. 82.

19. Asenjo y Artega, *Catastro*, p. 13; Ballesteros Muñoz, *Descripción y cultivo*, p. 26.

20. On schools, José Ballesteros Muñoz, *Guía comercial y agrícola de Puerto Rico*, p. 12. On journals, *Revista de Agricultura, Industria y Comercio*, 1888, pp. 52–61, 74, 97; 1889, pp. 8, 63, 92. On associations, *Revista*, 1890, p. 137; Fernando López Tuero, *Caña de azúcar*, pp. 75–76. On training jornaleros, del Valle Atiles, *Campesino puertorriqueño*, p. 100.

21. Federico Asenjo, *Páginas para los jornaleros de Puerto-Rico*, pp. 2–3, 51.

22. M. y J. Rosich, *Fabricación del azúcar mascabado en relación con las factorías centrales*, p. 19.

23. Manuel Fernández Umpierre, *Manual práctico de la agricultura de la caña de azúcar*, p. 195. These arguments were common throughout the Caribbean, as Ely, *Cuando reinaba*, pp. 594–97, demonstrates.

24. López Tuero, *Caña*, p. 75.

25. The Reglamento de Jornaleros of 1849 required that each worker carry with him at all times a *libreta* (notebook) in which were recorded his personal data and information regarding place of work, conduct, and current status with employer. The abuses committed in connection with this record-keeping device, as expounded by Gómez Acevedo in his *Organización y reglamentación*, proved the system ineffective and provided arguments for opponents to advo-

cate its abolition. On characteristics of the rural populace, Brau, *Clases jornaleras*, p. 25.

26. MacCormick, *Factorías centrales*, p. 10; Brau, *Clases jornaleras*, p. 50; Fernando López Tuero, *Estado moral de los factores de producción en Cuba y Puerto-Rico*, p. 9; López Tuero, *Economía rural*, pp. 10–11.

27. Trumbull White, *Our New Possessions . . . Four Books in One . . . A Graphic Account, Descriptive and Historical, of the Tropic Islands of the Sea Which Have Fallen Under Our Sway, Their Cities, Peoples and Commerce, Natural Resources and the Opportunities They Offer to Americans*, p. 399; Salvador Brau, *La campesina (Disquisiciones sociológicas)*, p. 36; *Report on Civil Affairs*, p. 38; MacCormick, *Artículos*, p. 55; Asenjo, *Páginas*, p. 53; Brau, *Clases jornaleras*, p. 29.

28. Del Valle Atiles, *Campesino puertorriqueño*, pp. 64–65; Brau, *Clases jornaleras*, p. 3.

29. Del Valle Atiles, *Campesino puertorriqueño*, p. 16; *Report on Civil Affairs*, p. 36.

30. Del Valle Atiles, *Campesino puertorriqueño*, p. 18; López Tuero, *Estado moral*, p. 14.

31. Brau, *Clases jornaleras*, pp. 38–40; López Tuero, *Economía rural*, p. 17.

32. Brau, *Clases jornaleras*, pp. 42–43, 46; López Tuero, *Economía rural*, pp. 5–7; *Report on Civil Affairs*, p. 36.

33. Brau, *Clases jornaleras*, pp. 31, 33–34, 37–38.

34. Ibid., pp. 25, 29; Brau, *Campesina*, pp. 19–25, 31, 36.

35. Del Valle Atiles, *Campesino puertorriqueño*, pp. 12, 13, 123; Brau, *Clases jornaleras*, pp. 46–47.

36. Brau, *Clases jornaleras*, pp. 36, 49; del Valle Atiles, *Campesino puertorriqueño*, pp. 88, 90, 91; Asenjo, *Páginas*, iii, iv.

37. On women, Brau, *Clases jornaleras*, pp. 29–30; Brau, *Campesina*, p. 10. On mixed schools, Brau, *Campesina*, pp. 7–8, 40, 45–47, 51.

38. Brau, *Campesina*, pp. xv, 1, 12–13, 15, 86; Herminio W. Santaella, *Nociones de agricultura, industria y comercio. Texto aprobado de Real Orden para todas las escuelas de primera enseñanza*, p. 74.

39. Asenjo, *Páginas*, pp. 28, 30, 46–47, 53.

40. Ibid., pp. 57, 61, 63, 69–73.

41. Ibid., pp. xii, xiii, 77.

42. Ibid., pp. 14; López Tuero, *Estado moral*, p. 7.

43. Asenjo, *Páginas*, pp. 7, 16, 18, 20, 21, 90, 96.

44. Fernando López Tuero, *Isla de Puerto Rico. La reforma agrícola*, pp. 169–74.

45. On "lack of capital," Asenjo y Arteaga, *Catastro*, p. 9. *Refaccionistas* were usually merchants who provided financing under a *contrato de refacción*, in which either the land itself was mortgaged or the product presold according to

expected market prices. The duration of the loan and repayment deadlines followed the sugar cycle closely, pointing to heavy dependence and high instability in the financial situation of the producer. On loans and terms, Asenjo y Arteaga, *Catastro*, p. 42.

46. *Derechos del propietario en cuanto se relaciona con la propiedad inmueble o sea nociones de derecho constitucional al alcance de todas las inteligencias por un abogado*, pp. 30–32; Asenjo y Arteaga, *Catastro*, pp. 7, 13, 19, 23, 43, 60.

47. Asenjo y Arteaga, *Catastro*, p. 13.

48. López Tuero, *Economía rural*, p. 34.

49. On international investors, MacCormick, *Factorías centrales*, p. 9. On the spirit of association, Federico Asenjo y Arteaga, *Estudios económicos. El comercio de la Isla y la influencia que en él ha de ejercer el Banco español de Puerto Rico*, pp. 44–47. On the 1877 project, AGPR, PN, José Ramón de Torres, box 66, 26 January 1877. On the Banco Español, White, *Our New Possessions*, p. 435. On a bank using native capital, Asociación de Agricultores de Puerto-Rico, *Acta de la junta general celebrada en 31 de julio de 1893 y documentos leídos en ella en cumplimiento de lo prevenido en los Estatutos y Reglamento*, p. 30.

50. Joaquín María Sanromá, *Puerto Rico y su hacienda*, p. 8; Román Baldorioty de Castro, *Bases para la fundación de un banco de emisión y descuento destinado principalmente a préstamos a la agricultura y el comercio, movilizando una parte de la riqueza rústica y urbana y promoviendo garantía provincial del interés*, p. 7; *Exposición presentada a la Comisión Colonial de Washington por los gremios de comerciantes, agricultores e industriales de Ponce*, p. 4; *Derechos del propietario*, pp. 30–32; Asenjo y Arteaga, *Catastro*, pp. 7, 19, 23, 43, 60.

51. Enrique Vijande, *La cuestión monetaria en Puerto Rico*, p. 29; MacCormick, *Artículos*, p. 15; Román Baldorioty de Castro, *Informe sobre la moneda mejicana*, pp. 6–7.

52. Vijande, *Cuestión monetaria*, pp. 12.

53. Sanromá, *Hacienda*, pp. 6, 25–26, 28–29, 91; *Revista*, 1888, pp. 10–11; Asociación de Agricultores, *Acta de la junta*, p. 5; *Exposición*, p. 14; Asenjo y Arteaga, *Catastro*, p. 44; López Tuero, *Estado moral*, pp. 53–54; López Tuero, *Economía rural*, pp. 106–7, 111; Baldorioty de Castro, *Bases para la fundación*, p. 14. Bonnín Orozco, "Las fortunas vulnerables," pp. 25–42, covers the ailments of the sugar industry and the reforms proposed.

54. *Boletín Mercantil*, 10 November 1871; MacCormick, *Factorías centrales*, xii.

55. White, *Our New Possessions*, p. 397; Fernando López Tuero, *Tratado de cultivos tropicales*, p. 121; Rosich, *Fabricación*, pp. 55–56.

56. Rosich, *Fabricación*, pp. 55–56; White, *Our New Possessions*, p. 396.

57. Rosich, *Fabricación*, pp. 55–56; *La Razón*, 30 May 1873; Baldorioty de Castro, *Bases para la fundación*, p. 4; Sanromá, *Hacienda*, p. 10.

58. On production increases, *Boletín Mercantil*, 10 November 1871; Asenjo y Arteaga, *Catastro*, p. 13. On white sugar, Rosich, *Fabricación*, p. 9. On profits, White, *Our New Possessions*, pp. 396, 397; *Report on Civil Affairs*, p. 38; MacCormick, *Factorías centrales*, pp. 24–25; Rosich, *Fabricación*, pp. 9, 55–56.

59. The United States became Puerto Rico's largest market throughout the nineteenth century, accounting for as much as 70 percent of sugar exported in the 1860s and 1870s. Fernández Méndez, *Historia cultural*, p. 244; *Estadística General del Comercio Exterior de la Isla de Puerto Rico*; *Report upon the Commercial Relations of the United States with Foreign Countries for the year(s)* ———.

60. Fernández Umpierre, *Manual práctico*, pp. 10–11, examines specifically the advantages of the beet sugar industry. MacCormick, *Factorías centrales*, p. 21; MacCormick, *Artículos*, p. 30; Rosich, *Fabricación*, p. 9; Fernández Umpierre, *Manual práctico*, p. 124; *La Razón*, 25 May 1873; and *Boletín Mercantil*, 18 August 1876, describe central projects.

61. *La Razón*, 10 July 1873; *Boletín Mercantil*, 6 July 1873.

62. MacCormick, *Factorías centrales*, pp. xi, 4, 94–97.

63. Ibid., pp. 36, 48; Enrique Delgado, *Proyecto para la creación de una empresa de factorías centrales en la isla de Puerto-Rico*, pp. 20, 43–44.

64. AGPR, PN, Demetrio Giménez y Moreno, box 250, 11 August 1882.

Chapter 3

1. Carlos Peñaranda, *Cartas puertorriqueñas, 1878–1880*, pp. 85–87, and M. Fernández Juncos, in *La Razón*, 15 May 1873, were two contemporary admirers of the project. Jaime Bagué y Ramírez, *Del ingenio azucarero patriarcal a la central azucarera corporativa: Glosa alrededor de las azucareras del año 1900*, lists three other centrales in the 1870s: Coloso in Aguada, Fortuna in Ponce, and Las Claras in Arecibo.

2. Manuel Ubeda Delgado, *Isla de Puerto Rico. Estudio histórico, geográfico y estadístico de la misma*, p. 139; Pedro San Miguel, "Tierra, trabajadores y propietarios: Las haciendas en Vega Baja, 1828–1865," pp. 8–12; Picó, *Nueva geografía*, pp. 386–94. Nitza Massini and Piedad Morayta of the Scientific Inventory Division of the Commonwealth Department of Natural Resources provided a 31,105-cuerda figure for the municipality of Vega Baja in 1978 from their computer records. Subtracting 6,000 cuerdas, as suggested by San Miguel (p. 8), a 25,105-cuerda figure is obtained for Vega Baja in the 1870s.

3. AMVB, "Relación de propiedad y bienes de Leonardo Igaravídez, que presenta Serapio Miticola, depositario judicial de los bienes del concurso necesario," box 1880C, doc. 72; Department of Natural Resources; San Miguel, "Tierra y trabajadores," p. 8. Given that the only population categories offered in AMVB, "Provincia de Puerto Rico. Pueblo de la Vega. Resúmen del

padrón general de habitantes de este territorio en la parte relativa a la clasifica-ción por cabeza de familia y demás condiciones sociales que a continuación se expresan," box 1885A, doc. 1, are male and female poor and wealthy heads-of-household and male and female non-heads-of-household less than and over 16 years of age, I have added the number of poor male heads-of-household to the number of non-heads-of-household over 16 to obtain the 2,574 figure by which I divided the 1,000-worker estimate (which must have included the jor-naleros of other haciendas absorbed by San Vicente) given in Peñaranda, *Car-tas*, p. 88. On the taxable income for San Vicente and Vega Baja, AMVB, "Villa de la Vega Baja. Año ecco. de 1883 a 84. Padrón general que com-prende todas las fincas rústicas de propiedad particular que existen en esta ju-risdicción el cual forma la junta pericial con vista de las declaraciones juradas presentadas por los dueños o representantes, y las alteraciones que en algunas de ellas ha tenido necesidad de practicar por constarle haberse obtenido mayor producción que la confesada", "Villa de la Vega. Contribuciones. Expediente relativo a la derrama de la contribución municipal para el año 1883–84. Re-parto parcial que se hace a la sección 2a de Pecuaria de la cantidad que le co-rresponde levantar en unión de las demás riquezas con arreglo a la renta imponible que cada uno disfruta," box 1883B; "Padrón general que com-prende el ganado vacuno, caballar y mular que existe en esta jurisdicción, con designación del que se halla exento del tributo por estar destinado a la agricul-tura," "Villa de la Vega. Año de 1887–88. Padrón General de las fincas rústi-cas, su valor y productos que forma la junta pericial para el repartimiento del año 1887 a 88," box 1887A, doc. 4. For the quote, Peñaranda, *Cartas*, p. 93.

4. AGPR, AT, SC, "Certificación expedida en relación de las cargas im-puestas sobre la Hacienda o Yngenio denominado 'Central San Vicente' dela jurisdicción de Vega Baja, como poseída por Don Leonardo Igaravídez, desde la instalación dela Antigua anotaduría de Hipotecas, ala fecha," box 71, doc. 975.

5. San Vicente centrifugal sugar was the highest grade of raw sugar, set at 96° on the Polariscope test. Peñaranda, *Cartas*, pp. 86–87.

6. George M. Rolph, *Something About Sugar. Its History, Growth, Manufac-ture and Distribution*, pp. 22–33; Peñaranda, *Cartas*, pp. 86–88; M. Fernández Juncos, in *La Razón*, 5 May 1873.

7. On the railways at San Vicente and on the island, Peñaranda, *Cartas*, p. 85; AMVB, "Relación de propiedad y bienes de Leonardo Igaravídez, que presenta Serapio Miticola, depositario judicial de los bienes del concurso necesario," box 1880C, doc. 72; Ramón Soler Fort, in *El Economista*, 17 May 1874; M. Fernández Juncos, in *La Razón*, 15 May 1873. On maritime trans-port, Peñaranda, *Cartas*, p. 84.

8. Peñaranda, *Cartas*, p. 88.

9. M. Fernández Juncos, in *La Razón*, 15 May 1873; Peñaranda, *Cartas*, p. 90.

10. AMVB, Presentación de azúcar de San Vicente, box 1879B, doc. 57, 15 February 1878; M. Fernández Juncos, in *La Razón*, 15 May 1873.

11. That San Vicente's equipment included Derosne evaporators and some of its product was white suggests that it was, in fact, putting out high-grade raw sugar. See note 7, chapter 2 for a brief explanation of the types of sugar produced in the Caribbean. For production statistics, see Peñaranda, *Cartas*, p. 88, and Coll y Toste, *Reseña del estado social*, p. 20; Bagué y Ramírez, *Ingenio azucarero*, p. 86. On Igaravídez, Ramón Soler Fort, in *El Economista*, 17 May 1874.

12. AGPR, PN, José Félix Lajara, box 766, 15 May 1865, suggests that Igaravídez's parents were not well-off since all assets were promptly sold by the family at his father's death, presumably to obtain cash. On Igaravídez's early commercial ventures, AGPR, PN, Demetrio Giménez y Moreno, box 206, 16 January 1866; box 213, 7 August 1869; *El Tiempo/"The Times."* No. 27, 31 January 1914. One wonders whether Igaravídez made his fortune smuggling slaves into Puerto Rico through St. Thomas in this period.

13. *El Tiempo/"The Times,"* No. 27, 31 January 1914.

14. AGPR, PN, José Félix Lajara, box 766, 13, 31 March, 27 May, 7 June, 7, 22 September, 22, 25 October 1865; box 768, 14 February, 26 August, 10 September 1867.

15. Even though there is a record of its existence, the document that relates Igaravídez's acquisition of a nobility title can no longer be found in the Vega Baja archive. AMVB, "Distrito electoral de Vega-Baja. Pueblo de Toa-Baja. Elección de un Diputado Provincial, verificada en los días 7, 8 y 9 de Abril de 1879. Diputado electo—Excmo. Sr. Marqués de Cabo Caribe por 74 votos," box 1879B, doc. 35; "Distrito electoral de Vega-Baja. Pueblo del Dorado. Elección de un Diputado Provincial verificada en los días 6 7 8 y 9 de Abril de 1879. Diputado electo—Excmo. Sr. Marqués de Cabo Caribe por 36 votos," box 1879B, doc. 36; *El Tiempo/"The Times,"* No. 27, 31 January 1914; Dulce María Tirado Merced, "Las raíces sociales del liberalismo criollo: El Partido Liberal Reformista (1870–1875)," p. 73.

16. The account of these transactions is complicated because of Bugella's previous personal commitments to his creditors. Vega's involvement is particularly obscure and it appears his role was only to manage the business. AGPR, PN, Demetrio Giménez y Moreno, box 218, 20 March 1872; box 221, 24 September 1873; Tirado Merced, "Raíces sociales," pp. 74–75.

17. AGPR, PN, Juan Ramón de Torres, box 49, 5, 10 May 1869; box 52, 9 March, 2 May, 27 October, 8 November 1871.

18. AGPR, PN, José Félix Lajara, box 771, 16 February 1872; box 772, 9 August 1874; Demetrio Giménez y Moreno, box 238, 5 July 1879.

19. AGPR, PN, Juan Ramón de Torres, box 50, 22 January 1870; box 65, 24 October 1876; José Félix Lajara, box 773, 1 April 1875; box 777, 24 May, 4 November 1878.

20. Details of the first refacción can be obtained in AGPR, PN, José Félix Lajara, box 770, 3, 14 May 1870. Those for haciendas Media-Luna and Flor del Valle are covered in AGPR, PN, Juan Ramón de Torres, box 52, 9 August 1871, and Demetrio Giménez y Moreno, box 218, 11 January 1872, respectively.

21. AGPR, PN, Juan Ramón de Torres, box 52, 15 April 1871; box 54, 26 March 1872; box 63, 24 March 1876; box 64, 2 June 1876; José Félix Lajara, box 770, 13 May 1870; Demetrio Giménez y Moreno, box 218, 4 May, 1 June 1872; box 220, 2 May 1873.

22. AGPR, PN, José Félix Lajara, box 768, 26 May, 16 June 1867.

23. AGPR, PN, José Félix Lajara, box 768, 23, 24 June 1867; box 770, 1 June 1870; Demetrio Giménez y Moreno, box 211, 1 August 1868; box 214, 5, 7 July 1870.

24. AGPR, PN, Demetrio Giménez y Moreno, box 220, 29 March 1873; Juan Ramón de Torres, box 67, 30 April 1877; Tirado Merced, "Raíces sociales," p. 76.

25. The terms of Jacinto López's will can be found in AGPR, PN, José Félix Lajara, box 765, 7 January 1864. The transactions leading to Igaravídez's control of Josefa Guadalupe's land can be reconstructed through AGPR, PN, Demetrio Giménez y Moreno, box 206, 12 January 1866; box 211, 21 July 1868; box 212, 21 May 1869; box 214, 8 July 1870; José Félix Lajara, box 777, 12 January 1878. Igaravídez's transactions with the cleric can be found in AGPR, PN, José Félix Lajara, box 767, 5 June, 15 October 1866; box 768, 14 January 1867; box 776, 15 October 1877; Juan Ramón de Torres, box 49, 23 February, 2 June 1869; Demetrio Giménez y Moreno, box 213, 2 December 1869; Mauricio Guerra, box 268, 7 June 1872. The only trace of María Luisa's sale to her brother is in *Devolución de la Central San Vicente a su legítimo poseedor y administrador. 2 de julio de 1889*, p. 4.

26. AGPR, PN, Demetrio Giménez y Moreno, box 214, 13 January, 27 July 1870; Juan Ramón de Torres, box 51, 3 December 1870; José Félix Lajara, box 773, 22 February, 18 March, 8 May 1875; box 776, 16 February 1877; box 777, 4 November 1878.

27. The hiring of skilled slaves for particular tasks is an aspect of slavery not yet fully examined by Puerto Rico historians. I have found other instances of this practice in Vega Baja, and it appears to be a common occurrence worthy of more detailed study. San Miguel, "Tierra y trabajadores," p. 31, offers figures for day laborers for 1845 and 1849.

28. Carlos Santana awaited Igaravídez's payment for his wife's share of San

Vicente in order to meet his obligations with Látimer y Cía. AGPR, PN, Demetrio Giménez y Moreno, box 212, 21 May 1869.

29. AGPR, PN, José Félix Lajara, box 770, 30 June 1870; box 772, 22 July 1874; box 775, 30 October, 13 December 1876; Demetrio Giménez y Moreno, box 214, 8 July 1870; box 218, 2 May 1872; box 221, 15 November 1873; box 227, 19 April 1876; Juan Ramón de Torres, box 51, 27 October 1870; AT, SC, "Certificación expedida en relación de las cargas impuestas sobre la Hacienda o Yngenio denominado 'Central San Vicente' dela jurisdicción de Vega Baja, como poseida por Don Leonardo Igaravídez, desde la instalación dela Antigua anotaduría de Hipotecas, ala fecha," box 71, doc. 975.

30. AGPR, PN, Demetrio Giménez y Moreno, box 208, 8 February 1867; box 214, 30 May 1870; box 216, 16, 21 February 1871; box 219, 5 September 1872; box 221, 7 August, 27 October 1873; Pedro R. Escalona, box 161, 9 August 1871; Juan Ramón de Torres, box 60, 14 January, 5 March 1875; box 67, 28 April 1877.

31. AGPR, PN, José Félix Lajara, box 769, 5 June 1869; box 758, 21 May, 29 December 1871; box 771, 20 February 1872, 16, 18 December 1873; box 773, 22 July 1875; box 775, 21 October, 5, 23 November 1876; box 777, 13 March 1878; Juan Ramón de Torres, box 51, 25 October 1870; box 52, 15 June, 3 July, 9 August, 21 December 1871; box 54, 1 June 1872; Demetrio Giménez y Moreno, box 221, 29 November 1873.

32. El Tiempo/"The Times," No. 27, 31 January 1914.

33. Hugh G. J. Aitken, ed., Explorations in Enterprise, pp. 7, 13; Arthur H. Cole, "An Approach to the Study of Entrepreneurship: A Tribute to Edwin F. Gay," in Explorations, ed. Aitken, p. 35.

34. Leland H. Jenks, "Approaches to Entrepreneurial Personality," in Explorations, ed. Aitken, pp. 88–90.

35. The purchase of these properties and other related matters appear in AGPR, PN as follows: Felicidad (José Félix Lajara, box 769, 5 June 1869; box 758, 21 May, 29 December 1871; box 771, 20 February 1872, 16, 18 December 1873; box 773, 22 July 1875; box 775, 21 October, 5, 23 November 1876; box 777, 13 March 1878; Juan Ramón de Torres, box 52, 15 June, 3 July, 9 August, 21 December 1871; box 54, 1 June 1872; Demetrio Giménez y Moreno, box 221, 29 November 1873). Santa Inés (Juan Ramón de Torres, box 49, 9 August 1869; box 52, 14 April 1871; box 69, 31 January 1878; Pedro R. Escalona, box 161, 8 August 1871). Fe (José Félix Lajara, box 775, 30 October, 13 December 1876; Demetrio Giménez y Moreno, box 227, 19 April 1876). Rosario (José Félix Lajara, box 773, 22 February, 18 March, 8 May 1875; box 776, 16 February 1877; box 777, 4 November 1878). Encarnación (Juan Ramón de Torres, box 67, 28 April 1877). Other purchases by Igaravídez included small plots (less than five cuerdas) of land contiguous to

San Vicente and owned by the Concepción family, as follows: José Félix La-jara, box 768, 12 August 1867; box 758, 19 October 1871; box 771, 16 February 1872; box 776, 31 March, 2 December 1877; box 777, 13 March 1878.

36. AGPR, PN, Juan Ramón de Torres, box 52, 4 April 1871.

37. AGPR, PN, Juan Ramón de Torres, box 63, 18 February 1876.

38. AGPR, PN, Demetrio Giménez y Moreno, box 221, 27 December 1873; box 235, 1 October 1878.

39. AGPR, OP, Serie Aguas, Derecho a aguas del Río Cibuco, box 412, doc. 25, 15 November 1851, 30 January, 8 February 1868, 29 July 1883, 28 June, 1, 27 July, 16 October 1886, 4 June 1887.

40. On the Banco, AGPR, PN, Juan Ramón de Torres, box 66, 26 January, 9 February 1877. On the Partido Conservador Templado, Tirado Merced, "Raíces sociales," pp. 72–73. On Igaravídez's Republican associations, *El Tiempo/"The Times*," No. 27, 31 January 1914. On his election to the Provincial Deputation, AMVB, "Distrito electoral de Vega-Baja. Pueblo de Toa-Baja. Elección de un Diputado Provincial, verificada en los días 7, 8 y 9 de Abril de 1879. Diputado electo—Excmo. Sr. Marqués de Cabo Caribe por 74 votos," box 1879B, doc. 35; "Distrito electoral de Vega-Baja. Pueblo del Dorado. Elección de un Diputado Provincial verificada en los días 6 7 8 y 9 de Abril de 1879. Diputado electo—Excmo. Sr. Marqués de Cabo Caribe por 36 votos," box 1879B, doc. 36; *El Tiempo/"The Times*," No. 27, 31 January 1914; Tirado Merced, "Raíces sociales," p. 73.

41. *Gaceta del Gobierno de Puerto-Rico*, 17 June 1873.

42. AMVB, Presentación de azúcar de San Vicente, box 1879B, doc. 57, 15 February 1878.

43. *El Tiempo/"The Times*," No. 27, 31 January 1914.

44. AGPR, PN, José Félix Lajara, box 768, 12 August 1867; box 758, 19 October 1871; box 771, 16 February 1872; box 776, 31 March, 2 December 1877; box 777, 13 March 1878.

45. Peñaranda, *Cartas*, pp. 91, 92–93; Bagué y Ramírez, *Ingenio azucarero*, p. 86.

46. AGPR, AT, SC, Jornales, box 71, doc. 963, 17, 24 November, 8 December 1883; PN, Juan Ramón de Torres, box 60, 14 January 1875.

47. AGPR, PN, Juan Ramón de Torres, box 52, 4 April 1871; box 60, 5 March 1875; José Félix Lajara, box 773, 4 February 1875.

Chapter 4

1. For a brief description of how exchanges took place in the absence of banks, see Adam Százdi, "Credit—without Banking—in Early Nineteenth-Century Puerto Rico," pp. 149–71. García Rodríguez also dedicates some paragraphs to the workings of the island's economic system in his *Primeros*

fermentos. Instruments of exchange varied only in the formality or ease with which the process was initiated. Although a draft bill was drawn by means of a letter upon a line of credit arranged with another person or firm, it served the same purpose and behaved in the same way as would an informal promissory note and a slightly more businesslike voucher.

2. A note originated with the underwriter, that is, with the person who issued the obligation and signed the document itself. The guarantor committed himself to providing the money at the time it was due if the underwriter failed to do so. In order to cash the note, the person in whose favor it was issued—the first beneficiary—had to endorse it. He or she could, however, endorse it in somebody else's favor—to pay an old debt or acquire some item—and thus transfer the power to cash it to that person, the holder. Since notes could change hands many times, then, the final holder could require the money from all those who had been beneficiaries in the past and from the underwriter and guarantor. *Código de Comercio. Decretado, Sancionado y Promulgado en 30 de mayo de 1829*, Articles 452, 465, and 534.

3. *Código de Comercio*, Libro Segundo, Título Noveno, Sección Duodécima: Del recambio y resaca, Articles 549–57.

4. For Sturges & Co., AGPR, PN, Juan Ramón de Torres, box 49, 8 October 1869; box 61, 28 August 1875. For Cail y Cía., AGPR, PN, Demetrio Giménez y Moreno, box 221, 27 December 1873; box 235, 1 October 1878. For Ancel et fils, AGPR, PN, Demetrio Giménez y Moreno, box 221, 23 December 1873; box 228, 11 August 1876. For Vázquez Ramos and Alfonzo, AGPR, PN, Demetrio Giménez y Moreno, box 227, 19 April 1876; Juan Ramón de Torres, box 67, 8 April 1877.

5. Joseph Earl Sweigart, "Financing and Marketing Brazilian Export Agriculture: The Coffee Factors of Río de Janeiro, 1850–1888," pp. 111, 116.

6. AGPR, PN, Demetrio Giménez y Moreno, box 213, 10 August 1869; box 221, 27 November 1873; box 229, 11 September 1876; box 234, 24 August 1878; box 235, 10 September 1878; box 238, 2 August 1879.

7. Hermann Max, *El valor de la moneda. La función del dinero. La función del crédito. La función de los cambios*, Part 2, La función del crédito, pp. 143–239.

8. Witness the fact that, even though limited liability companies existed in Puerto Rico (for example, the Sociedad Anónima de Crédito Mercantil and the Caja de Ahorros), merchants and landholders chose to form partnerships, conceivably to facilitate business through the use of their names.

9. AGPR, AT, SC, Documentos relacionados a la quiebra, box 31, doc. 441, 26 November 1880.

10. Clifford Stevens Walton, *The Civil Law in Spain and Spanish-America, including Cuba, Puerto Rico and the Philippine Islands, and the Spanish Civil Code in force, annotated and with references to the Civil Codes of Mexico, Central and*

South America, with a History of all the Spanish Codes, and Summary of Canonical Laws, of the Principal Fueros, Ordenamientos, Councils and Ordenanzas of Spain from the Earliest Times to the Twentieth Century, including the Spanish, Mexican, Cuban and Puerto Rican Autonomical Constitutions, and a History of the Laws of the Indies, Articles 1912, 1916.

11. Darthes Hnos. appears as Igaravídez's creditor for 137,610 pesos in table 1 of Ramos Mattei, *Hacienda azucarera*, p. 30. On the declaration of bankruptcy and its consequences, see AGPR, AT, SC, Documentos relacionados a la quiebra, box 31, doc. 438, 4 January, 4 August 1880; doc. 441, 26 November 1880; Relación del proceso de quiebra, box 50, doc. 709, 3 March 1882; SG, "Expediente sobre impedimento de los Jueces de esta Capital y de los abogados residentes para conocer la quiebra de la Caja de Ahorros de San Juan de Puerto-Rico y otros negocios," box 16, doc. 9, 8 January 1880.

12. AGPR, AT, SCr, "Testimonio de varios lugares de la causa criminal seguida contra D. Leonardo Igaravídez mandado compulsar en virtud de apelación del Pror. Duprey en el incidente de prisión que fue oido en un solo efecto. Juzgado de la Insta. de San Francisco," box 1, 3 November 1881; *Código de Comercio*, Articles 1005–7.

13. Table 1 of Ramos Mattei, *Hacienda azucarera*, p. 30, and Tirado Merced, "Raíces sociales," p. 82, state that Igaravídez owed the Caja de Ahorros 195,000 pesos. AGPR, AT, SCr, Documentos sin clasificar, box 325 or 4(?).

14. For Igaravídez's claims, AGPR, AT, SCr, "Testimonio de varios lugares de la causa criminal seguida contra D. Leonardo Igaravídez mandado compulsar en virtud de apelación del Pror. Duprey en el incidente de prisión que fue oido en un solo efecto. Juzgado de la Insta. de San Francisco," box 1, 3 November 1881; SC, Documentos relacionados a la quiebra, box 31, doc. 438, 4 January 1880. For his creditors' claims, AGPR, AT, SC, Documentos relacionados a la quiebra, box 31, doc. 438, 4 August 1880; Relación del proceso de quiebra, box 50, doc. 709, 3 March 1882.

15. AMVB, "Relación de propiedad y bienes de Leonardo Igaravídez, que presenta Serapio Miticola, depositario judicial de los bienes del concurso necesario," box 1880C, doc. 72; Peñaranda, *Cartas puertorriqueñas*, p. 88; Bagué y Ramírez, *Ingenio azucarero*, p. 86.

16. AGPR, OP, Asuntos Varios, Cónsul francés a gobernador-general, box 88A, doc. 121, 30 July 1881, 4 January 1884.

17. AGPR, AT, SC, Documentos relacionados a la quiebra, box 31, doc. 447, 25, 30 August 1881.

18. On Francisco de Diego, AGPR, AT, SC, Desembolsos hechos por Francisco de Diego, box 48, doc. 673, 27 August, 3, 7, 12, 15 September, 20 October, 11, 12, 16 November 1881, 19, 21, 28 January, 11 February, 18

September, 27 November 1882. On five other creditors, AGPR, AT, SC, Relación del proceso de quiebra, box 50, doc. 709, 3 March 1882.

19. Under the Audiencia Territorial (the highest court of appeals) were the district courts of first instance (the highest of which was in San Juan) and a series of municipal courts—*juzgados de instrucción*—that tried small and simple cases. Since Igaravídez was a merchant in San Juan, his case was seen in the court of first instance of the capital; smaller accusations originating in Vega Baja, however, could interfere with the proceedings. José Trías Monge, *El sistema judicial de Puerto Rico*, p. 39; AGPR, AT, SG, "Expediente sobre impedimento de los Jueces de esta Capital y de los abogados residentes para conocer la quiebra de la Caja de Ahorros de San Juan de Puerto-Rico y otros negocios," box 16, doc. 9, 15 December 1879, 8, 17 January 1880. On the president of the Audiencia, AGPR, AT, SC, Recusación del presidente de la Real Audiencia, box 40, doc. 560, 15, 22 June, 9, 21 August 1883, 15 January 1884. On accusations against Igaravídez, AGPR, AT, SCr, "Testimonio de varios lugares de la causa criminal seguida contra D. Leonardo Igaravídez mandado compulsar en virtud de apelación del Pror. Duprey en el incidente de prisión que fue oido en un solo efecto. Juzgado de la Insta. de San Francisco," box 1, 3 November 1881.

20. AGPR, AT, SC, Desembolsos hechos por Francisco de Diego, box 48, doc. 673, 20 October, 11 November 1881. AGPR, AT, SC, Relación del proceso de quiebra, box 50, doc. 709, 14, 17 January, 23, 30 March, 20 May 1882; Recusación del presidente de la Real Audiencia, box 40, doc. 560, 15, 22 June, 9, 21 August, 17 November, 6 December 1883, 15 January 1884; OP, Serie Aguas, Derecho a aguas del Río Cibuco, box 412, doc. 25, 6 September 1883.

21. Charles Jones, "Commercial Banks and Mortgage Companies," pp. 40–42.

22. Tomás Raya, in *El Boletín Mercantil*, 14 November 1879; *El Boletín Mercantil*, 16, 19 November 1879; Enrique Gadea, in *El Boletín Mercantil*, 21, 28 November 1879; *El Agente*, 6 January 1880.

23. On sugar prices, Michael J. Gonzales, *Plantation Agriculture and Social Control in Northern Peru, 1875–1933*, pp. 36–37. On the town council, AMVB, "Villa de la Vega. año 1886–87. Expediente de quejas producidas en contra del señalamiento de productos que han servido de base para el repartimiento de la contribución territorial del citado año," box 1886C, doc. 20, 16 July 1886; Petición para descontinuar apremio, box 1885D, doc. 38, 13 January 1885. On the workers' debt, AMVB, "Pueblo de Vbaja. Expediente de apremio seguido contra los jornaleros de esta jurisdicción en cobro de los 48 cvos. que adeuden por contribución del año 1880 a 1881," box 1889E, doc. 55.

24. AGPR, DP, Administración Municipal, box 1, 8 November 1848, 28 September 1873, (date unreadable) 1876, 16 December 1877, 13 June 1879.

25. Serapio Miticola, for example, hired a lawyer to convince the court of his need for more than the 40,000 peso-loan approved in late 1880. AGPR, PN, Demetrio Giménez y Moreno, box 242, 29 November 1880; box 246, 8 March, 13 April 1881; AT, SC, Documentos relacionados a la quiebra, box 31, doc. 447, 15, 16, 22, 23 December 1880, 20 April, 9, 11, 31 May, 2, 3 June 1881.

26. *Memoria leida en la reunión de acreedores de Don Leonardo Igaravídez que tuvo efecto en 17 de julio de 1888, presidida por el Señor Don Augusto de Cottes, Presidente de la Comisión elegida por aquéllos al celebrar el convenio que puso fin a la quiebra del Señor Igaravídez, para vigilar su observancia e intervenir en su cumplimiento,* 17 July 1888, Clauses 14–24 of agreement, pp. 3–4, 5.

27. Ibid., p. 5.

28. *Documentos que debieron leerse en la reunión de acreedores de Don Leonardo Igaravídez convocada para el 17 de noviembre de 1888, por la Comisión Interventora del cumplimiento del Convenio, celebrado por aquéllos y que no tuvo efecto por falta de número bastante de concurrentes,* 17 November 1888, pp. 18–19, 21–22; *Reunión de acreedores,* 17 July 1888, pp. 7, 8–9.

29. AMVB, "Expediente de Apremio contra Don Leonardo Igaravídez," box 1888A, doc. 8, 15 March 1888; AGPR, AT, SG, Recusación del juez en varios casos, box 31, doc. 11, 22 December 1888, 19 January 1889; "Expediente instruido a instancia de Don Pablo Marién Pror. apoderado de D. Julián E. Blanco, en solicitud de que se nombre un Juez especial para que conozca de la Causa que se sigue en el Juzgado de Vega-baja, sobre estafa," box 32, doc. 13, 22 July 1889.

30. Julián E. Blanco y Sosa (1830–1905), as a founding member of the Partido Liberal Reformista and deputy to the Cortes in 1871, was an influential personality in island politics and active in agricultural associations and commercial companies. Federico Ribes Tovar, *Historia cronológica de Puerto Rico. Desde el nacimiento de la isla hasta el año 1973,* pp. 248–49, 319.

31. Creditors were privileged once their claims were recognized and given precedence over others by the receivership trustees following the guidelines of the Commercial and Civil Codes. The four types of creditors were: *dominicales,* those who held a property title over moveable goods; *hipotecarios,* those who held mortgages over real estate, including refaccionistas; *escritutarios,* those whose claim was registered in a deed; and *comunes,* others with claims over any other moveable or real property. The first two kinds of creditors could abstain from the decisions of the concurso without losing the right to pursue their claims at a later date. *Código de Comercio,* Libro Cuarto, Título Octavo: "De la

graduación y pago de los acreedores," Articles 1113–36, 1155; Walton, *Civil Code*, Articles 1917, 1920, 1922–25.

32. *Reunión de acreedores*, 17 July 1888, pp. 11-12; *Comisión interventora*, 17 November 1888, pp. 5, 7–8.

33. AMVB, Petición para rebaja de contribuciones, box 1888D, doc. 42; "Alcaldía Municipal de Vega-Baja. año de 1889. Diligencias instruidas con motivo de un escrito dirigido al ayuntamiento por Don Julio Pérez relativo a las contribuciones impuestas a la Hacienda Encarnación," box 1889E, doc. 66; Protesta sobre embargo de 30 cuerdas, box 1889E, doc. 67; "Alcaldía Municipal de Vega-Baja. año de 1889. Diligencias instruidas con motivo de una consulta que el Ayuntamiento acordó e hiciera al Lcdo. Don Rafael López Landrón relativa a la central San Vicente," box 1889E, doc. 68; "Alcaldía municipal de Vega-Baja. año de 1889. Diligencias instruidas con motivo de un escrito dirigido al Ayuntamiento por Don Julio Pérez en su carácter de apoderado de Don Julián E. Blanco, administrador de la Central San Vicente (o) por Don Julián E. Blanco, administrador de la Central San Vicente," box 1889E, docs. 69–74; "Febrero 5 del año 1888. Expediente de apremio contra la Sucesión de D. Leonardo Igaravídez. Cabo Caribe," box 1889E, doc. 75; "Notificando a los interesados (Sucesores de D. Leonardo Igaravídez, Da. Dolores Náter de Fernández, Sucesión López Landrón y Don Juan Rodríguez) de la Central San Vicente sobre expropiación de terrenos a dicha corporación," box 1889F, doc. 103; "Administrador de la Hacienda Felicidad (200 cuerdas embargadas) pide prórroga para el pago de contribuciones vencidas," box 1889F, doc. 107; "Provincia de Pto Rico. Villa de Vega-baja. año de 1892. Sobre escrito de queja presentado contra la contribución territorial por Dn Julián E. Blanco, como admor. de la Central San Vicente," box 1892D, doc. 82.

34. *Comisión interventora*, 15 November 1888, pp. 11–12, 14–15; *Devolución de la Central San Vicente a su legítimo poseedor y administrador. 2 de julio de 1889*, 28 May 1889, pp. 22–23; *Los últimos sucesos de la Central "San Vicente." Circular y documentos que la Comisión elegida por los acreedores de don Leonardo Igaravídez dirije a dichos acreedores para su conocimiento. Abril de 1889*, 22 February 1899, pp. 1–2, 5–6.

35. AGPR, AT, SC, Gallart y Forgas contra Sucesión Igaravídez, box 5, doc. 32, 8 October 1869, 28 August 1875, 15 January 1884, 22 June, 6, 12, 14, 18 July, 3 November 1888, 4, 21 January, 7 March 1889; *Reunión de acreedores*, 17 July 1888, p. 10.

36. AGPR, AT, SG, Recusación del juez en varios casos, box 31, docs. 8, 12, 14; *Ultimos sucesos*, 31 March 1889, pp. 8–11, 17–18; *Devolución*, Note, p. 24; 4 July 1889, pp. 3–6.

37. AMVB, Miguel Landrón López solicita lista de esclavos, box 1887B,

doc. 11, 3 January 1887; *Comisión interventora*, 17 November 1888, pp. 19–20; AMVB, "Expediente de apremio contra D. Leonardo Igaravídez," box 1888A, doc. 8, 15 March 1888; *Reunión de acreedores*, 17 July 1888, pp. 9–10.

38. *Ultimos sucesos*, 31 March 1889, pp. 12–14; 5 April 1889, p. 25.

39. Ibid., 31 March 1889, pp. 15–19; *Devolución*, Note, pp. 24–25.

40. *Ultimos sucesos*, 31 March 1889, p. 19; 6 April 1889, iv; AMVB, "El administrador de la Central San Vicente da una relación de animales que han desaparecido de dicha Hacienda y pide al Alcalde le ayude en la recuperación de dichos animales," box 1889F, doc. 104; *Devolución*, 4 July 1889, p. 25.

41. AGPR, AT, SC, "Certificación expedida en relación de las cargas impuestas sobre la Hacienda o Yngenio denominado 'Central San Vicente' dela jurisdicción de Vega Baja, como poseida por Don Leonardo Igaravídez, desde la instalación dela Antigua anotaduría de Hipotecas, ala fecha," box 71, doc. 975, 16 October, 19 November, 12 December 1891, 4, 17, 18 February, 12 April, 17 August 1892. Another successful sugar producer, Hacienda La Esperanza, was auctioned off in 1888 after the death of José Ramón Fernández, the well-known conservative Marqués de la Esperanza. See *El Clamor del País*, 3 March 1888.

42. Gonzales, *Plantation Agriculture*, esp. chap. 2, "Planters and Capital," pp. 24–41.

Chapter 5

1. Steve J. Stern, *Peru's Indian Peoples and the Challenge of Spanish Conquest. Huamanga to 1640*, pp. 35–38, 72–73, 183.

2. Sidney W. Mintz, "Cañamelar. The Subculture of a Rural Sugar Plantation Proletariat," p. 351.

3. Tom Bottomore, ed., *A Dictionary of Marxist Thought*. For a similar treatment of the absence of conflict see Stern, *Peru's Indian Peoples*, pp. 11–13.

4. Walter Rodney, *A History of the Guyanese Working People, 1881–1905*, pp. 41–44, and Picó, *Libertad y servidumbre*, pp. 82, 158–59, offer contrasting views on the bargaining possibilities of estate workers.

5. When abolition was declared on 22 March 1873, freedmen and women were required to sign three-year contracts with a person of their choice. Island historians are still in the process of determining whether these agreements, which generally made no provisions for medical care, clothing, or working tools, were signed with exmasters and what instruments of coercion, if any, were used by the planters to bind their work force.

6. Unless otherwise stated, all conclusions in this chapter stem from a statistical analysis of 593 cases chosen randomly among a universe of 889 persons who worked in San Vicente during 16 sample weeks that cover both zafra and tiempo muerto (high and low season) in 1879, 1883, and 1885 and

who also appeared in at least one other primary source. These data were drawn from the following sources: AGPR, AT, SC, Jornales, box 71, docs. 963, 964; Documentos relacionados a la quiebra, box 31, doc. 451; temporary box T80-116, Juicios Verbales, 1879, 1883, and 1885; AMVB, "Datos suministrados por los comisionados de barrio para formar tres estados que comprenden el número de habitantes de este partido con expresión de sus clases, condiciones, estados y sexos según lo dispuesto en la superior circular no. 119 de 3 de enero de 1860," box 1860D, doc. 25; "Pueblo de Vega Baja. año de 1870. Barrios de Pugdo. Adentro, del Pueblo, de Cibuco, de Yeguada, de Almirante Norte," box 1870, doc. 1; "Indice alfabético del padrón gral. de jornaleros," box 1870, doc. 2; "Copia del padrón de esclavos de esta jurisdicción," box 1873A, doc. 20; "Contratos de Libertos," box 1873B, doc. 60; "Pueblo de Vega-Baja. Sección 2a. Ejercicio de 1880–81. Agricultura menor y pecuaria. Evaluaciones parciales practicadas por el ayuntamiento de este pueblo en unión de los síndicos elejidos por cada una de las secciones de contribuyentes que han de levantar el repartimiento general autorizado por el artículo 135 de la Ley para cubrir el déficit del presupuesto municipal del corriente año económico," box 1880, doc. 1; "Pueblo de Vega Baja. Contribución Territorial para el año 1880–81. Riqueza Agrícola. Cultivo de fincas propias o arrendadas. Declaraciones juradas," box 1880, doc. 5; "Relación de los artesanos de este término municipal que presenta el síndico del gremo Don Valentín Resi agrupados y clasificados sus jornales," "Relación de los braceros que constituyen la sección 6a de contribuyentes y que con arreglo a lo dispuesto por el Aymto de conformidad con lo que prescrive la base 6a de la regla 2a del Arto 135 de la Ley deben figurar en el repartimiento general de este año con la tercera parte de la suma que puedan alcanzar por término medio de su haber durante el año calculado a razón de tres reales diarios en veinte y cuatro días laborables de cada mes. Dicho cálculo constituye una renta imponible para cada uno de la suma de 36 pesos anuales. año ecco de 1883 á 84," "Villa de la Vega. Contribuciones. Expediente relativo a la derrama de la contribución municipal para el año 1883–84. Reparto parcial que se hace a la sección 2a de Pecuaria de la cantidad que le corresponde levantar en unión de las demas riquezas con arreglo a la renta imponible que cada uno disfruta," "Villa de la Vega Baja. Año ecco. de 1883 á 84. Padrón parcial que comprende la riqueza Agrícola de este término municipal con expresión de sus valores y productos para la derrama de la contribución territorial del mencionado año. Padrón general que comprende todas las fincas rústicas de propiedad particular que existen en esta jurisdicción, el cual forma la Junta pericial con vista de las declaraciones juradas presentadas por los dueños o representantes, y las alteraciones que en algunas de ellas ha tenido necesidad de practicar por constarle haberse obtenido mayor producción que la confesada," box 1883B; "Padrón general que comprende el ganado vacuno, caballar y mular que existe en esta jurisdicción, con designación del que se halla exento del tributo por estar destinado a la agricultura," "Villa de la Vega. año de 1887–88. Padrón General de las fincas rústicas su valor y productos que forma la junta pericial para el repartimiento del año 1887 á 88," box 1887A, doc. 4; "Pueblo de Vega-Baja. Artesanos y jornaleros. año económico de 1887 á 88. Relación de las utilidades que calculan a los contribuyentes por este concepto en el repartimiento general del expresado año, formado por los síndicos de esta Sección," box 1887A, doc. 6; Apremios por contribuciones, box 1889E, docs. 52, 54, 59, 61, 77; "Pueblo de Vbaja. Expediente de apremio seguido contra los jornaleros de esta jurisdicción en cobro de los 48 cvos. que adeuden por contribución del año 1880 a 1881," box 1889E, doc. 55; "Villa de Vega Baja. año de 1890. Ngdo. de cárcel. Expediente formado sobre cumplimiento de condena impuesta por la superioridad al preso (name) de esta cárcel," box 1890C, docs. 57, 58, 60, 63, 64; "Expediente sobre cumplimiento de condena del preso (name)," box 1891F, docs. 137, 140, 150, 151, 156, 157, 159, 162, 172, 181, 184.

7. Although 54 percent of the total sample worked in only one of these years, 34 percent were listed as workers in two years and almost 13 percent in all three. Of those that worked in the nine weeks chosen from August 1879 to March 1880, 36 percent worked for more than three weeks. In 1883, 46 percent of the workers performed their duties in two or more of three November weeks. In 1885, 50 percent worked in three or more of the four weeks selected from August to December.

8. Of those individuals whose race is known (315), 61 percent were listed as *negro, mulato, pardo,* or *moreno.* Although racial categories vary according to the type of documentation used, it is usually inferred that negros and morenos were unmixed black, whereas mulatos and pardos were mixtures of varying degrees. Unfortunately, the values accorded these distinctions are not evident to historians, while it is clear that they reflect a rigid social hierarchy, as San Miguel, *El mundo,* pp. 139–41, points out. Given the large number of cases in which race is extrapolated through civil status (slave or free), for the sake of simplicity I refer to all persons of color as "nonwhite."

9. Gonzales, *Plantation Agriculture,* p. 58, explains the impact of mechanized ploughing on the coordination of agricultural and industrial functions.

10. Employees and workers would have to wait two months and four weeks, respectively, for arrangements to be made. De Diego would "pay," for four weeks and on a daily basis, all or part of the *jornal* in articles to be paid for by San Vicente with subsequent sugar sales. AGPR, AT, SC, Documentos relacionados a la quiebra, box 31, doc. 447, 31 May 1881. The reaction of San Vicente's workers can be contrasted to that of their Caribbean counterparts in Rodney, *History of Guyanese Working People,* p. 33; Manuel Moreno Fraginals, "El token azucarero cubano," in *La historia como arma y otros estudios sobre escla-*

vos, ingenios y plantaciones, pp. 145–61; and Carlos Buitrago Ortiz, *Los orígenes históricos de la sociedad precapitalista en Puerto Rico (Ensayos de etnohistoria puertorriqueña)*, p. 29.

11. Ramos Mattei, *Hacienda azucarera*, p. 24, states that San Vicente's slaves numbered 201 in 1864. Just prior to abolition, however, Igaravídez is listed as the owner of 65 slaves. AMVB, "Copia del padrón de esclavos de esta jurisdicción," box 1873A, doc. 20.

12. So rare was an instance of failure to pay wages in 1889 that a group of workers gathered before the Vega Baja town hall to demand compensation. *Ultimos sucesos*, 31 March 1889, p. 21.

13. For the municipality of Vega Baja as a whole, however, San Miguel, *El mundo*, p. 145, states that there were twice as many whites as nonwhites in skilled, "urban" occupations.

14. AMVB, Contratos de Libertos, box 1873B, doc. 60.

15. AGPR, AT, SC, Jornales, box 71, doc. 963, 17, 24 November, 8 December 1883; PN, Juan Ramón de Torres, box 60, 14 January 1875.

16. *Memoria leida en la reunión de acreedores de Don Leonardo Igaravídez*, 17 July 1888, pp. 11–12; AGPR, AT, SC, Documentos relacionados a la quiebra, box 31, doc. 447, 31 May 1881.

17. AMVB, "Expediente sobre Colonias Agrícolas y Aldeas. Villa de Vegabaja. año 1886," box 1886D, doc. 33, 1, 6, 18 June, 7 September 1886.

18. The quote is from Peñaranda, *Cartas puertorriqueñas*, p. 93. Cubano Iguina, "Trade and Politics," p. 173, describes the effort to establish worker colonies all over the island.

19. William A. Green, *British Slave Emancipation. The Sugar Colonies and the Great Experiment, 1830–1865*, pp. 245–60; Michael Craton, *Searching for the Invisible Man. Slaves and Plantation Life in Jamaica*, pp. 23–24; Michael Craton, James Walvin, and David Wright, *Slavery, Abolition and Emancipation. Black Slaves and the British Empire*, pp. 326–27; Douglas Hall, *Five of the Leewards, 1834–1870. The Major Problems of the Post-Emancipation Period in Antigua, Barbuda, Montserrat, Nevis and St. Kitts*, pp. 40, 44–51; Eric Foner, *Nothing But Freedom. Emancipation and Its Legacy*, pp. 21–25, 37–38.

20. Dietz, *Economic History*, pp. 31–34.

21. The percentage increase and decrease were calculated using four zafra and four tiempo muerto weeks from the original sample. AGPR, AT, SC, Jornales, box 71, docs. 963, 964; Documentos relacionados a la quiebra, box 31, doc. 451.

22. Scarano, "Slavery and Free Labor," pp. 553–63; Andrés Ramos Mattei, "El liberto en el régimen de trabajo azucarero de Puerto Rico, 1870–1880," in *Azucar y esclavitud*, ed. Andrés A. Ramos Mattei, pp. 91–124; San Miguel, *El mundo*, pp. 120, 135–37.

23. The slaves Igaravídez freed between 1867 and 1872 bought their free-

dom, which was probably promised them by their previous owner, Igaravídez's second wife's husband. Together with at least four purchases before 1873, these legal transactions point to ambivalent—perhaps shrewd—approaches to the issue of the new wage labor force. *El Tiempo/"The Times,"* No. 27, 31 January 1914, gives credence to Igaravídez's progressive stance. The manumission cases can be located in AGPR, PN, José Félix Lajara, box 768, 28 March 1867; box 769, 3 November 1869; box 770, 20 June, 3 July 1870; box 758, 9 April 1871; box 771, 5 July 1872. The slave purchases can be found in José Félix Lajara, box 769, 15 June 1868; Juan Ramón de Torres, box 49, 25 August 1869; box 50, 7 March 1870.

24. García Rodríguez, *Primeros fermentos*, and Andrés Ramos Mattei, *Los libros de cuentas de la hacienda Mercedita, 1861–1900. Apuntes para el estudio de la transición hacia el sistema de centrales en la industria azucarera en Puerto Rico*, however, both describe a process of "proletarianization"—loss of access to land, population resettlement, and a new mentality—as a result of mechanization and the establishment of centrales.

25. Sidney W. Mintz, "The Culture History of a Puerto Rican Sugar Cane Plantation, 1876–1949," and *Worker in the Cane. A Puerto Rican Life History.*

26. Louis A. Pérez, Jr., "Vagrants, Beggars, and Bandits: Social Origins of Cuban Separatism, 1878–1895," portrays lawlessness as social protest. Rebecca J. Scott, "Comparing Emancipations: A Review Essay," also refers to the obstacles that the state might encounter in its efforts to promote or revoke traditional entitlements. For contrasting views in the coffee areas of Puerto Rico, see Luis Edgardo Díaz Hernández, *Castañer. Una hacienda cafetalera en Puerto Rico (1868–1930)*, pp. 57–63, and Laird W. Bergad, *Coffee and the Growth of Agrarian Capitalism in Nineteenth-Century Puerto Rico*, p. 140.

27. The progressive reduction in "breathing space" that Raymond Williams, *The Country and the City*, convincingly traces for late eighteenth-century England is not evident here. E. P. Thompson's variant of class consciousness as a process through which a group evaluates a new situation by traditional moral values is much more appropriate to describe the limited impact of Central San Vicente on its workers. See his "Time, Work-Discipline and Industrial Capitalism," and "The Moral Economy of the English Crowd in the Eighteenth Century."

28. Mintz, "Culture History."

Chapter 6

1. Ramos Mattei, *Hacienda azucarera*, pp. 29, 35, explains the "structural crisis" of the 1870s in much the same way as did agricultural reformers in the nineteenth century. This view has been reinforced by Moreno Fraginals, *El ingenio*, vol. 2, p. 93. I challenge this interpretation in "La transición en el Caribe: Reflexiones en torno a *Between Slavery and Free Labor*," pp. 152–53.

2. Production costs and product yields, in fact, varied greatly according to the fertility of the soil. *Almanaque de la Isla de Puerto-Rico 1891*, pp. 102–3.

3. For examples of how Caribbean planters evaluated their particular situation based on their perception of external conditions, see Christian Schnakenbourg, *Histoire de l'industrie sucrière en Guadeloupe aux XIXe. et XXe. siècles. Vol. I. La crise du système esclavigiste (1835–1847)*, p. 201, and Franc Baez Evertsz, *Azúcar y dependencia en la República Dominicana* p. 25.

4. Ana Maria dos Santos, "Agricultural Reform and the Idea of 'Decadence' in the State of Rio de Janeiro, 1870–1910," treats similar issues for Brazil.

5. For a comparative perspective on centralization see Eisenberg, *Sugar Industry*; Ely, *Cuando reinaba*; Moreno Fraginals, "Plantations in the Caribbean"; Fe Iglesias, "The Development of Capitalism in Cuban Sugar Production, 1860–1890"; David Watts, *The West Indies: Patterns of Development, Culture and Environmental Change since 1492*, pp. 490–501. The quote is from Watts, *West Indies: Patterns of Development*, p. 498.

6. Scarano, "Slavery and Free Labor," p. 560.

7. The psychological and material importance of landowning during the shift to central-owning has been suggested by Schnakenbourg, *Histoire de l'industrie sucrière*, p. 226; Gadiel Perruci, *A República das Usinas. Um Estudo de História Social e Económica do Nordeste: 1889–1930*, pp. 113–14; Franciso M. Zeno, *Influencia de la industria azucarera en la vida antillana y sus consecuencias sociales*, pp. 43–44; Eisenberg, *Sugar Industry*, p. 220; Franklin W. Knight, "Origins of Wealth and the Sugar Revolution in Cuba, 1750–1850," pp. 231–54. Jenks, "Approaches to Entrepreneurial Personality," in *Explorations*, ed. Aitken, pp. 80–92, pays particular attention to the various roles an entrepreneur plays in different social and economic contexts.

8. Suggestive views of class relations and conflict appear in Thompson, *English Working Class*, "Time, Work-Discipline," "Moral Economy"; Gareth Stedman Jones, *Outcast London. A Study in the Relationship between Classes in Victorian Society*; and Williams, *Country and City*. For the "nonwestern world," see Sidney W. Mintz, "The Rural Proletariat and the Problem of Rural Proletarian Consciousness," pp. 291–326; and for Cuba, Ramiro Guerra y Sánchez, *Sugar and Society in the Caribbean. An Economic History of Cuban Agriculture*.

9. For contrasting views of the twentieth-century sugar industry, see Dudley Smith and William M. Requa, *Puerto Rico Sugar Facts*, and Harvey S. Perloff, *Puerto Rico's Economic Future*. Morales Carrión, ed., *Puerto Rico*, pp. 152, 165, 173–74, 209, 216–17, 230, 233, 242, 244, 261, 269, and Luis M. Geigel and Bartolomé M. Morell, *Crédito agrícola refaccionario. El mercadeo de productos agrícolas en Puerto Rico*, pp. 4–5, 10–12, deal with the transition from an agricultural to an industrial economy.

Glossary

apremio–legal proceeding for the collection of payment due, usually taxes.

Audiencia Territorial–established in 1831 under the presidency of the captain-general, the functions of its members—a regent, scribe, prosecutor, and a number of magistrates and relators—became judicial in nature by the 1860s, when it was transformed into the highest court of appeals in the colony.

ayuntamiento–town council; local decision-making body in each municipality, made up of the population's better known and more influential citizens.

bagasse–dry fiber that remains after juice has been extracted from the cane.

barrio–neighborhood, municipal ward.

bocoy–unit of volume, approximately 13–15 quintales.

central–sugar factory to which planters sent their cane to be ground and manufactured in exchange for 5 to 6 percent of the weight of the raw material in sugar.

colono–agricultural settler who entered into a contractual relationship with the owner of the land he or she cultivated.

concurso de acreedores–judicial agreement by which an insolvent debtor's assets were applied to the payment of outstanding obligations to creditors. Voluntario is that agreed to by both debtor and creditors; necesario is compulsory, ordered by the court.

convenio–agreement with the force of a contract.

cuerda–unit of land measurement, roughly equivalent to an acre.

Diputación Provincial–advisory body established for the colony in the 1812 Spanish constitution and revived in the liberal periods of colonial rule. In 1870, its members, elected by district, had a wide range of powers with respect to both governor and ayuntamiento, which permitted the Diputación to serve as a decentralizing agent.

escudo–currency in use in Puerto Rico prior to 1870, roughly equivalent to half a peso.

facultades omnímodas–extraordinary powers granted to island governors during the Latin American wars of independence and reasserted in 1825 and 1837 for security reasons. The arbitrary rule of colonial authorities, sanctioned by the crown on these occasions, was a permanent feature of Puerto Rico's nineteenth century.

guardia civil–public security body established in 1869 and again in 1874 to safeguard Spain's rule on the island. Made up mostly of peninsular Spaniards, it carried out extreme political repression after the restoration of the monarchy in Spain.

hacienda–large landed estate, characterized in Puerto Rico by a mixed free and slave work force, the production of mainly sugar and coffee for the export market, and a dependence on imports of machinery and some food staples.

jíbaro–small, self-sufficient landowner, most of whose production was for internal consumption.

jornalero–wage worker.

juicio verbal–judicial proceeding, in which oral allegations—usually small claims—by interested parties before a lay judge took the place of more formal accusations with the intervention of attorneys.

libreta–literally, notebook, in which were recorded a wage worker's personal data and information regarding place of work, conduct, and current status with employer.

peninsulares–Spaniards who were born in the metropolis (as opposed to American-born Spaniards)

peseta–about .20 peso.

peso–currency in use in Puerto Rico after 1870, roughly equivalent to a U.S. dollar.

plaza–town square, usually surrounded by buildings housing civil and military authorities, the church, and important merchant houses; the center of business, social, and political activities.

quiebra–bankruptcy proceeding to determine the status and manage the business of one whose debits were more than his or her assets. Quiebra culpable results from bad management, careless investment, and disorderly excesses; quiebra fraudulenta is caused by the merchant's willful misuse or misrepresentation of funds available to cover expenses in an attempt to cheat creditors.

quintal–unit of weight, equal to 100 lbs.

quita y espera–legal provision by which a person's creditors agreed to lower the amount to be paid and extend the deadline for payment.

Real Cédula de Gracias–Ferdinand VII's decree upon his return to the throne of Spain in 1814 granting Puerto Rico the right to trade with friendly nations, to import machinery duty-free, and to take in Catholic foreigners as residents. Puerto Rico's growth in the early nineteenth century has been traditionally attributed to this ruling.

refacción–contract that provided a landowner with the capital to finance the running or upkeep expenses of a hacienda. Refaccionistas, usually merchants, offered these short-term loans (six months to a year) at an interest rate of 12 to 18 percent yearly.

Reglamento de Jornaleros–semicoerced wage labor mechanism established in 1849 and designed to keep track of the employment status of those who could not support themselves from the production of their lands or through property income.

socio comanditario–silent partner who puts up the capital in a business enterprise but does not exercise direct management.

socio gestor administrador–managing partner who runs day-to-day business in a company.

tiempo muerto–low season, roughly from July to December, during which new cane is planted and machinery repaired.

zafra–cane-cutting and sugar-manufacturing season, roughly from January to June.

Selected Bibliography

Archival Materials

Archivo General de Puerto Rico (AGPR), Audiencia Territorial (AT), Serie Civil (SC).

AGPR, AT, Serie Criminal (SCr).

AGPR, AT, Sala de Gobierno (SG).

AGPR, Diputación Provincial (DP), Administración Municipal.

AGPR, Obras Públicas (OP), Serie Aguas.

AGPR, OP, Serie Asuntos Varios.

AGPR, Protocolos Notariales (PN), Juan Ramón de Torres; Demetrio Giménez y Moreno; José Félix Lajara; Pedro R. Escalona; Mauricio Guerra.

AGPR, temporary box T80-116, Juicios Verbales, 1879, 1883, and 1885.

Archivo Municipal de Vega Baja (AMVB).

Printed Primary Sources

El Agente.

Agricultural Resources and Capabilities of Porto Rico. House of Representatives, 56th Congress, 2d Session, Document No. 171, 1900.

Almanaque de la Isla de Puerto Rico 1891. Publicado por la Revista de Agricultura, Industria y Comercio. Puerto Rico: Imprenta de Acosta, 1890.

Asenjo, Federico. *Páginas para los jornaleros de Puerto-Rico.* Puerto Rico: Libreria de "Las Bellas Artes," 1879.

Asenjo y Arteaga, Federico. *El catastro de Puerto-Rico. Necesidad de su formación y posibilidad de llevarlo a cabo.* Puerto Rico: Carlos B. Meltz, 1890.

———. *Estudios económicos. El comercio de la Isla y la influencia que en él ha de ejercer el Banco español de Puerto Rico.* Puerto Rico: Imprenta Militar, 1862.

Asociación de Agricultores de Puerto-Rico. *Acta de la junta general celebrada en 31 de julio de 1893 y documentos leidos en ella en cumplimiento de lo prevenido en los Estatutos y Reglamento.* Puerto Rico: Sucesión de José Julián Acosta, 1893.

Baldorioty de Castro, Román. *Bases para la fundación de un banco de emisión y descuento destinado principalmente a préstamos a la agricultura y el comercio, movilizando una parte de la riqueza rústica y urbana y promoviendo garantía provincial del interés.* Puerto Rico: Imprenta de Acosta, 1871.

———. *Informe sobre la moneda mejicana (Unión mercantil e industrial de Ponce).* Puerto Rico: Tipografía "La Civilización," 1883.

Ballesteros Muñoz, José. *Descripción y cultivo de la caña de azúcar, formada con notas adquiridas sobre el terreno en diez y ocho años de práctica.* Caracas: Tip. El Pregonero, 1899.

———. *Guía comercial y agrícola de Puerto Rico.* Mayagüez: n.p., 1894?.

Boletín Mercantil de Puerto-Rico (Organo del Partido de los españoles sin condiciones).

Brau, Salvador. *La campesina (Disquisiciones sociológicas).* Puerto Rico: Imprenta de José González Font, 1886.

———. *Las clases jornaleras de Puerto-Rico. Su estado actual, causas que lo sostienen y medios de propender al adelanto moral y material de dichas clases. Memoria premiada en el Certamen del Ateneo Puerto-riqueño.* Puerto Rico: Imprenta del "Boletín Mercantil," 1882.

———. *Ensayos. Disquisiciones sociológicas.* Río Piedras: Editorial Edil, 1972.

Código de Comercio. Decretado, Sancionado y Promulgado en 30 de mayo de 1829. Nueva edición aumentada con la Ley de Enjuiciamiento sobre los negocios y causas de comercio. Decretada y promulgada en 24 de julio de 1830. Edición Oficial de Real Orden. Madrid: Oficina de D. L. Amarita, 1856.

Coll y Toste, Cayetano. *Reseña del estado social, económico e industrial de la Isla de Puerto-Rico al tomar posesión de ella los Estados-Unidos.* Puerto Rico: La Correspondencia, 1899.

Córdova, Pedro Tomás de. *Memorias geográficas, históricas, económicas y estadísticas de la Isla de Puerto Rico.* San Juan: Imprenta del Gobierno, 1831–33.

Delgado, Enrique. *Proyecto para la creación de una empresa de factorías centrales en la isla de Puerto-Rico.* Puerto Rico: Establecimiento Tipográfico de Acosta, 1881.

Derechos del propietario en cuanto se relaciona con la propiedad inmueble o sea nociones de derecho constitucional al alcance de todas las inteligencias por un abogado. Mayagüez: Imprenta de "El Progreso," 1895.

Devolución de la Central San Vicente a su legítimo poseedor y administrador. 2 de julio de 1889. Puerto Rico: Imprenta y Librería de Acosta, 1889.

Documentos que debieron leerse en la reunión de acreedores de Don Leonardo Igaravídez convocada para el 17 de noviembre de 1888, por la Comisión Interventora del cumplimiento del Convenio, celebrado por aquéllos y que no tuvo efecto por falta de número bastante de concurrentes. Puerto Rico: Imprenta y Librería de Acosta, 1888.

El Economista.

Estadística general del comercio exterior de la provincia de Puerto Rico. San Juan: Imprenta de Dalmau, 1837–41; Imprenta de Gimbernat, 1843–47; Imprenta de Márquez, 1849–54; Imprenta de Acosta, 1855–90.

Exposición presentada a la Comisión Colonial de Washington por los gremios de comerciantes, agricultores e industriales de Ponce. Ponce: Tip. del "Correo de Puerto-Rico," 1899.

Fernández Umpierre, Manuel. *Manual práctico de la agricultura de la caña de azúcar.* Puerto Rico: Imprenta del "Boletín Mercantil," 1884.

Gobierno y Capitanía General de Puerto Rico. *Comunicación dirijida al Ministro de Ultramar sobre ausilios que podrían concederse por el gobierno de S.M. para favorecer el establecimiento de factorías centrales.* Puerto Rico: Gobierno General de la isla de Puerto Rico, Impr. y Librería de Acosta, 1881.

Instituto Geográfico y Estadístico. *Censo de la población de España, según el empadronamiento hecho el 31 de diciembre de 1860 por la Dirección General del Instituto Geográfico y Estadístico.* Madrid: Imprenta de la Dirección General del Instituto Geográfico y Estadístico, 1861, pp. 774–97.

López Tuero, Fernando. *Caña de azúcar.* Puerto Rico: Tipografía del "Boletín Mercantil," 1895.

———. *Estado moral de los factores de producción en Cuba y Puerto-Rico.* Madrid: Librería de Fernando Fe, 1896.

———. *Isla de Puerto Rico. Estudios de economía rural.* Puerto Rico: Imprenta del "Boletín Mercantil," 1893.

———. *Isla de Puerto Rico. La reforma agrícola.* San Juan: Tipografía del "Boletín Mercantil," 1891.

———. *Tratado de cultivos tropicales.* Puerto Rico: Imprenta del "Boletín Mercantil," 1896.

MacCormick, Santiago. *Artículos publicados en el periodico "El Asimilista," debidos a la pluma del Sr. D. Santiago MacCormick con motivo de otros propios del Sr. D. Manuel Fernández Umpierre, dados a la luz en el "Boletín Mercantil".* Puerto Rico: Imprenta de "El Asimilista," 1884.

———. *Factorías centrales en Puerto-Rico. Informe dado a la Excma. Diputación Provincial sobre el sistema de las factorías centrales para la elaboración del azúcar;*

sobre la utilidad y conveniencia de esas empresas, y sobre los medios de plantearlas en escala grande y general por toda esta Provincia. Por el comisionado al efecto D. Santiago Mac-Cormick. Puerto Rico: Est. tipográfico del "Boletín Mercantil," 1880.

Maymí Cruells, Francisco. *¿Canje tenemos? Crisis segura. Colección de artículos publicados por el periódico El País del 22–30 de octubre y del 1–6 de noviembre de 1895.* Puerto Rico: Sucesion de José J. Acosta, 1897.

Memoria leida en la reunión de acreedores de Don Leonardo Igaravídez que tuvo efecto en 17 de julio de 1888, presidida por el Señor Don Augusto de Cottes, Presidente de la Comisión elegida por aquéllos al celebrar el convenio que puso fin a la quiebra del Señor Igaravídez, para vigilar su observancia e intervenir en su cumplimiento. Puerto Rico: Imprenta y Librería de Acosta, 1888.

Peñaranda, Carlos. *Cartas puertorriqueñas, 1878–1880.* 1885; rpt. San Juan: Editorial "El Cemí," 1967.

La Razón.

Report of Brig. Gen. Geo. W. Davis, U.S.V., on Civil Affairs of Puerto Rico, 1899. Washington, D.C.: Government Printing Office, 1900.

Report on the Census of Porto Rico, 1899. Washington, D.C.: War Department, Government Printing Office, 1900.

Report upon the Commercial Relations of the United States with Foreign Countries for the year(s)_____. Washington, D.C.: Government Printing Office, 1876–80, 1880/81–1884/85.

Revista de Agricultura, Industria y Comercio. Puerto Rico: Imprenta del "Boletín Mercantil."

Romeu, Rafael. *Leyes de arrendamiento y desahucio de la Península, Cuba y Puerto-Rico, con notas para su mejor inteligencia y un formulario para su exacto cumplimiento de los juzgados municipales y de paz.* Madrid: Imprenta de Alejandro Gómez Fuentenebro, 1879.

Rosich, M. y J. *Fabricación del azúcar mascabado en relación con las factorías centrales.* Ponce: Tipografia Baldorioty, Marina y Aurora, 1902.

Salaberri Lescum, Enrique. *Año 1889. Puerto Rico, Vega Baja. Fabricación de azúcar por el maestro azucarero D. Enrique Salaberri Lescum. Folleto dedicado a los maestros de azúcares y a los hacendados.* Puerto Rico: Tip. de "La Integridad Nacional," 1889.

Sanromá, Joaquín María. *Puerto Rico y su hacienda.* Madrid: Imprenta de T. Fortanet, 1873.

Santaella, Herminio W. *Nociones de agricultura, industria y comercio. Texto aprobado de Real Orden para todas las escuelas de primera enseñanza.* Coamo, P.R.: Imprenta El Alba, 1898.

El Tiempo/"The Times" (Periódico diario excepto los domingos, el único que se publica en inglés y en español). San Juan: "The Times Publishing Company," No. 27, 31 January 1914.

Ubeda Delgado, Manuel. *Isla de Puerto Rico. Estudio histórico, geográfico y estadístico de la misma.* Puerto Rico: Establecimiento tip. del Boletín, 1878.

Los últimos sucesos de la Central "San Vicente." Circular y documentos que la comisión elegida por los acreedores de don Leonardo Igaravídez dirije a dichos acreedores para su conocimiento. Abril de 1889. Puerto Rico: Imprenta y Librería de Acosta, 1889.

del Valle Atiles, Francisco. *El campesino puertorriqueño. Sus condiciones físicas, intelectuales y morales, causas que las determinan y medios para mejorarlas.* Puerto Rico: Tipografía de José González Font, 1887.

Vendrell, Adolfo. *La caña de azúcar: Nociones sobre su cultivo y trabajo industrial.* Puerto Rico: Taller Tipográfico del Asilo de Beneficencia, 1892.

Vijande, Enrique. *La cuestión monetaria en Puerto Rico.* Madrid: Tipografía de Manuel Ginés Hernández, 1899.

White, Trumbull. *Our New Possessions . . . Four Books in One . . . A Graphic Account, Descriptive and Historical, of the Tropic Islands of the Sea Which Have Fallen Under Our Sway, Their Cities, Peoples and Commerce, Natural Resources and the Opportunities They Offer to Americans.* Book 2. Boston: J. Q. Adams, 1898.

Secondary Sources

Abbagnano, Nicola. "Positivism." *The Encyclopedia of Philosophy.* New York: Macmillan, 1967.

Adamson, Alan H. *Sugar without Slaves. The Political Economy of British Guiana, 1838–1904.* New Haven, Conn.: Yale University Press, 1972.

Aguilar Monteverde, Alonso. *Dialéctica de la economía mexicana. Del colonialismo al imperialismo.* 5th ed. Mexico: Editorial Nuestro Tiempo, S.A., 1974.

Aitken, Hugh G. J., ed. *Explorations in Enterprise.* Cambridge, Mass.: Harvard University Press, 1965.

Artola, Miguel. *La burguesía revolucionaria (1808–1869).* Historia de España Alfaguara V. Madrid: Alianza Editorial, 1973.

Báez Evertsz, Franc. *Azúcar y dependencia en la República Dominicana.* Santo Domingo: Editora de la Universidad Autónoma de Santo Domingo, 1978.

Bagué y Ramírez, Jaime. *Del ingenio azucarero patriarcal a la central azucarera corporativa: Glosa alrededor de las azucareras del año 1900.* Mayagüez: Colegio de Agricultura y Artes Mecánicas, 1968.

Baldrich, Juan José. *Sembraron la no siembra. Los cosecheros de tabaco puertorriqueños frente a las corporaciones tabacaleras, 1920–1934.* Río Piedras: Ediciones Huracán, 1988.

Baralt, Guillermo A. *Esclavos rebeldes. Conspiraciones y sublevaciones de esclavos en Puerto Rico (1795–1873)*. Río Piedras: Ediciones Huracán, 1981.

Baran, Paul A., and Paul M. Sweezy. *Monopoly Capital: An Essay in the American Economic and Social Order*. Great Britain: Penguin Books, 1966.

Bath, Richard C., and Dilmus D. James. "Dependency Analysis of Latin America: Some Criticisms, Some Suggestions." *Latin American Research Review* (hereafter, *LARR*) 11, 3 (1976): 3–38.

Beachey, R. W. *The British West Indies Sugar Industry in the Nineteenth Century*. Oxford: Basil Blackwell, 1957.

Beckford, George L. *Persistent Poverty. Underdevelopment in Plantation Economies of the Third World*. New York: Oxford University Press, 1972.

Benítez, José A. *Las antillas: Colonización, azúcar e imperialismo*. Havana: Casa de las Américas, 1977.

Bergad, Laird W. "Agrarian History of Puerto Rico, 1870–1930." *LARR* 13, 3 (1978): 63–67.

———. *Coffee and the Growth of Agrarian Capitalism in Nineteenth-Century Puerto Rico*. Princeton, N.J.: Princeton University Press, 1983.

———. "Towards Puerto Rico's Grito de Lares: Coffee, Social Stratification, and Class Conflicts, 1828–1868." *Hispanic American Historical Review* (hereafter *HAHR*) 60, 4 (November 1980): 617–42.

Besouchet, Lidia. *Maúa y su época*. Buenos Aires: Ediciones "América Económica," 1940.

Best, Lloyd A. "Outlines of a Model of Pure Plantation Economy." *Social and Economic Studies* 17, 3 (September 1968): 283–327.

Blanco, Tomás. *Prontuario histórico de Puerto Rico*. 3d ed. Mexico, D.F.: Editorial Clásica, 1946.

Bonnín Orozco, María Isabel. "Las fortunas vulnerables: Comerciantes y agricultores en los contratos de refacción de Ponce, 1865–1875." Master's thesis, University of Puerto Rico at Río Piedras, 1984.

Bottomore, Tom, ed. *A Dictionary of Marxist Thought*. Cambridge, Mass.: Harvard University Press, 1983.

Buitrago Ortiz, Carlos. *Haciendas cafetaleras y clases terratenientes en el Puerto Rico decimonónico*. Río Piedras: Editorial de la Universidad de Puerto Rico, 1982.

———. *Los orígenes históricos de la sociedad precapitalista en Puerto Rico (Ensayos de etnohistoria puertorriqueña)*. Río Piedras: Ediciones Huracán, 1976.

Cano, Wilson. *Raízes da concentracão industrial em São Paulo*. Río de Janeiro and São Paulo: DIFEL/Difusão Editorial, 1977.

Cardoso de Mello, João Manuel. *O Capitalismo Tardio. Contribuição a revisão crítica da formação e do desenvolvimento da economia brasileira*. São Paulo: Editôra Brasiliense, 1982.

Carr, Raymond. *Puerto Rico: A Colonial Experiment.* New York: Vintage Books, 1984.

Cassirer, Ernst. "El positivismo y su ideal de conocimiento histórico. Hipólito Taine." In *De la muerte de Hegel a nuestros días (1832–1932). El problema del conocimiento en la filosofía y en la ciencia modernas,* No. 4, pp. 295–308. Translated by Wenceslao Roces. 2d ed. Mexico City: Fondo de Cultura Económica, 1974.

Cepero Bonilla, Raúl. *Azúcar y abolición. Apuntes para una historia crítica del abolicionismo.* Havana: Editorial Cénit, 1948.

Chamberlain, John. *The Enterprising Americans: A Business History of the United States.* New York: Harper & Row, 1963.

Cole, Arthur H. *Business Enterprise in its Social Setting.* Cambridge, Mass.: Harvard University Press, 1959.

Coll y Toste, Cayetano, ed. *Boletín histórico de Puerto Rico.* 14 vols. San Juan: Tip. Cantero, Fernández, 1914–27.

Colón, E. D. *Datos sobre la agricultura en Puerto Rico antes de 1898.* San Juan: Tip. Cantero, Fernández, 1930.

Comellas, José Luis. *Los moderados en el poder, 1844–1854.* Madrid: Escuela de Historia Moderna, 1970.

Comte, Auguste. "Los tres estados de la inteligencia humana." *Principios de Filosofía Positiva.* Translated by Jorge Lagarrigue. Santiago: Librería del Mercurio, 1875. Rpt. in *Problemas de la filosofía. Textos filosóficos clásicos y contemporáneos,* edited by Luis O. Gómez and Roberto Torretti, pp. 653–58. Río Piedras: Editorial Universitaria, 1975.

Craton, Michael. *Searching for the Invisible Man. Slaves and Plantation Life in Jamaica.* Cambridge, Mass.: Harvard University Press, 1978.

Craton, Michael, James Walvin, and David Wright. *Slavery, Abolition, and Emancipation. Black Slaves and the British Empire.* London: Longman Group Limited, 1976.

Crist, R. E. "Sugar Cane and Coffee in Puerto Rico: The Role of Privilege and Monopoly in the Expropriation of the Jíbaro." *American Journal of Economics and Sociology,* 7 (January 1948): 173–84.

Cruz Monclova, Lidio. *Historia de Puerto Rico (Siglo XIX).* 3 vols. Río Piedras: Editorial Universitaria, 1957.

Cubano Iguina, Astrid T. "Economía y sociedad en Arecibo en el siglo XIX: los grandes productores y la inmigración de comerciantes." In *Inmigración y clases sociales en el Puerto Rico del siglo xix,* edited by Francisco A. Scarano, pp. 67–124. Río Piedras: Ediciones Huracán, 1981.

———. "Trade and Politics in Nineteenth-Century Puerto Rico." Ph.D. dissertation, Princeton University, 1988.

Curet, José. *De la esclavitud a la abolición: Transiciones económicas en las haciendas azucareras de Ponce, 1845–1873.* Río Piedras: Centro de Estudios de la Realidad Puertorriqueña, 1979.

―――. *Los amos hablan. Unas conversaciones entre un esclavo y su amo, aparecidas en el Ponceño, 1852–53.* Río Piedras: Editorial Cultural, 1986.

Dean, Warren. "The Planter as Entrepreneur: The Case of São Paulo." *HAHR* 46, 2 (May 1966): 138–52.

―――. *Río Claro: A Brazilian Plantation System, 1820–1920.* Stanford, Calif.: Stanford University Press, 1976.

Deerr, Noel. *The History of Sugar.* 2 vols. London: Chapman and Hall Ltd., 1949.

Díaz Hernández, Luis Edgardo. *Castañer. Una hacienda cafetalera en Puerto Rico (1868–1930).* Río Piedras: Editorial Edil, 1983.

Díaz Soler, Luis M. *Historia de la esclavitud negra en Puerto Rico.* Río Piedras: Editorial Universitaria, 1974.

Dietz, James L. *Economic History of Puerto Rico. Institutional Change and Capitalist Development.* Princeton, N.J.: Princeton University Press, 1986.

Edson, Hubert. *Sugar: From Scarcity to Surplus.* New York: Chemical Publishing, 1958.

Eichner, Alfred S. *The Emergence of Oligopoly. Sugar Refining as a Case Study.* 1969. Rpt. Westport, Connecticut: Greenwood Press, 1978.

Eisenberg, Peter L. *The Sugar Industry in Pernambuco. Modernization Without Change, 1840–1910.* Berkeley: University of California Press, 1974.

Ely, Roland T. *Cuando reinaba su majestad el azúcar. Estudio histórico-sociológico de una tragedia latinoamericana: el monocultivo en Cuba. Origen y evolución del proceso.* Buenos Aires: Editorial Sudamericana, 1963.

Fernández Mendez, Eugenio. *Historia cultural de Puerto Rico, 1493–1968.* 3d ed. San Juan: Ediciones "El Cemí," 1971.

Ferrer, Aldo. *La economía argentina. Las etapas de su desarrollo y problemas actuales.* 10th ed. Mexico City and Buenos Aires: Fondo de Cultura Económica, 1975.

Ferreras Pagán, J. *Biografía de las Riquezas de Puerto Rico: Riqueza Azucarera.* 2 vols. San Juan: Tipografía de Luis Ferreras, 1902.

Figueroa, Javier. *Diccionario histórico-biográfico.* Vol. 14 of *La Gran Enciclopedia de Puerto Rico.* Madrid: Ediciones R, 1976.

Figueroa Mercado, Loida. *History of Puerto Rico. From the beginning to the [sic] 1892.* New York: Anaya Book, 1972.

Florescano, Enrique, ed. *Haciendas, latifundios y plantaciones en América Latina.* Mexico City: Siglo Veintiuno, 1975.

Foner, Eric. *Nothing But Freedom. Emancipation and Its Legacy.* Baton Rouge: Louisiana State University Press.

Fradera, Josep. "Aproximación al colonialismo liberal español, 1833–1868."

Paper presented before the Department of History, University of Puerto Rico at Río Piedras, 1988.

García, Gervasio L., and A. G. Quintero Rivera. *Desafío y solidaridad. Breve historia del movimiento obrero puertorriqueño.* Río Piedras: Ediciones Huracán, 1982.

García Ochoa, María Asunción. *La política española en Puerto Rico durante el siglo XIX.* Río Piedras: Editorial de la Universidad de Puerto Rico, 1982.

García Rodriguez, Gervasio L. *Primeros fermentos de organización obrera en Puerto Rico, 1873–1898.* Río Piedras: Centro de Estudios de la Realidad Puertorriqueña, 1974.

Gautier Dapena, José A. *Trayectoria del pensamiento liberal puertorriqueño en el siglo XIX.* San Juan: Instituto de Cultura Puertorriqueña, 1975.

Gayer, Arthur D., Paul T. Homan, and Earle K. James. *The Sugar Economy of Puerto Rico.* New York: Columbia University Press, 1938.

Geigel, Luis M., and Bartolomé M. Morell. *Crédito agrícola refaccionario. El mercadeo de productos agrícolas en Puerto Rico.* San Juan: Sección de Publicación de Impresos, Departamento de Instrucción, 1950?.

Genovese, Eugene D. *The World the Slaveholders Made. Two Essays in Interpretation.* New York: Pantheon Books, 1969.

Gil-Bermejo García, Juana. *Panorama histórico de la agricultura en Puerto Rico.* Seville: Escuela de Estudios Hispano-Americanos & Instituto de Cultura Puertorriqueña, 1970.

Gómez Acevedo, Labor. *Organización y reglamentación del trabajo en el Puerto Rico del siglo XIX (Propietarios y jornaleros).* San Juan: Instituto de Cultura Puertorriqueña, 1970.

Gonzales, Michael J. *Plantation Agriculture and Social Control in Northern Peru, 1875–1933.* Austin: University of Texas Press, 1985.

González, Lydia Milagros, and Angel G. Quintero Rivera. *La otra cara de la historia. La historia de Puerto Rico desde su cara obrera.* Vol. 1: 1800–1925. Parte I: Album de fotos de la clase obrera puertorriqueña. Río Piedras: Centro de Estudios de la Realidad Puertorriqueña, 1984.

González Vales, Luis. "Towards a Plantation Society (1860–1866)" and "The Challenge to Colonialism (1866–1897)." In *Puerto Rico. A Political and Cultural History,* edited by Arturo Morales Carrión, pp. 79–125. New York: W. W. Norton, 1983.

Graham, Richard. *Britain and the Onset of Modernization in Brazil, 1850–1914.* Cambridge Latin American Studies, No. 4. Cambridge: University Press, 1972.

Green, William A. *British Slave Emancipation. The Sugar Colonies and the Great Experiment, 1830–1865.* Oxford: Clarendon Press, 1976.

Guerra y Sánchez, Ramiro. *Sugar and Society in the Caribbean. An Economic*

History of Cuban Agriculture. Translated by Marjory M. Urquidi. New Haven, Conn.: Yale University Press, 1964.

Hall, Douglas. *Five of the Leewards, 1834–1870. The Major Problems of the Post-Emancipation Period in Antigua, Barbuda, Montserrat, Nevis, and St. Kitts*. St. Laurence, Barbados: Caribbean Universities Press, 1971.

———. *Free Jamaica, 1838–1865. An Economic History*. New Haven, Conn.: Yale University Press, 1959.

Hays, Samuel P. *The Response to Industrialism, 1885–1914*. Chicago: University of Chicago Press, 1957.

Hennessy, C. A. M. *The Federal Republic in Spain. Pi y Margall and the Federal Republican Movement, 1868–1874*. Oxford: Clarendon Press, 1962.

Herrero, José Antonio. *La mitología del azúcar: Un ensayo en la historia económica de Puerto Rico, 1900–1970*. Río Piedras: Centro de Estudios de la Realidad Puertorriqueña, 1977(?).

Hostos, Adolfo de. *Diccionario histórico bibliográfico comentado de Puerto Rico*. Barcelona: Academia Puertorriqueña de la Historia and Industrias Gráficas Manuel Pareja, 1976.

Fe Iglesias. "The Development of Capitalism in Cuban Sugar Production, 1860–1900." In *Between Slavery and Free Labor: The Spanish-Speaking Caribbean in the Nineteenth Century*. Johns Hopkins Studies in Atlantic History and Culture, edited by Manuel Moreno Fraginals, Frank Moya Pons, and Stanley L. Engerman, pp. 54–75. Baltimore: The Johns Hopkins University Press, 1985.

Jackson, F. E., ed. *The Representative Men of Porto Rico*. n.p., F. E. Jackson & Son, 1910.

Jones, Charles. "Commercial Banks and Mortgage Companies." In *Business Imperialism, 1840–1930. An Inquiry Based on British Experience in Latin America*, edited by D. C. M. Platt, pp. 17–52. Oxford: Clarendon Press, 1977.

Jones, Gareth Stedman. *Outcast London. A Study in the Relationship between Classes in Victorian Society*. Oxford: Clarendon Press, 1971.

Keith, Robert. "Encomienda, Hacienda and Corregimiento in Spanish America: A Structural Analysis." *HAHR* 51, 3 (August 1971): 431–46.

Keith, Robert G., ed. *Haciendas and Plantations in Latin American History*. New York: Holmes & Meier, 1977.

Kiernan, V. G. *The Revolution of 1854 in Spanish History*. Oxford: Clarendon Press, 1966.

Kirkland, Edward C. *Industry Comes of Age: Business, Labor and Public Policy, 1860–1897*. Economic History of the United States, Vol. 6. New York: Holt, Rinehart and Winston, 1961.

Klarén, Peter F. *Modernization, Dislocation and Aprismo. Origins of the Peruvian*

Aprista Party, 1870–1932. Institute of Latin American Studies Monograph Series, No. 32. Austin: University of Texas Press, 1973.

Knight, Franklin W. *The Caribbean. The Genesis of a Fragmented Nationalism.* 1978. Rpt. New York: Oxford University Press, 1980.

————. "A Colonial Response to the Glorious Revolution in Spain: The 'Grito de Yara'." In *La revolución de 1868: Historia, Pensamiento, Literatura,* edited by Clara E. Lida and Iris M. Zavala, pp. 196–209. New York: Las Americas Publishing Company, 1970.

————. "Origins of Wealth and the Sugar Revolution in Cuba, 1750–1850." *HAHR* 57, 2 (May 1977): 231–54.

Knight, Wyllis R. "Agriculture." In *The Structure of American Industry: Some Case Studies,* edited by Walter Adams, pp. 1–29. 4th ed. New York: Macmillan, 1971.

Lalinde Abadía, Jesus. *La administración española en el siglo XIX puertorriqueño (Pervivencia de la variante indiana del decisionismo castellano en Puerto Rico).* Seville: Escuela de Estudios Hispano-Americanos, Universidad de Sevilla, 1980.

Leddy Phelan, John. "Authority and Flexibility in the Spanish Imperial Bureaucracy." *Administrative Science Quarterly* 5, 1 (June 1960): 47–65.

Le Riverend Brusone, Julio. "Sobre la industria azucarera de Cuba durante el siglo XIX." *Trimestre Económico* 11, 1 (1944): 52–70.

Lewis, Gordon K. *Puerto Rico: Freedom and Power in the Caribbean.* New York: Monthly Review Press, 1963.

Liss, Peggy K. *Atlantic Empires. The Network of Trade and Revolution, 1713–1826.* Baltimore: The Johns Hopkins University Press, 1983.

Lockhart, James. "Encomienda and Hacienda: The Evolution of the Great Estate in the Spanish Indies." *HAHR* 49, 3 (August 1969): 411–29.

López, Adalberto. "Socio-Politico Developments in a Colonial Context: Puerto Rico in the Nineteenth Century." In *Puerto Rico and the Puerto Ricans: Studies in History and Society,* edited by Adalberto López and James Petras, pp. 42–86. New York: John Wiley and Sons, 1974.

López Domínguez, Francisco. "Origen y desarrollo de la industria azucarera en Puerto Rico." *Revista de Agricultura de Puerto Rico* 19, 3–6 (September–December 1927): 103–7, 167–73, 222–24, 287–89.

Lynch, John. *The Spanish American Revolutions 1808–1826.* New York: W. W. Norton, 1986.

Mandle, Jay R. *The Plantation Economy. Population and Economic Change in Guyana, 1838–1960.* Philadelphia: Temple University Press, 1973.

Martínez Cuadrado, Miguel. *La burguesía conservadora (1874–1931).* Historia de España Alfaguara 6. Madrid: Alianza Editorial, 1974.

Martínez de Carrerá, Teresita. "The Attitudes of Influential Groups of Colonial Society towards the Rural Working Population in Nineteenth-Century Puerto Rico, 1860–73." *Journal of Caribbean History* 12 (1979): 35–54.

Martínez Vergne, Teresita. "New Patterns for Puerto Rico's Sugar Workers: Abolition and Centralization at San Vicente, 1873–1892." *HAHR* 68, 1 (February 1988): 45–74.

———. "La transición en el Caribe: Reflexiones en torno a *Between Slavery and Free Labor.*" *Historia y Sociedad* 2 (1989): 148–84.

Max, Hermann. *El valor de la moneda. La función del dinero. La función del credito. La función de los cambios.* Buenos Aires: Joaquín Almendros, 1970.

Mintz, Sidney W. "Cañamelar. The Subculture of a Rural Sugar Plantation Proletariat." In *The People of Puerto Rico. A Study in Social Anthropology,* edited by Julian H. Steward, Robert A. Manners, Eric R. Wolf, Elena Padilla Seda, Sidney W. Mintz, and Raymond L. Scheele, pp. 314–417. Urbana: University of Illinois Press, 1956.

———. "The Culture History of a Puerto Rican Sugar Cane Plantation, 1876–1949." *HAHR* 33, 2 (May 1953): 224–51.

———. "Labor and Sugar in Puerto Rico and in Jamaica, 1800–1850." *Comparative Studies in Society and History* 1, 3 (March 1959): 273–83.

———. *Petits cultivateurs et prolétaires ruraux dans la région des caraïbes.* Collection de réimpression du centre de recherches caraïbes 3. Montreal: Université de Montréal, 1967?.

———. "The Role of Forced Labour in Nineteenth-Century Puerto Rico." *Caribbean Historical Review,* no. 2 (December 1951): 134–51.

———. "The Rural Proletariat and the Problem of Rural Proletarian Consciousness." *Journal of Peasant Studies* 1, 3 (April 1974): 291–326.

———. *Worker in the Cane. A Puerto Rican Life History.* New Haven, Conn.: Yale University Press, 1960.

Morales Carrión, Arturo. *Auge y decadencia de la trata negrera en Puerto Rico (1820–1860).* San Juan: Centro de Estudios Avanzados de Puerto Rico y el Caribe & Instituto de Cultura Puertorriqueña, 1978.

Moreno Fraginals, Manuel. *El ingenio. Complejo económico social cubano del azúcar.* 3 vols. Havana: Editorial de Ciencias Sociales, 1978.

———. *La historia como arma y otros estudios sobre esclavos, ingenios y plantaciones.* Barcelona: Editorial Crítica, 1983.

———. "Plantations in the Caribbean: Cuba, Puerto Rico, and the Dominican Republic in the Late Nineteenth Century." In *Between Slavery and Free Labor: The Spanish-Speaking Caribbean in the Nineteenth Century.* Johns Hopkins Studies in Atlantic History and Culture, edited by Manuel Moreno Fraginals, Frank Moya Pons, and Stanley L. Engerman, pp. 3–21. Baltimore: The Johns Hopkins University Press, 1985.

Moreno Fraginals, Manuel, Frank Moya Pons, and Stanley L. Engerman, eds. *Between Slavery and Free Labor. The Spanish-Speaking Caribbean in the Nineteenth Century*. Johns Hopkins Studies in Atlantic History and Culture. Baltimore: The Johns Hopkins University Press, 1985.

Mörner, Magnus. "The Spanish American Hacienda: A Survey of Recent Research and Debate." *HAHR* 53, 2 (May 1973): 183–216.

Nistal Moret, Benjamin. "La contratación de los libertos de Manatí: 1873–1876." *Revista del Instituto de Cultura Puertorriqueña* 16, 61 (October–December 1973): 51–59.

————. *Informe histórico sobre la hacienda "La Esperanza": Formación y desarrollo hasta 1894*. San Juan: Fideicomiso de Conservación de Puerto Rico, 1979.

Ortiz, Fernando. *Contrapunteo cubano del tabaco y el azúcar*. Havana: Consejo Nacional de Cultura, 1983.

Ortiz Cuadra, Cruz M. "Crédito y azúcar: Los hacendados de Humacao ante la crisis del dulce, 1865–1900." Master's thesis, University of Puerto Rico at Río Piedras, 1985.

Overman, Charles T. "Rise and Fall of the Henrietta: 1827–1918." *Revista/Review Interamericana* 14, 4 (Winter 1974–75): 493–505.

Pérez, Louis, Jr. "Vagrants, Beggars, and Bandits: Social Origins of Cuban Separatism, 1878–1895." *American Historical Review* 90, 5 (December 1985): 1092–1121.

Pérez de la Riva, Juan. "La contradicción fundamental de la sociedad colonial cubana: Trabajo esclavo contra trabajo libre." *Economía y Desarrollo* 2 (April–June 1970): 144–54.

Perloff, Harvey S. *Puerto Rico's Economic Future*. Chicago: University of Chicago Press, 1950.

Perruci, Gadiel. *A República das Usinas. Um Estudo de História Social e Econômica do Nordeste: 1889–1930*. Río de Janeiro: Editôra Paz e Terra, 1978.

Picó, Fernando, S.J. *Amargo café (Los pequeños y medianos caficultores de Utuado en la segunda mitad del siglo XIX)*. Río Piedras: Ediciones Huracán, 1981.

————. *Libertad y servidumbre en el Puerto Rico del siglo XIX (Los jornaleros utuadeños en vísperas del auge del café)*. Río Piedras: Ediciones Huracán, 1979.

————. *Los gallos peleados*. Río Piedras: Ediciones Huracán, 1983.

————. *Historia general de Puerto Rico*. Río Piedras: Ediciones Huracán, 1986.

————. *1898. La guerra después de la guerra*. Río Piedras: Ediciones Huracán, 1987.

Picó, Rafael. *Nueva geografía de Puerto Rico: Física, económica, social*. Río Piedras: Editorial Universitaria, 1969.

Prado, Caio, Júnior. *Esbôço dos fundamentos da teoria econômica*. 2d ed. São Paulo: Editôra Brasiliense, 1960.

Quintero Rivera, A. G. "Background to the Emergence of Imperialist Capitalism in Puerto Rico." In *Puerto Rico and the Puerto Ricans: Studies in Society and History*, edited by Adalberto López and James Petras, pp. 87–117. New York: John Wiley and Sons, 1974.

––––––. *Historia de unas clases sin historia* (*Comentarios críticos al* País de cuatro pisos). Cuadernos "Avances para discusión" 6. Río Piedras: Centro de Estudios de la Realidad Puertorriqueña, 1983.

Ramos Mattei, Andrés. *Los libros de cuentas de la hacienda Mercedita, 1861–1900. Apuntes para el estudio de la transición hacia el sistema de centrales en la industria azucarera en Puerto Rico*. Río Piedras: Centro de Estudios de la Realidad Puertorriqueña, 1975.

––––––. *La hacienda azucarera. Su crecimiento y crisis en Puerto Rico (Siglo XIX)*. Río Piedras: Centro de Estudios de la Realidad Puertorriqueña, 1981.

––––––, ed. *Azúcar y esclavitud*. Río Piedras: Universidad de Puerto Rico, 1982.

Reyes, María M. "Los juicios verbales celebrados en el pueblo de Manatí en 1864." *Anales de Investigación Histórica* 1, 1 (January–March 1974): 93–106.

Ribes Tovar, Federico. *Historia cronológica de Puerto Rico. Desde el nacimiento de la isla hasta el año 1973*. New York: Plus Ultra Educational Publishers, 1973.

Rivera Medina, Eduardo, and Rafael L. Ramírez, eds. *Del cañaveral a la fábrica. Cambio social en Puerto Rico*. Río Piedras: Ediciones Huracán, 1985.

Rodney, Walter. *A History of the Guyanese Working People, 1881–1905*. Baltimore and London: The Johns Hopkins University Press, 1981.

Rolph, George M. *Something About Sugar. Its History, Growth, Manufacture and Distribution*. San Francisco: John J. Newbegin, 1917.

de la Rosa, Luis. "Los fondos documentales en el Archivo General de Puerto Rico." Paper presented at the Congress on Puerto Rican Local History, Inter-American University, San Germán, 28 February

Safford, Frank. "Significación de los antioqueños en el desarrollo económico colombiano. Un examen crítico de las tesis de Everett Hagen." *Anuario Colombiano de Historia Social y de la Cultura* (1966): 49–71.

San Miguel, Pedro. "Tierra, trabajadores y propietarios: Las haciendas en Vega Baja, 1828–1865." *Anales de Investigación Histórica* 6, 2 (1979): 1–51.

––––––. *El mundo que creó el azúcar. Las haciendas en Vega Baja, 1800–1873*. Río Piedras: Ediciones Huracán, 1989.

Santiago de Curet, Ana Mercedes. "Crédito, moneda y bancos en Puerto Rico durante el siglo XIX." Master's thesis, University of Puerto Rico at Río Piedras, 1978.

dos Santos, Ana Maria. "Agricultural Reform and the Idea of 'Decadence' in the State of Río de Janeiro, 1870–1910." Ph.D. dissertation, University of Texas at Austin, 1984.

Scarano, Francisco. "Slavery and Free Labor in the Puerto Rican Sugar Economy: 1815–1873." In *Comparative Perspectives on Slavery in New World Plantation Societies*, edited by Vera Rubin and Arthur Tuden, pp. 553–63. Annals of the New York Academy of Sciences. Vol. 292. New York: Academy of Sciences, 1977.

———. *Sugar and Slavery in Puerto Rico. The Plantation Economy of Ponce, 1800–1850.* Madison: University of Wisconsin Press, 1984.

Schnakenbourg, Christian. *Histoire de l'industrie sucrière en Guadeloupe aux XIXe. et XXe. siècles.* Vol. I. La crise du système esclavigiste (1835–1847). Paris: Editions L'Harmattan, 1980.

Schwartz, Stuart B. *Sugar Plantations in the Formation of Brazilian Society. Bahia, 1550–1835.* Cambridge: University Press, 1985.

Scott, Rebecca J. "Gradual Abolition and the Dynamics of Slave Emancipation in Cuba, 1868–86." *HAHR* 63, 3 (August 1983): 449–78.

———. *Slave Emancipation in Cuba. The Transition to Free Labor, 1860–1899.* Princeton, N.J.: Princeton University Press, 1985.

———. "Comparing Emancipations: A Review Essay." *Journal of Social History* 20, 3 (Spring 1987): 565–83.

———. "Exploring the Meaning of Freedom: Postemancipation Societies in Comparative Perspective." *HAHR* 68, 3 (August 1988), 407–28.

Sheridan, Richard B. "Sweet Malefactor: The Social Costs of Slavery in Jamaica and Cuba, 1807–1854." *Economic History Review*, 2d series, 29, 2 (May 1976): 236–58.

Smith, Dudley, and William M. Requa. *Puerto Rico Sugar Facts.* Washington, D.C.: Association of Sugar Producers of Puerto Rico, 1939.

Stein, Stanley J., and Barbara H. Stein. *The Colonial Heritage of Latin America. Essays on Economic Dependence in Perspective.* New York: Oxford University Press, 1970.

Stern, Steve J. *Peru's Indian Peoples and the Challenge of Spanish Conquest. Huamanga to 1640.* Madison: University of Wisconsin Press, 1982.

Sweigart, Joseph Earl. "Financing and Marketing Brazilian Export Agriculture: The Coffee Factors of Río de Janeiro, 1850–1888." Ph.D. dissertation, University of Texas at Austin, 1980.

Százdi, Adam. "Credit—Without Banking—in Early Nineteenth Century Puerto Rico." *The Americas* 19, 2 (October 1962): 149–71.

Taylor, William B. *Landlord and Peasant in Colonial Oaxaca.* Stanford: Stanford University Press, 1972.

Thompson, E. P. *The Making of the English Working Class.* New York: Vintage Books, 1966.

———. "The Moral Economy of the English Crowd in the Eighteenth Century." *Past and Present* 50 (February 1971): 76–136.

————. "Time, Work-Discipline and Industrial Capitalism." *Past and Present* 38 (December 1967): 56–97.

Tirado Merced, Dulce María. "Las raíces sociales del liberalismo criollo: El Partido Liberal Reformista (1870–1875)." Master's thesis, University of Puerto Rico at Río Piedras, 1981.

Trías Monge, José. *El sistema judicial de Puerto Rico*. Río Piedras: Editorial Universitaria, 1978.

Tuñón de Lara, Manuel. "El problema del poder en el sexenio 1868–1874." In *La revolución de 1868: Historia, Pensamiento, Literatura*, edited by Clara E. Lida and Iris M. Zavala, pp. 138–82. New York: Las Americas Publishing Company, 1970.

Van Young, Eric. "Mexican Rural History since Chevalier: The Historiography of the Colonial Hacienda." *LARR* 18, 3 (1983): 5–62.

Vilar, Pierre. *Crecimiento y desarrollo. Economía e historia. Reflexiones sobre el caso español*. Barcelona: Ediciones Ariel, 1964.

————. *El modo de producción como concepto fundamental para la construcción histórica*. Colombia: Ediciones Nuestra América, 1979.

Vogt, Paul L. *The Sugar Refining Industry in the United States. Its Development and Present Condition*. Series on Political Economy and Public Law, No. 21. Philadelphia: University of Pennsylvania, 1908.

Walton, Clifford Stevens. *The Civil Law in Spain and Spanish-America, including Cuba, Puerto Rico and the Philippine Islands, and the Spanish Civil Code in force, annotated and with references to the Civil Codes of Mexico, Central and South America, with a History of all the Spanish Codes, and Summary of Canonical Laws, of the Principal Fueros, Ordenamientos, Councils and Ordenanzas of Spain from the Earliest Times to the Twentieth Century, including the Spanish, Mexican, Cuban and Puerto Rican Autonomical Constitutions, and a History of the Laws of the Indies—Recopilación de Leyes de los Reynos de las Indias, by Clifford Stevens Walton, Doctorando, University of Madrid, Licentiate of the University of Havana, Member of the Bar of the Supreme Court of the United States and of the Bar of the District of Columbia, Associate of the Institut de Droit International, and Corresponding Member of the Sociedad Geografía y Estadística de México*. Washington, D.C.: W. H. Lowdermilk, 1900.

Watts, David. *The West Indies: Patterns of Development, Culture and Environmental Change since 1492*. Cambridge: Cambridge University Press, 1987.

Wessman, James W. "Division of Labour, Capital Accumulation and Commodity Exchange on a Puerto Rican Sugar Cane Hacienda." *Social and Economic Studies* 27, 4 (December 1978): 464–80.

————. "The Sugar Cane Hacienda in the Agrarian Structure of Southwestern Puerto Rico in 1902." *Revista/Review Interamericana* 8, 1 (Spring 1978): 99–115.

————. "Theory of Value, Labor Process and Price Formation: A Study of a Puerto Rican Sugarcane Hacienda." *American Ethnologist* 7, 3 (August 1980): 479–92.

Williams, Raymond. *The Country and the City*. New York: Oxford University Press, 1973.

Wolf, Eric R., and Sidney W. Mintz. "Haciendas and Plantations in Middle America and the Antilles." *Social and Economic Studies* 8, 3 (September 1957): 380–412.

Woodward, Ralph Lee, Jr., ed. *Positivism in Latin America, 1850–1900. Are Order and Progress Reconcilable?* Lexington: D.C. Heath, 1971.

Zea, Leopoldo. *Positivism in Mexico*. Translated by Josephine H. Schulte. Austin: University of Texas Press, 1974.

Zeno, Franciso M. *Influencia de la industria azucarera en la vida antillana y sus consecuencias sociales*. San Juan: Tip. La Correspondencia, 1935.

Index

Teresita Martínez-Vergne, a native of Puerto Rico, taught at the University of Puerto Rico in Río Piedras before she joined the History Department of Macalester College in St. Paul, Minnesota.

Library of Congress Cataloging-in-Publication Data

Martínez-Vergne, Teresita.
    Capitalism in colonial Puerto Rico: Central San Vicente
in the late nineteenth century / Teresita Martínez-Vergne.
       p.   cm. — (University of Florida social sciences monograph; 78)
    Includes bibliographical references and index.
    ISBN 0-8130-1110-8
    1. Sugar trade—Puerto Rico—History—19th century. 2. Central
San Vicente (Sugar factory)—History. 3. Sugar factories—Puerto
Rico—History—19th century. I. Title. II. Series: University of
Florida monographs. Social sciences; no. 78.
  HD9114.P82M37   1992   91-28358
  338.1'7361'09729509034—dc20   CIP